FACE TO FACE:

THE UNVEILING OF JESUS CHRIST

FACE TO FACE:
THE UNVEILING OF JESUS CHRIST

AN EXPLORER'S PRELUDE TO THE BOOK OF REVELATION

MICAH PAUL GAYLOR

Face to Face: The Unveiling of Jesus Christ
By Micah Paul Gaylor
Copyright © 2023 Micah Paul Gaylor
Second Edition, 2025

Edited by: Rebecca Hershberger and Sandy Landry
Cover art: Adobe Stock
Cover design by: Micah Paul Gaylor
Book layout by: Micah Paul Gaylor
Chapter title artwork by: Jamie Gaylor

International Standard Book Number: 979-8-9877560-3-4
Ebook ISBN: 979-8-9877560-5-8
Hardcover ISBN: 979-8-9877560-4-1

Library of Congress Cataloging-in-Publication Data: An application to register this book for cataloging has been submitted to the Library of Congress.

Bolding in scripture quotations was added by the author for emphasis only.

DEDICATION

To my Lord Jesus:

I've used Your gifts to produce this simple offering. May it be a pleasing fragrance, whether You desire the aroma to reach a few, or many, or You alone.

To my wife, Jamie:

My greatest honor in this life is getting to experience every wilderness and wellspring, every trial and treasure of the journey, hand-in-hand with you. Let's savor this particular milestone, and then walk toward the next season with greater wisdom and a fresh twinkle in our eyes.

TABLE OF CONTENTS

Author's Note

This passion project has consumed my imagination and much of my free time for the last 25 years, and its seed was planted even earlier. Back in high school, I watched my dad get excommunicated from two churches over zealous (and sometimes belligerent) arguments about eschatology. That's a story for another time, but the pain of watching those events drove me deep into the Word of God as I sought to understand a subject that had caused such intense debate and division.

Fast forward to shortly after college. Different state, different church. I was married, had four young kids, and was part of a small but devoted church in northern Vermont. After a few years, the church bought a large piece of property in the mountains and took a left-hand turn down Doomsday-Prepper Lane. Fueled by fear and a twisted view of discipleship, the leaders began gaslighting parishioners into building a homesteading compound in preparation for the "end times."

In response to that troubling development, I redoubled my study of scripture, desperately searching for a deeper understanding of God's heart, hoping to find the strength to extricate myself and my family from an increasingly codependent Church group full of our closest friends and mentors. That's when I first encountered Jesus *in* the text of the Book of Revelation, beyond theories and doctrines, in a way that transformed my fear into faith, enlarged my perspective of God, empowered my resolve, and utterly changed the course of my life. We left soon after and never looked back.

That is only a small part of a larger story, but it gives you a sense of my deep connection with Revelation. I'm no scholar. I have no seminary experience to draw from, but I've studied and loved the Word of God for decades, and I've discovered a liberating grace in the Book of Revelation that must be shared.

Beyond that, I have also drunk from many Christian streams throughout my life. I've experienced the flavors of various denominations and nourished spirit and soul at the wells of diverse ministries to gain a well-rounded perspective.

None of that should make me more or less trustworthy than whatever the Holy Spirit witnesses to your heart as you read. But I am honored to present to you my own unique blend of old and new wines to delight and enlighten your palette and expand your capacity to know Jesus Christ.

Micah Paul Gaylor
September 2024

CHAPTER 1

UNCOVERING THE PATH

or - "Let's get this stuff out of the way!"

T he world is in turmoil. A malaise of deep darkness is increasing around the globe. Everywhere we look, the foundations of civilization are shaking. In many ways, it feels like reality itself is under attack, and a foreboding horizon suggests even greater distress in the future.

Many Christians are turning toward biblical end-times prophesy for comfort in these trying times. This is a positive step, but comfort isn't going to usher in the kingdom of God. Whether Jesus tarries for another five years, fifty years, or five hundred years, the people of God are called to do more than just survive these times. We are called to thrive; to build when everything else crumbles; to love when fear and hatred abound; to grow when others shrink back. We were made for these times. Or better yet, these times were made for us. We need every second of the shaking, the trials, the tribulations, and the travail if we are to become the resplendent Bride and perfect counterpart our coming King deserves. But these present and future circumstances will only produce the desired transformation if we embrace them from the proper perspective.

Perspective is why I'm writing this series. This is more than an academic exercise of eschatological exegesis, and it certainly isn't "Revelation for Dummies," though please keep reading if you were looking for either of those! Whatever your expectations, if you read with an open mind and a tender heart, you may find yourself transformed by something more powerful than facts and enraptured by Someone more glorious than knowledge.

I know this from experience. I began writing these books seeking biblical truth, and twenty years later I find myself on a much more fulfilling journey with the Living Word. I've also discovered a whole lot of exciting biblical truth along the way. But I'm not here as an expert "high priest" of the truth. Think of me as an experienced companion here to guide you to streams of living water where so many others have only found dark and lifeless paths through Revelation.

> We are called to thrive; to build when everything else crumbles; to love when fear and hatred abound; to grow when others shrink back. We were made for these times. Or better yet, these times were made for us.

My goal is to enlarge your perspective of God with colors and facets you've never seen. To weave together familiar Bible verses into a breathtaking tapestry. One that reveals complex textures and living hues that awaken your spirit and compel you forward. But more than anything, I present this series as a simple invitation to "come and see," to experience, and to participate in the Unveiling of Jesus Christ. The Spirit and the Bride say, "Come!"

PREPARATION AND PERSPECTIVE

Going forward, I will often leverage the metaphor of an epic quest to describe our journey through Revelation. The metaphor itself is a visualization tool, helpful in organizing some complex ideas in your mind. And that's important because reaching our goal will require combining a vast array of biblical concepts. The only way to do that is to walk through the material in a methodical, step-by-step progression, holding multiple truths together in our minds as we build toward the end goal. You know, just like a quest!

As you may imagine, any journey through Revelation contains impossibly treacherous terrain, murky landmarks, and confounding paths shrouded in doubt and fear. At least, that's how it may look from here, standing on the edge of an impenetrable forest of cryptic prophecies, searching for a treasure not yet fully defined. You may already sense the hope of glory hidden deep inside, but how do you find the entrance, let alone navigate the internal labyrinth to obtain the mysterious prize?

You are reading a study on the book of Revelation, so I don't need to convince you of the worthiness of this venture, but you may be wondering how we plan to flourish where many have failed before us.

The first and most important answer is perspective. We can't hope to understand God's intention for the book of Revelation if we are not intimately familiar with the bigger story that Revelation consummates. So before we even think about entering the forest for our quest, we need to enlarge our grid for understanding God's end-times plan. That's the perspective we'll be focusing on in this book.

To that end, as we stand on the outskirts of this staggering adventure, our first task is to clean up the fallen brush left by previous travelers who sought to carve their own corridor rather than searching for the one blazed by the Creator. We need to clear away the clutter before we see His intended entrance. Then we will spend most of our time in this book expanding our perspective by getting acquainted with a divine map of our quest. Finally, we'll end the book by braving the first few steps into the forest to spy out the path ahead in preparation for book 2.

Along the way, we'll answer some fundamental questions: Where are we? Where are we going? And how do we get there? In many ways, these questions allude to the substance of this first book, and they will help establish a proper perspective for success.

If you are as excited as I am to dive into the book of Revelation, the prospect of dedicating an entire book to preparation may feel superfluous, but I promise that this investment will pay dividends down the road. We must be on the same page, using the same map, starting from the same place, striving for the same destination. In reality, this groundwork will not only prepare us for the journey, but it will also enhance our longing for the treasure as it cultivates our capacity to receive the magnitude of its transformational qualities.

Now, put on your gloves and help me deal with three specific fallen branches that threaten to block our view. Think of them as common misconceptions about the book of Revelation. Perhaps you are already familiar with these errors and know how to avoid them. Either way, we'll pull them off to the side, toss them in the fire, and move on without ceremony. No need to belabor their origin or speculate about their purpose. And don't worry if the silhouette of their fiery demise remains in your memory for a while; the journey ahead should remove all doubt of their lifeless nature.

OBSTACLE NUMBER 1: FOCUS

> The Revelation of Jesus Christ, which God gave Him to show to His bond-servants, the things which must soon take place; and He sent and communicated it by His angel to His bond-servant John, who testified to the word of God and to the testimony of Jesus Christ, even to all that he saw. Blessed is he who reads and those who hear the words of the prophecy, and heed the things which are written in it; for the time is near.
> —*REVELATION 1:1-3*

These verses are a consuming fire that can make quick work of any fallen brush. We'll eventually carry them with us like a torch to light our path, but for now let's just bask in the glow of the first five words: "The Revelation of Jesus Christ." These words are the first key to the book of Revelation and are the best place to start. The word *revelation* is translated from the Greek word *apokalupsis*, from which we derive our English word *apocalypse*. It is a word with enormous cultural and religious baggage. Where we're going, we won't have time or room for baggage, so let's toss it into the fire.

The meaning of *apokalupsis* is to uncover, to reveal, or to unveil. The root of the Greek word has the connotation of removing a veil or a cover from something that is hidden. I prefer the imagery of unveiling for its intimate quality, and because it synchronizes beautifully with so many other threads that weave throughout the book of Revelation. The Revelation of Jesus Christ is, quite literally, the Unveiling of Jesus Christ. It is neither a revelation about Jesus nor a revelation in which Jesus is the central figure. *He* is the revelation. All prophetic experiences contained in Revelation facilitate His unveiling.

That means it is not the revealing of the antichrist. It is not a prophecy about future cataclysms and perilous times. It is not about worldwide destruction and judgment and great tribulation. It is the Unveiling of Jesus. I cannot overstate this simple concept. Focus is key here. If our focus is right, all of these other thoughts can fall into their rightful place in the background. If our focus is wrong, we won't even be on the right journey, let alone arrive at the right destination.

OBSTACLE NUMBER 2: PURPOSE

> The Revelation of Jesus Christ, **which God gave Him to show to His bond-servants ...**
> —*REVELATION 1:1A*

Notice that the Unveiling was given to Jesus by the Father. It is for Christ to reveal Himself. It is not somebody else revealing Jesus. It is Jesus revealing Jesus. This is important because it is an act of intentional intimacy. It is an act of love designed to reproduce glorious results.

Also, notice that the Unveiling is designed for a specific target audience. The concept of bondservants is another multilayered theme that we will unpack later. For now, I'll just mention that a bondservant serves out of love and freedom rather than fear and requirement. Beyond that, it is enough to recognize that the casual observer will not benefit from the book of Revelation. It is not a passive book for those on the sideline. The purpose is not knowledge for the sake of information. The purpose is illumination for transformation.

Years ago, while struggling to write a particular chapter of this book, a friend helped me see the difference between reading Revelation for the sake of information and reading it for transformation. He challenged me to approach this project through the lens of *principles* instead of truth. Principles? Instead of truth? What does that even mean?

> The Revelation of Jesus Christ is, quite literally, the Unveiling of Jesus Christ. It is neither a revelation about Jesus nor a revelation in which Jesus is the central figure. *He* is the revelation.

Truths and principles are closely related and often intertwined, like the connection between soul and spirit, or knowledge and wisdom, or the letter of the law and the spirit of the law. I like to think of truths as static and finite data points: One plus one equals two; the earth revolves around the sun; God is love; Jesus rose again at dawn on a Sunday. Truths are important. They are the raw building blocks of observable reality. If we don't know and love the truth, we can't hope to understand principles.

Principles are dynamic, infinite relationships between truths. I like to think of principles as expressions of God's divine character sown into the canvas of creation at the dawn of time. They are the glue that holds truths (and therefore reality) together. A more practical and precise description comes from Arthur Burk, who defines principles as "universal, non-optional, cause and effect relationships."[1]

I wrestled with this paradigm for a long time because I love the truth and I'm an engineer. My struggle to look beyond data points was great. But I trusted my friend's wisdom and started digging for principles instead of just truths. Gradually, some Scriptures started opening up to me in new ways, and that's when a number of my favorite chapters in this book were birthed. It was a practical object lesson for me about the power of perspective to limit or enhance our experience of Christ's unveiling.

Don't worry if the difference between truth and principle feels ambiguous or unimportant at this point. Clarity will increase as you keep reading. My goal is to provide you with some tools to help you flourish on the journey ahead. Many of those tools will be principles, while some will be the raw materials of truth that we find along the way. Think of the difference between teaching you how to fish (principles) and merely giving you the fish (truth).

That distinction is especially important for the book of Revelation because seeking truths can lead to knowledge of events, but seeking principles leads to transformation. And transformation is the ultimate purpose of Revelation.

OBSTACLE NUMBER 3: RESPONSE

> **Blessed is he who reads and those who hear** the words of the prophecy, **and heed** the things which are written in it; for the time is near.
> —*REVELATION 1:3*

The book of Revelation is meant to be a blessing to those who read, understand, *and heed its message.* If we read with the wrong focus (the first obstacle) we won't properly understand the purpose of the message (the second obstacle), and then we're unlikely to respond—or heed—in a way that leads to the promised blessing. If our focus is the antichrist, or war, or famine, or great tribulation, then any attempt to respond will be defiled by fear, and we will miss the mark by preparing for survival or some other lesser thing.

On the other hand, if our focus is the Unveiling of Jesus, our response will be one of growing passion, and an increasingly purified, emancipated, and overcoming love. That is because the blessing of heeding the book of Revelation is not survival, or protection, or escape. As we will see, the blessing is getting to experience the Unveiling, and that means the complete transformation of all things, first in us, and then through us.

People get too hung up on when the book of Revelation will come to pass, or looking through history to find if any events have already transpired. This isn't wrong, but let's not miss the main point:

> The Revelation of Jesus Christ, which God gave Him to show to His bondservants, **the things which must soon take place ...**
> —*REVELATION 1:1*

> Blessed is he who reads and those who hear the words of the prophecy, and heed the things which are written in it; **for the time is near.**
> —*REVELATION 1:3*

Although these words were written almost two thousand years ago, the time was near then and the time is near now. The time is always near because it is an active invitation to participate with Jesus in His Unveiling, and thereby bring it to pass:

> Since all these things are to be destroyed in this way, what sort of people ought you to be in holy conduct and godliness, **looking for and hastening the coming of the day of God ...**
> —*2 PETER 3:11-12*

Will we be the generation that receives the blessing of heeding Christ's Unveiling? Will we hasten the coming of the day of God? What that means and how we do that will become clearer as we move forward. For now, let's take a quick look at the end of the book to see what the right response looks like. Don't worry, this sneak peek is spoiler-free:

> The Spirit and the bride say, "Come." And let the one who
> hears say, "Come." And let the one who is thirsty come; let
> the one who wishes take the water of life without cost.
> —*REVELATION 22:17*

At the end of the book of Revelation, there is no fear or interceding for mercy. The bond-servants—seen now as a passionate Bride—are energized and yearning for the events of Revelation to transpire. When they cried out, "Come!" it was not only a reference to the physical return of Jesus, but also an invitation to all those who are thirsty to come and partake freely of the water of life that is contained in the message of Jesus' unveiling. In other words, the Bride had experienced the unveiling of Jesus and was now fully participating in it!

INVOCATION

Father, before we embark on this journey we ask you to clear away the ideas and assumptions, the fears and misconceptions, and anything else that limits our view or hinders our focus. We want to hear, to understand, to respond, and to participate in the unveiling of Jesus. Amen.

CHAPTER 2

ORIENTATION

or - "Which way is up?!"

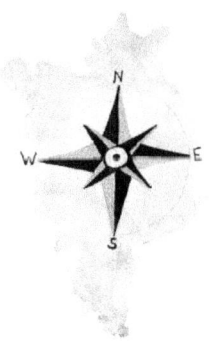

N ow that we have an uncluttered view of the forest edge, let's take a moment to get our bearings. Where are we? Where are we going? How do we get there? Answering these questions will clear our mind to see the ancient entrance hidden in plain sight.

Fortunately, God has provided a map for directions. And what a map it is! This is no ordinary, static document. It resembles a tapestry with living colors and intricate textures that reflect the glorious themes of His journey. The journey is the Unveiling, and its map is fashioned from materials as mysterious as the book of Revelation and as exotic as the Song of Solomon, with each thread perfectly woven to draw us down the path with breathless anticipation.

This map will reveal the entrance and guide every step of our journey, but first, we need to find our current position. It would be utterly foolish to get lost before we start just because we're holding the map upside down or backward. Our orientation begins with a familiar verse from the writer of the book of Revelation:

> See how great a love the Father has bestowed on us, that we should be called children of God; and such we are. For this reason the world does not know us, because it did not know Him. Beloved, now we are children of God, and it has not appeared as yet what we will be. **We know that when He appears, we will be like Him, because we will see Him just as He is.** And everyone who has this hope fixed on Him purifies himself, just as He is pure.
> —*1 JOHN 3:1-3*

Simple, concise, and powerful. Like the cardinal points on a map, John's statement provides the necessary orientation for understanding the Unveiling.

WHERE ARE WE?

We *are* loved by the Father. We *are* children of God. Yes, those are elementary truths, but like the point on a map that says "you are here," these simple truths provide essential bearings for every subsequent step. We must be grounded in the love of the Father before we begin. We *must* see how great a love He has given to us as His children, regardless of what we have done, or are doing, or will do. Our entire journey is an expression of His love, and every signpost, every event, every blessing, every detour, opposition, and apparent distraction must be viewed from the perspective of the Father's love, or we will depart from the path and fall short of our destination.

As a point of reference, consider the sequence modeled by Jesus:

> Immediately coming up out of the water, He saw the heavens opening, and the Spirit like a dove descending upon Him; and a voice came out of the heavens: "You are My beloved Son, in You I am well-pleased."
> —Mark 1:10-11

This proclamation of the Father's love was spoken for Jesus' benefit before He began His earthly ministry. If Jesus Himself needed to hear this in a dramatic, unmistakable fashion, how much more should this be the foundation of our journey?

That Jesus was called "My beloved *Son*" at that time and not "My beloved *Child*" is a distinction that will take on enormous significance in the coming chapters. But even now, at the beginning of our journey, take a moment to marvel at the fact that we *start* as children of God and go from there. *Now* we are children of God. That free gift of ultimate acceptance before we've done a single thing to deserve it is fundamentally simple and unfathomably immense. And in both of those ways, it is the perfect seed of what we will become. As a seed it contains raw, unpacked DNA yet looks nothing like the mature state. It contains the essence of what will come but not the final form.

The fact that we are called to a state beyond children does not subtract from the vastness of what it means to be children of God. We will spend our entire lives unpacking that truth, and the awe of its essence will remain with us for eternity. As beginnings go, that is mind-blowing! But there is something more. Children mature. In God's design, they eventually leave their father and mother and cleave to their spouse and the two become one flesh. Seeds grow. Eventually they no longer just consume resources for themselves but reproduce seed-bearing fruit of their own. Both of these analogies are at once appropriate and wholly inadequate to describe the journey we are on and the destination God has intended for us. This journey is a romance wrapped in a mystery, disguised as a tragedy before the foundation of the world.

> Our entire journey is an expression of His love, and every signpost, every event, every blessing, every detour, opposition, and apparent distraction must be viewed from the perspective of the Father's love, or we will depart from the path and fall short of our destination.

WHERE ARE WE GOING?

Or what will we become? John tantalizes with clues while maintaining the mystery: "It has not appeared as yet what we will be. We know that when He appears, we will be like Him ..." So, we don't know the exact form of what we will be because such a thing has never been fully seen and fully understood, but we do know that we will be like Jesus. Not *like* Jesus in the way that a picture of a person is *like* the actual person, but we will be *just like* Jesus. Just as He is. His journey will be our journey. His form will be our form. His essence will be our essence. That means we will eventually be like the glorified Christ, not just Christ as

> This journey is a romance wrapped in a mystery, disguised as a tragedy before the foundation of the world.

He was on earth, and we will follow His path to get there.

This is a massive theme that we'll revisit from multiple angles and reinforce with a plethora of examples from Scripture throughout this book. For now, as we focus on getting our bearings, it is important just to recognize that there is a call to something higher and that we are not there yet.

HOW DO WE GET THERE?

Or more fundamentally, do we need to *do* anything to get there? Does the destination come to us, or do we go to the destination? We've already seen that the book of Revelation requires a response (or a heeding), and John hints at the same: "When He appears we will be like Him, because we will see Him just as He is. And everyone who has this hope fixed on Him purifies himself, just as He is pure."

Wait, what?! These seem to be two competing concepts held in tension. On one hand, the catalyst for our transformation is "when He appears." That's not something we do; it's something Jesus does. His appearance is what transforms us. But then John turns around and puts the responsibility on us: "Everyone who has this hope fixed on Him purifies himself, just as He is pure."

So which is it? Obviously, the answer is both. His appearance transforms us, but we are only transformed as we see Him as He is. His appearance *will* happen, but it is not a foregone conclusion that we will see Him as He is when He appears, which is why the exhortation is to fix our hope on Him *now*, and thus embrace a process that progressively purifies our vision and prepares us for His appearing. The clear implication is that we must be engaged in the process or we will fall short of the goal:

Now, little children, abide in Him, so that when He appears, we may have confidence and not shrink away from Him in shame at His coming.
　　—1 JOHN 2:28

Therefore, do not throw away your confidence, which has a great reward. For you have need of endurance, so that when you have done the will of God, you may receive what was promised. For, "yet in a very little while, He who is coming will come, and will not delay. But My righteous one shall live by faith; and if he shrinks back, My soul has no pleasure in him." But we are not of those who shrink back to destruction, but of those who have faith to the preserving of the soul.
　　—HEBREWS 10:35-39

Again and again in Scripture there is a promise, a process, and a required response, and it is from that perspective that we will view our map. Whether these are new concepts to you or basic, foundational Christianity, I encourage you to move forward with an attitude of expectation and wonder. Intellectual assent does not transform any more than talking about a map gets us to our destination. These truths are invitations, and they require the response of intimate engagement and active participation.

Arriving at our ultimate destination is no certainty. We will always be children of God. That is already our essence. It was a free gift and it will never be rescinded. But maturity requires our free will to engage with God and His principles. And as we shall see, the principle of His appearing is not just a singular, one-time event, but rather a progressive unveiling that draws, and purifies, and prepares, and transforms. We will not arrive without the journey...

Oh look, there's the entrance straight ahead! Can you see it now?

CHAPTER 3

THE CRIMSON THREAD - PART 1

or - "Where do I focus?!"

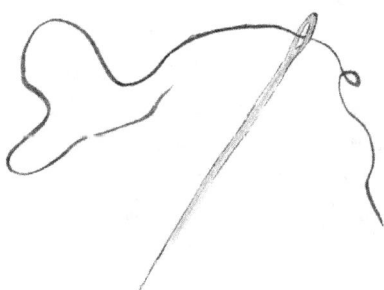

We finally see the entrance to the path ahead, and we're holding our map correctly. What's next? Now I want to draw your attention to one of the map's special features. See the border around the map's edge? Look closely. It's a single crimson thread that frames the entire journey.

Why does our map need such a peculiar border, you ask? Other materials may have worked, but only this crimson thread is grand enough to contain the full majesty of the Revelation of Jesus Christ. Without a frame, or worse, with the wrong frame, our ability to fully appreciate the map would suffer. And like any good frame, this one also sets the proper boundaries, accentuates the masterpiece, and focuses the eye where the artist intended.

In a moment we'll inspect those boundaries to better understand the enormous scope of our journey, but first, we need to familiarize ourselves with the nature and craftsmanship of the crimson thread itself.

What single thread could possibly frame Christ's Unveiling? The answer is found in a familiar passage:

> "The sower went out to sow his seed; and as he sowed, some fell beside the road, and it was trampled under foot and the birds of the air ate it up. Other seed fell on rocky soil, and as soon as it grew up, it withered away, because it had no moisture. Other seed fell among the thorns; and the thorns grew up with it and choked it out. Other seed fell into the good soil, and grew up, and produced a crop a hundred times as great." As He said these things, He would call out, "He who has ears to hear, let him hear."
>
> His disciples began questioning Him as to what this parable meant. And He said, **"To you it has been granted to know the mysteries of the kingdom of God,** but to the rest it is in parables, so that seeing they may not see, and hearing they may not understand. Now the parable is this: **the seed is the word of God.**
> —*LUKE 8:5-11*

The Parable of the Sower is a common sermon topic preached from many pulpits and Sunday school classrooms. The seed is the Word of God sown into human hearts to produce the fruit of the kingdom of God. It is a straightforward illustration with powerful implications for our daily lives, and yet beneath the surface hides a profound principle about the nature of God's plan for creation.

We typically think of the sower as Jesus and the seed as the gospel. Or, the sower is the Father, and the seed is the incarnated Christ. Both perspectives are true, but let's zoom way out and view this parable through a wider lens.

Jesus suggested that the Parable of the Sower was specifically designed to reveal the mysteries of His kingdom to His disciples. Sound familiar? It resembles the salutation of the book of Revelation: "The revelation of Jesus Christ, which God gave Him to show to His bond-servants, the things which must soon take place ..." In both cases, we have the Living Word—the very mystery of God Himself—revealing the principles and process that will lead to the life of God being fully manifested in us and through us. And that process started before the dawn of time.

What was the first clue Jesus gave for understanding the Parable of the Sower? "The seed is the word of God." Think about that for a minute. Think about what a seed is and what it does. Think about its lifecyle. Over the next few chapters we will unpack the spiritual significance of the lifecycle of a seed because the seed nature of the Word of God is the primary key to understanding the mysteries of the kingdom, all of which are hidden in Christ. Of course, Jesus *is* the Word of God, so the lifecycle of the seed is the perfect frame to view the masterpiece of Christ's Unveiling. This is because it speaks to the process of everything God planned to do, has done, is doing, and will do through Christ.

I realize we just switched from crimson threads to seed lifecycles, but that's okay. After all, they are metaphors for the same process. Just as the lifecycle of a seed goes from implantation to growth to outward fruit, so the crimson thread follows the many stages of God's seed—the Word—from eternity past to the end of time.

FOUR CORNER STAKES

With all of that in mind, we are now ready to follow the single crimson thread, which is the seed of the Word of God, around our map to see how it frames the entirety of God's eternal plan and culminates in Christ's Unveiling. This will be a long and winding road, so we'll start with an overview before jumping into the details.

To help us wrap our minds around this thread, imagine that we have unrolled our map and nailed it to a nearby oak tree. Each nail is like a tiny stake driven into the four corners of the map, just inside the borders of the crimson thread. The stakes provide maximum stability while we perform our inspection, and they also give us reference points for following the thread. If we imagine that each of these four stakes is also a scriptural truth that brings further shape and clarity to God's plan for His Seed, then we can use the stakes to easily trace the crimson thread around the map until we arrive back at the beginning with a full view of the frame.

Figure 1 provides a visual of this hypothetical construct to give the analogy footing in your mind:

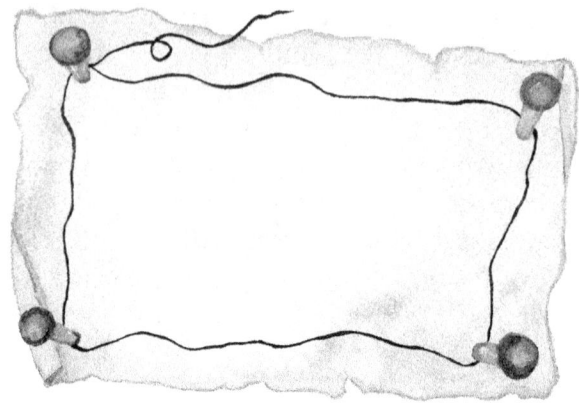

— Figure 1 —

As we move forward, I'll reference these stakes periodically to remind you what aspect of the seed we're discussing, but don't worry about remembering the names of the stakes. Just follow the logical path of the crimson thread and it will all come together in the end.

1ST STAKE - THE ORIGIN

The thread begins at our first stake, where the origin and DNA of the seed are established:

> In the beginning was the Word, and the Word was with God, and the Word was God. He was in the beginning with God. All things came into being through Him, and apart from Him nothing came into being that has come into being. In Him was life, and the life was the Light of men. The Light shines in the darkness, and the darkness did not comprehend it.
> —*JOHN 1:1-5*

Jesus was the initial seed sown at the dawn of creation. He was outside of creation, one with the Father and the Holy Spirit, and was then sown as the Word of God into creation, producing life, light, everything that came with it, and everything that came after. In every sense, creation was through Him and for Him. These truths are self-evident from the text, but have you ever wondered *why*? Why did the Father use the

Son (as the Word) to create everything? Why was it *through* Him? There were an infinite number of ways that God could have created the universe. Why follow this specific process? And more importantly, what does that choice tell us about God and His purpose? The answers to those questions begin to take shape as we follow the thread to the next stake.

2ND STAKE - THE PURPOSE

The second stake hints at the purpose of the seed:

> He is the image of the invisible God, the **firstborn of all creation**. For by Him all things were created, both in the heavens and on earth, visible and invisible, whether thrones or dominions or rulers or authorities—all things have been created through Him and for Him. He is before all things, and in Him all things hold together. He is also the head of the body, the church; and He is the beginning, the **firstborn from the dead,** so that He Himself will come to have first place in everything.
> —*COLOSSIANS 1:15-18*

In this passage, Jesus is described as the "firstborn" in two very different, yet related, contexts. He is the Firstborn of the original creation, and He is the Firstborn of the new creation. We'll unpack this concept in a later chapter because it has tremendous implications for the Unveiling. For now, just note that the idea of the firstborn is directly related to the lifecycle of a seed. Nothing is ever born that wasn't first sown as a seed. The fact that there is a *first*born implies that other offspring are meant to follow the pattern of the Firstborn.

We know from John 3:16 that Jesus is "the only begotten Son of God," meaning that He is the only divine seed sown directly by God, but this seed was meant to eventually bear the fruit of many other sons who will carry the same divine essence as the original seed. In that way, the title of firstborn springs out of Christ's role as the Word of God sown at the dawn of creation, and it implies that the initial seed had a goal beyond the first creation.

The seed of the Word of God went back to work after His inaugural seventh-day sabbath. That is why the Word of God is "living and active"

(Hebrews 4:12); "it is a lamp to our feet and a light to our path" (Psalm 119:105); and "it proceeds from the mouth of God and does not return without accomplishing its purpose" (Isaiah 55:11). All of these attributes signal that the Genesis creation story only represented the initial planting of the seed, and that the seed would have to germinate and grow until it formed the mature plant—that is to say, until the fullness of time when the Word took on human flesh as the incarnated Christ. Only then could the mature seed, the Word of God, plant Himself one final time as the seed of a brand new creation that contained the DNA of God's ultimate intention.

3RD STAKE - THE CATALYST

As the thread rounds the third stake, we find the catalyst that will unpack the seed's purpose:

> Truly, truly, I say to you, unless a grain of wheat falls into the earth and dies, it remains alone; but if it dies, it bears much fruit.
> —*JOHN 12:24*

Christ's earthly ministry and work on the cross were the crux of God's plan and the inflection point of eternity. By planting Himself in death He shed the shell of the first creation, and by rising again He became the root of a brand-new creation. But notice that the ultimate goal of a seed is not only to grow to maturity but also to bear fruit that contains more seed that can likewise grow to maturity. In other words, a seed is not meant to remain alone. And it is that aspect of the seed's lifecycle that best frames Christ's unveiling at the end of the age. Everything that transpires in the book of Revelation is the inevitable result of Jesus Christ, the mature root of the new creation, bringing forth fruit that contains His essence in the form of more seed.

4TH STAKE - THE FRUIT

The fourth and final stake contains an immense ocean of revelation about the seed nature of God's Word and His ultimate plan for creation, and it closes the loop by redirecting the thread back to the beginning:

But now Christ has been raised from the dead, the **first fruits of those who are asleep**. For since by a man came death, by a man also came the resurrection of the dead. For as in Adam all die, so also in Christ all will be made alive. But each in his own order: Christ the first fruits, after that those who are Christ's at His coming, then comes the end, when He hands over the kingdom to the God and Father, when He has abolished all rule and all authority and power.

For He must reign until He has put all His enemies under His feet. The last enemy that will be abolished is death. FOR HE HAS PUT ALL THINGS IN SUBJECTION UNDER HIS FEET. But when He says, "All things are put in subjection," it is evident that He is exempted who put all things in subjection to Him. When all things are subjected to Him, then the Son Himself also will be subjected to the One who subjected all things to Him, so that God may be all in all.
—*1 CORINTHIANS 15:20-28*

Similar in some ways to the title of Firstborn, the idea of first fruits is even more directly tied to the lifecycle of the seed, and as we'll see shortly, it all revolves around God's plan to no longer remain alone. The resurrected Christ is the first fruit of God's plan, the prime example of what the original seed sown at the dawn of creation was meant to produce. The rest of the fruit will come to maturity during the period of Christ's Unveiling. But even that is not the end of the plan.

While describing God's endgame, Paul mentions two fascinating and related concepts: "the last enemy that will be abolished is death," and "then the Son Himself also will be subjected to the One who subjected all things to Him, so that God may be all in all." Keep these phrases in the back of your mind as we move forward, letting them inspire questions. For in-

Everything that transpires in the book of Revelation is the inevitable result of Jesus Christ, the mature root of the new creation, bringing forth fruit that contains His essence in the form of more seed.

stance: Where did death come from? Why is it the last enemy? And what does it mean for God to be "all in all"?

A CLOSER LOOK

That was a ten-thousand-foot overview of the crimson thread's general shape. Now we need to bring it closer to better examine the texture. Settle in, get comfortable, and give yourself time to savor the intricate detail, the unparalleled craftsmanship, and the immense splendor God has wrought from such a simple material. The more we grasp the majesty of this frame, the clearer our perspective will grow for comprehending the map, and the greater our anticipation for the Unveiling will flourish.

Comfortable? Good, now let's go back to the start. John chapter 1 says, "In the beginning was the Word, and the Word was with God, and the Word was God." That was our first stake. But to understand its significance we need to go all the way back to the beginning—the familiar creation account in Genesis—to derive more clues about God's original motivation for planting, the field He chose, and the DNA of the seed Himself. All of these clues together will inform the pattern of the seed's lifecycle:

> In the beginning God created the heavens and the earth. The earth was formless and void, and darkness was over the surface of the deep, and the Spirit of God was moving over the surface of the waters. Then God said, "Let there be light"; and there was light.
> —GENESIS 1:1-3

"In the beginning God"—this opening phrase represents the motivation for everything that follows. Before creation, there was only God. In *The Divine Romance*, a book that has deeply influenced my perspective on this topic, Gene Edwards described God before creation as "the ALL." There was nothing outside of the Godhead in that time before all time and eternity, for He was everything. There were no heavens and earth, no hell, no good or evil. There was just the I AM. As far as we understand, He was Father, Son, and Holy Spirit, perfectly harmonious within every aspect of Himself, and yet alone. He was the Only. The One. Perhaps not lonely, but certainly alone. And though He wouldn't make it clear until the sixth day of creation, His prime motivation was to have a suitable companion—one who was outside of Himself. One who could both share His nature and help expand His kingdom beyond Himself.

THE BLANK CANVAS

"In the beginning God created"—from that place of aloneness, the I AM decided to create. The very concept of anything existing outside of the ALL was a necessary paradox with a singular solution: the Artist needed a blank canvas that existed outside of Himself if He was to create something that was not the I AM. He needed an arena for the process.

And so God stepped back, ever so slightly, creating a space for something other. The result was not so much a creation, but rather a void. A formless void. And in accordance with His intention, this void—this blank canvas of the deep—had no matter, or energy, or substance, or order of any kind. It was a paradox. It was darkness. It was chaos. It was empty, dimensionless nothingness. It wasn't even really a thing, any more than darkness is a thing. It was simply the absence of God, because it was the space from which He had temporarily receded.

This initial darkness was not yet good or evil, though it had the capacity to hold either. It had no will of its own, but its very existence represented the potential for free will, because it meant that there could be a will outside of God's will. And in that way, it was the perfect setting for God's masterpiece—the only backdrop against which He could form the type of companion He desired.

So the Artist brooded over His blank canvas, staring intently into the void, utterly unfazed by the emptiness. His nature absolute, His character immovable, His goodness inexorable, He prepared a statement that would reverberate into reality with all the colors of His essence.

SOWING THE SEED

And "then God said, 'Let there be LIGHT.'" He didn't just plant light as a seed; He planted His Word, and out of the Word sprang Light. He wasn't just sowing a concept or an idea; He was sowing the Son, Himself, His essence, His order, His life into the empty, orderless, lifeless canvas. And on this canvas, His Word would no longer be the only or the ALL, for His seed now existed alongside that which was not Him. This too was necessary.

His Word caused light to shine out of darkness, and that very act created the concept of good and evil. For the first time light and darkness existed, side-by-side, as two separate essences on the same canvas. And this contrast was another element essential for forming a suitable companion.

With light came everything necessary for light to exist in what would later become the heavenly and earthly realms of creation. This included time, space, the fundamental laws of science and nature, and all of the moral and spiritual principles that would govern the universe. All of these were expressions of the essence of the Word spoken onto the canvas of nothingness on the first day, and they too now stood in direct contrast to the essence of the void. As such, they formed the building blocks for the remaining days of creation and the foundation of God's plan.

So the Artist brooded over His blank canvas, staring intently into the void, utterly unfazed by the emptiness. His nature absolute, His character immovable, His goodness inexorable, He prepared a statement that would reverberate into reality with all the colors of His essence.

CHAPTER 4

THE CRIMSON THREAD - PART 2

or - "Alone for a reason"

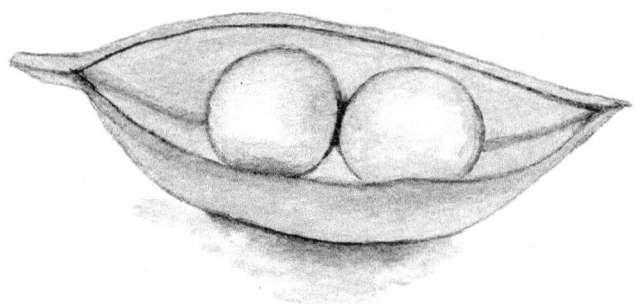

I f the first stake introduced the essence of the seed of the Word of God, the path of the thread around the second stake reveals the purpose and pattern of the seed's work. Remember our key verse:

> He is the image of the invisible God, the **firstborn of all creation**. For by Him all things were created, both in the heavens and on earth, visible and invisible, whether thrones or dominions or rulers or authorities—all things have been created through Him and for Him. He is before all things, and in Him all things hold together. He is also the head of the body, the church; and He is the beginning, the **firstborn from the dead,** so that He Himself will come to have first place in everything.
> —*COLOSSIANS 1:15-18*

I've already mentioned the concept of the firstborn, and we're not going to unpack it further in this chapter. Instead, I want to focus on the progression of the seed of the Word of God after the initial building blocks of creation were established on the first day. Each day of creation contains endless insights into His character and the nature of His plan, but in the interest of time, we are going to jump forward to the sixth day of creation where we find clues specific to His plan for the human race, who are the crown of His creation and the prototype for the companion He desires. And because there are so many facets of truth contained in these passages, we are going to narrow our focus even further by using the following verse as a lens:

> Nevertheless death reigned from Adam until Moses, even over those who had not sinned in the likeness of the offense of **Adam, who is a type of Him who was to come.**
> —*ROMANS 5:14*

Adam was a type, or shadow, of Jesus Christ. That means Adam's story bears a striking, though inexact, resemblance to Christ's story. Like a shadow approximates the caster, or a seedling hints at the essence of the mature plant, the pattern of Adam's life, pre-fall, portends the core attributes of Christ's nature and purpose.

The best way to understand God's ultimate plan for creation is to look directly at the life of Christ in the gospels, and we'll do plenty of that in later chapters, but the primordial drama surrounding the creation of Adam and Eve provides an uncluttered overview of God's plan that aligns perfectly with the frame of our map:

> Then the LORD God formed man of dust from the ground, and breathed into his nostrils the breath of life; and man became a living being. The LORD God planted a garden toward the east, in Eden; and there He placed the man whom He had formed.
> —*GENESIS 2:7-8*

> Then the LORD God took man and put him into the garden of Eden to cultivate it and keep it. The LORD God commanded the man, saying, "From any tree of the garden you may eat freely; but from the tree of the knowledge of good and evil you shall not eat, for in the day that you eat from it you will surely die."

> Then the LORD God said, "**It is not good for the man to be alone; I will make him a helper suitable for him**." Out of the ground the LORD God formed every beast of the field and every bird of the sky, and brought them to the man to see what he would call them; and whatever the man called a living creature, that was its name. The man gave names to all the cattle, and to the birds of the sky, and to every beast of the field, but for Adam there was not found a helper suitable for him.
> —*GENESIS 2:15-20*

"It is not good for man to be alone." Up until this point God had called each phase of His creation "good." Through the first six days, everything was exactly as He wanted, perfectly representing His will, congruent with His Word. Even in the middle of the sixth day, after creating all the beasts of the field, God saw that it was good. But then God created Adam and initially left him alone—a state that He explicitly stated was *not* good. Why?

Have you ever wondered why God created Adam first? Why not create Adam and Eve together and present them to each other? Would that have been "good"? Did God forget something? Did He change His mind? Was Adam flawed in some way? Was God simply establishing a gender hierarchy? No, there is a much deeper message in God's sequencing, and it has little to do with gender roles and nothing to do with male chauvinism.

To explain what I mean, I need to start by planting a few more seeds. The first is that the very nature of male and female predates the universe. Everything God creates is an expression of His own nature, and male and female are no exception. I'm not saying that God is both male and female in the sense of physical gender, but rather if

> The primordial drama surrounding the creation of Adam and Eve provides an uncluttered overview of God's plan that aligns perfectly with the frame of our map.

you boil down the essence of male and female to their fundamental ingredients, you'll find two sets of spiritual principles that have their origin in God's nature. In the simplest possible terms, it relates to the giving and receiving postures of God, though the crudeness of that description is inadequate.

Said another way, God designed true masculinity into His creation to reflect His giving, initiating, and building nature, and He designed true femininity to reflect His receiving, responding, and waiting nature. We'll return to this concept in a later chapter because it is a foundational element in the Unveiling of Jesus. For now, just keep in mind that male and female are equally important expressions of God's divine nature.

Second, we need to understand that Adam was created with both aspects of male and female in his essence. So was Eve. Yes, the physical expression of gender in their DNA was irrefutably binary: Adam's body was designed as an expression of maleness, and Eve's body was designed as an expression of femaleness. Their physical genders were genetically fixed by the Creator. But they were also triune beings created in the image of God, and as such their spirits carried both male and female expressions of God's nature:

> So God created man in His own image, in the image of God He created him; **male and female He created them.**
> —GENESIS 1:27

"Male and female He created them." That's a loaded statement with many facets and potential interpretations. We're not going to take the time to peel back all of its layers right now, but at the very least it suggests that Adam, who was created in the image of God, was created both male and female, even *before* Eve was formed. Again, I'm not talking about Adam's physical gender, nor am I suggesting human sexuality is fluid. I'm just saying that expressions of both male and female aspects of God's nature were deeply embedded in Adam from the beginning.

Please stick with me if you are struggling to follow my logic or if you find this unorthodox application of gender disconcerting. The rest of this chapter should clarify my intention. Recognizing the divine principles *behind* the concepts of male and female is vital to understanding God's sequencing, and it reveals something profound about the purpose and pattern of God's seed, of which Adam was a type.

ADAM'S ALONENESS

Back to the creation story. God created Adam and then left him alone just long enough to experience the depth and meaning of that aloneness. Why?

And why do this with Adam and not the rest of creation? There is no record of male coming before female with the animals. The fifth and sixth days of creation established a level playing field for God's expression of gender in the animal kingdom: male and female animals were created together, with separate yet complimentary functions that would have to join together to be fruitful and multiply. But with mankind, the physical male was explicitly created first and alone. Why?

Remember, God Himself was alone. Before creation, He was the ALL. He was perfect, complete, and in pure harmony within Himself, but He was alone in His uniqueness. There was nothing outside of Him, and He must have decided that it was not good. And that's what the whole drama of creation was about. That's why He conceived of the void and sowed Himself in seed form as the Word—the essence of the pre-incarnate Christ—into the nothingness. That is why six days of creation were made to build upon each other, finally culminating in the crown of His creation: a man formed in His image and likeness.

Adam was designed to represent God in His aloneness. He was created in God's image, and he too was perfect and complete in the sense that he was everything that he was supposed to be at that time. Yet in that place, Adam surveyed the earth and found nothing that matched him. He saw that every living thing was designed to reproduce, but nothing on earth was equal or compatible with his essence. There were myriad subordinate creatures designed for his rule, but nothing on his level. God was there as the Word, but God was wholly "other." God was spirit; Adam was flesh and bone *with* a spirit. God was divine, eternal, and higher in every way than Adam's temporal existence. Yes, Adam was designed for fellowship with God, but that fellowship was limited from the beginning by Adam's limits. In the deepest sense, Adam was alone. And that meant that God was still alone because despite being created in His image, Adam could not possibly be a suitable, compatible helper for the Word.

THE DIVINE DIVIDE

Not only was Adam alone, but he was also utterly incapable of fulfilling His original purpose as long as he remained alone. Think about God's command to mankind at the end of the sixth day:

> God blessed them; and God said to them, "Be fruitful and multiply, and fill the earth, and subdue it; and rule over the fish of the sea and over the birds of the sky and over every living thing that moves on the earth."
> —*GENESIS 1:28*

Adam and Eve were designed and commissioned first to reproduce, and then as their numbers grew, they were to learn how to take the order and beauty that God had instituted in the garden and replicate it throughout the untamed earth. In other words, they were made to extend the kingdom of God across the natural realm. It was a monumental calling.

Their ultimate purpose also went far beyond that original earthly mandate, but we won't get into that yet. For now just notice that in Adam's initial state, before Eve, there was no way for him to fulfill his original purpose, and this too was a reflection of the Divine condition—an intentional revelation of God's nature and plan so immensely important that He chose to sow it like a mystery into the very fabric of humanity at the dawn of creation. Through Adam, God was making a statement about Himself. Are you catching some of the ramifications yet?

I understand if some of this is difficult to accept. How could an infinite, omnipotent, omniscient God be alone? And how could He possibly need His own suitable companion to help Him experience fulfillment by being fruitful and multiplying? These are legitimate questions, but the answers should crystallize as we move forward with the story. God wasn't done foreshadowing, and His solution to Adam's predicament would become the silhouette of the Creator's glorious cosmic strategy.

THE CHASM CROSSED

God's plan required creating risk where none existed. To the outside observer, it would look like the most foolish gambit—an unspeakable, ill-advised mistake—but He was supremely confident that His Word would accomplish everything intended. Like a grandmaster playing seven-dimensional chess against a monkey, the outcome was never in doubt. Yes, there would be free will and adversity and an opponent to deal with, but these were essential variables in His desired endgame. And so without hesitation, knowing that it would not be understood until much later, God revealed the crux of His game plan with a peculiar omen:

> So the LORD God caused a deep sleep to fall upon the man, and he slept; then He took one of his ribs and closed up the flesh at that place. And the LORD God fashioned into a woman the rib which He had taken from the man, and brought her to the man.
>
> The man said, "This is now bone of my bones, and flesh of my flesh; she shall be called Woman, because she was taken out of Man."
>
> **For this cause a man shall leave his father and his mother, and shall cleave to his wife; and they shall become one flesh.**
> —GENESIS 2:21-24

Finally, Eve was created, not so much as something completely new and different, but as something carefully and intimately drawn from Adam's being. In a sense, Eve's essence had already existed within Adam; she just needed to be separated out. And it *was* a separation. Some might disagree, but I believe Adam was forever altered by this surgery. Eve was "taken from" Adam. The Hebrew word translated as rib also has the connotation of "side," as if to say that God took out one side of Adam and formed it into Eve. Before Eve, Adam was complete but had no way of fulfilling the commission that God intended to give to mankind because He had no way of being fruitful and multiplying to fill and subdue the earth. After the deep sleep, Adam could only fulfill his commission when he was side by side, con-

I n Adam's initial state, before Eve, there was no way for him to fulfill his original purpose, and this too was a reflection of the Divine condition...

nected, and united with Eve. This too was an intentional picture of God's own situation.

Of course, God could have formed both Adam and Eve from the dust at the same time and breathed into both of their nostrils the breath of life. It certainly would have been simpler, easier, and less messy. Why choose this specific method? There must have been more to it than simply illustrating His own aloneness. Why the incremental process, and the deep sleep and surgery? Why all the drama?

Perhaps one simple reason is this: If God had created both Adam and Eve as separate beings from the beginning, there would be nothing to draw them together beyond the utility of fulfilling their commission. They would both be free-will beings with separate origins and nothing inherent to unite them. Sure, they could have chosen to work together, and even to procreate together, but God's goal was that Adam would cleave to His wife and the two would "become one flesh." This meant so much more than just procreation. They were meant to be a part of each other, sharing the same essence, and therefore forever drawn back together, to complete each other, and to become whole through the unity of diversity. Separate but one by design *and* choice. Two separate free wills perfectly united through self-sacrificial love. And this too was a shadow of God's ultimate plan for creation. In this act of drawing one from the other, the Creator was not only solving Adam's aloneness, but He was also previewing the process and principle He would use to solve His own aloneness. He was alluding to the objective of His seed.

FREE TO BECOME ONE

Adam had to fall into a deep sleep before Eve could be pulled from his essence, and when he awoke, Eve was presented to him as the only thing in the universe with whom he could become one flesh. This, of course, is a picture of Christ having to pass through death so that the Church could be pulled from His side. But notice the specific sequence of Eve's formation:

> So the LORD God caused a deep sleep to fall upon the man, and he slept; then He took one of his ribs and closed up the flesh at that place. The LORD God fashioned into a

woman the rib which He had taken from the man, and brought her to the man.
—GENESIS 2:21-22

First, there was the deep sleep. Then the removal of the rib. Then God closed up the flesh. Then He fashioned Eve from the rib. Only then did He bring her to Adam. This all suggests that Adam's deep sleep only lasted long enough for God to remove the rib and close up the flesh. It seems that, at this point, God formed Eve somewhere far enough away from Adam that He would then have to bring her to Adam when the job was done. Why does this matter? It means that the fashioning of Eve was a process—perhaps a lengthy one—that was sequentially separate from Adam's sleep.

The fashioning of Christ's suitable companion is also a process that started after His resurrection and is still ongoing. Even now the Body of Christ is being formed into a compatible helper—a pure and spotless Bride—but there will eventually come a time when the fashioning is complete. Only then will we be presented to Jesus perfect and complete, ready to become one spiritual flesh with the Creator. That is part of the mystery that Paul referred to in his famous statement about marriage:

> So husbands ought also to love their own wives as their own bodies. He who loves his own wife loves himself; for no one ever hated his own flesh, but nourishes and cherishes it, just as Christ also does the church, because we are members of His body. FOR THIS CAUSE A MAN SHALL LEAVE HIS FATHER AND HIS MOTHER, AND SHALL CLEAVE TO HIS WIFE; AND THEY SHALL BECOME ONE FLESH. This mystery is great; but I am speaking with reference to Christ and the church.
> —EPHESIANS 5:28-32

Remember what Adam said when he first saw Eve: "Bone of my bones and flesh of my flesh!" This statement is so deep, with implications so stunning that we'll have to wait until we get deeper into the book of Revelation to fully unpack it. The creation of a suitable companion is one of the central themes of Revelation because the unveiling of the Bride of Christ is fundamental to the unveiling of Jesus Himself. Some aspects of Christ can only be seen through His suitable companion. And that was God's goal all along. All of creation—the formless void, free will, death, heaven and earth, good and evil, angels and demons, sin—they were all essential, inevitable elements for bringing forth a Bride *from* and *for* the Son; not just so that God will no longer be alone, but also so that His Word can fulfill His ultimate purpose.

> The creation of a suitable companion is one of the central themes of Revelation because the unveiling of the Bride of Christ is fundamental to the unveiling of Jesus Himself.

If you're anything like me, you may be wondering why God would have to go through any kind of drama to find a suitable companion, let alone fulfill His self-appointed purpose for being. Couldn't He just snap His fingers and create one? Or say the word and make it so? I think He probably could if He wanted a robot. But without the void of something outside of God, without separating light from darkness and the resulting concepts of good and evil, there could be no exercise of free will. And without these things, any companion would essentially be a robot or a slave. Certainly not a counterpart to share in and increase His rule. Freedom is an essential part of God's essence, so a suitable helper must be of like kind *and* free.

He also wasn't interested in creating another "big-G" God—if such a thing is even logically possible. Can the uncreated Creator even create *another* uncreated Creator? Perhaps that is another reason why Adam had to be formed before Eve. Regardless, His goal was a suitable companion—a helper derived from His essence—separate, compatible, and free to be drawn to Him like an inseparable lover, so that the two could willingly become one flesh. And like Eve, this companion was meant to be a joint heir that would not only reflect His divine nature but also reveal the most beautiful aspects of His essence—aspects that would have otherwise remained internal, inaccessible, and hidden from the world!

CHAPTER 5

THE CRIMSON THREAD - PART 3

or - "An impossible, inevitable endgame"

So what exactly is God's ultimate purpose, beyond forming a Bride? We've already alluded to the idea that God desired to express His nature outside of Himself, and we've seen that desire echoed in His command to Adam and Eve to be fruitful and multiply, to fill the earth and subdue it. But what is God's endgame? Where is it all leading, and how do we get there?

The answers will come into view as we follow the crimson thread around our third and fourth stakes. Remember, in the last two chapters, we unrolled our map and staked it to a tree before tracing the thread around the first two stakes. These are mere contrivances to anchor the major themes of God's master plan around the allegorical map we are building. The one that will help us chart a course through the book of Revelation. But if you are finding it too abstract or cumbersome to trace an imaginary crimson thread around four hypothetical stakes, please don't get too hung up on the metaphor. Just focus on following the path of the seed of the Word of God from beginning to end as we continue to follow it through the Scriptures.

Now let's pick up our thread at the third stake by returning to the original concept of the seed because therein lies the principle that God is using to derive His companion and to fulfill His purpose to become fruitful and multiply His kingdom:

> Truly, truly, I say to you, unless a grain of wheat falls into the earth and dies, it remains alone; but if it dies, it bears much fruit.
> —*JOHN 12:24*

Before we unpack one of the underlying principles of this verse, let's acknowledge the most obvious implication. If you think of Jesus before the crucifixion as a seed representing pre-fallen Adam, then Christ's death on the cross was the action that caused this seed to be planted into the earth. When He rose from the dead with His resurrected "new creation" body, it was as if the seed had shed its original form and finally reached its full potential as the mature tree.

That is why Scripture refers to the resurrected Christ as both "the second man and the last Adam" (1 Corinthians 15:45-47). He represents what humanity was always destined to become: the ultimate summation of the spiritual and natural into the perfect blend of divinity and humanity. And although His resurrection also provided the rib from which His suitable helper would be formed, there remains a process of fashioning that is now almost two thousand years in the making.

That was the obvious part. Now let's go a bit deeper to understand the catalytic mechanism of death described in this verse. Yes, new life springs from death, but the question often ignored is why? Why was death a necessary instrument for deriving His suitable companion? We can't just say "because of sin." Yes, sin entered the world through one man, and death through sin (Romans 5:12). Yes, the wages of sin is death, and therefore Christ had to die on the cross to atone for the sin of humanity, but the seed nature of the Word of God is a fundamental principle of the universe that preceded those things. So we need to look further back. Why did God design the seed to require a type of death before reproduction? More importantly, why did God initiate creation by planting His Word as a seed, therefore requiring the universe to follow the principle of the seed to reach maturity? The answer to that question is the substance of the crimson thread, and it is a profound statement about the nature of reality and the very essence of God Himself.

DEATH ON PURPOSE

Look again at Christ's statement about the grain of wheat: *unless* a grain of wheat falls … but *if* it dies, it bears much fruit. At the statement's core is a simple "if/then" statement of choice that harkens back to the dawn of creation. Choice is key here. Before the beginning, God decided that *if* He didn't want to remain alone, *then* He would have to make room for free will and something other than Himself to exist. In other words, if He wanted a companion, then there would first have to be self-sacrifice.

With that choice, God was establishing the required ingredients for the One to become two: He would voluntarily restrain His sovereignty to make room for a suitable companion with her own free will. There was no other way that was congruent with His nature. It was a magnificent demonstration of self-sacrifice born out of perfect love. And out of that decision, the void was formed.

Some may find this concept controversial, but I see no way around it: God chose to limit His own sovereignty. His essence outside of creation remained undiminished, but within the context of the blank canvas that would contain creation, room had to be made for free will that could violate His own.

At its heart, the principle of the seed is all about free will. To be clear, when I talk about free will, I am referring to our ability to *have* a will that is separate and autonomous from God's will, not our ability to *act* on that will. We don't always have freedom to *do*, but we always have freedom to *will*. Solomon described it this way:

> A man's heart plans his way, but the LORD directs his steps.
> —*PROVERBS 16:9 (NKJV)*

God did not abandon His sovereignty when He gifted mankind with free will, but He was agreeing to factor the free will choices of others into the execution of His sovereign plan. It was an impossible challenge that only His character could surmount. Like a maestro skillfully weaving a symphony of unimaginable complexity and singular beauty from the discordant melodies and mistuned instruments of a billion unskilled musicians intent on marching to their own rhythm, He was willing to embrace temporary chaos for an opportunity to manifest the full glory of His transcendent nature.

And the formless, lifeless void was the key. It represented both the potential and risk of free will. It is debatable whether the void itself was initially evil, but it certainly implied the possibility of death and darkness because it was, by design, separate from God's life and light. It was no accident that creation began with God speaking the seed of His Word into this void. His Word is the expression of His will, and so His Word would enter the void, wrestle with it, and form from it the building blocks of our reality. He was not afraid to embrace the risk, trusting His Word to demonstrate the perfect immutability of His divine character in the most anti-God environment possible.

By starting with the formless void, God was able to personally demonstrate the type of character and choices that it would take to exercise free will in a life-giving, abundant, productive way. This was imperative because He knew that free will exercised in any way that was incongruent with His character could only produce the discord of death instead of harmonious life.

This is an immensely important point that warrants exposition because many Christians have a fundamentally flawed view of God's sovereignty. One which has led to a basic misunderstanding of God's heart, especially as it relates to what it means for us to submit ourselves to God's will. As a natural result, some have developed unbalanced and destructive doctrines about many other kinds of submission described in the Bible, misconstruing what it really means for Christians to submit to their leaders, or for wives to submit to their husbands, or just about any other relationship where the Bible ostensibly commands one will to be subject to another.

I offer a few simple questions that capture the heart of my perspective: Why would God give mankind free will if He was just going to turn around and demand that we submit every choice to Him? Is that free will, or is that merely the *illusion* of free will? Does He really want to dictate our choices? And did He really design any other human relationship to dictate our choices?

OBEDIENCE AND INITIATIVE

These questions are pertinent and practical and transcend mere philosophical debate. We must wrestle with God's purpose and plan for human free will if we are to overcome in the days ahead and experience the transforming power of Christ's Unveiling. To that end, rather than trying to provide definitive answers to some of life's deepest questions, I invite your spirit to ruminate on the subject of God's intention for human will through the simple lens of parenthood.

A good parent gives clear and firm instructions to a young child on a variety of topics: How to make the bed. How to load the dishwasher. How to cross the street safely. Take these piano lessons. Do your math homework before playing video games. Standard stuff, right? But what kind of parent plans out every detail of their child's play time? At 9 A.M. you'll build this cabin from these Lincoln Logs; at 10:15 A.M. you'll draw a horse in a field with burnt sienna, pacific blue, and fern green crayons; at 10:45 A.M. we'll play Go Fish together, and you're only allowed to ask me if I have a three, a five, or a seven in that order.

Too outlandish? Then what kind of parent dictates their high school graduate's college choices, demands they follow a particular career path, or arranges their marriage to a spouse of the parent's choice?

Ridiculous, right?! Most people would recoil at the thought of such unhealthy and abusive control. We intuitively understand that good parenting is the art of progressively reducing the force of our own will and influence so that the child can grow in self-discovery, creativity, and maturity. We provide bright safety guidelines that recede over time. Great parents purposefully introduce age-appropriate amounts of risk into the child's life to encourage initiative, not stifle it.

Doesn't our Heavenly Father do the same? He is not an insecure helicopter parent hovering nearby out of fear for our safety. Neither does He need the validation of our obedience and good behavior. He is a wise Father

> Why would God give mankind free will if He was just going to turn around and demand that we submit every choice to Him? Is that free will, or is that merely the *illusion* of free will?

who knows the power of adversity to grow us up. He's not looking to dictate our every move, because our obedience is not His end goal. The more mature we grow, the less clear and specific His instructions become. Submission to God's will is more about alignment with His principles than being led around by the hand like a little child.

Each of us has areas in our life where God still needs to be highly directive to protect us from our immaturity and naïveté. And when He presents us with new "age-appropriate" challenges, clearer instructions are sometimes necessary. Sometimes those instructions come in the form of communication, and sometimes they come in the form of walls and gates and obstacles that protect or silently direct. But always His goal is to legitimize our identity as sons in the mold of the Firstborn rather than reinforce a position of slavery. We are meant to grow up in all areas so that we don't require constant intervention or instruction to be fruitful. The Father is not afraid of our initiative. His greatest joy comes from seeing our creativity unleashed within the frame of His design.

Following the leading of the Holy Spirit in submission to God's will is not about compliance with some predetermined set of instructions meant to control our choices and determine our actions. It's about learning His heart, understanding His nature, seeing His character, and then being conformed to that character over time as we attempt to emulate Him through the trials and tribulations of life. And He gives wide latitude for our free will to learn that kind of obedience within the framework of circumstances that He faithfully orchestrates for our benefit. He's not looking for people who do what they are told. He's looking for people who want to know Him and be like Him. That is the foundation for the highest expressions of free will that bring Him the greatest pleasure.

Isn't that the example Christ gave us?

> Therefore Jesus answered and was saying to them, "Truly, truly, I say to you, the Son can do nothing of Himself, unless it is something He sees the Father doing; for whatever the Father does, these things the Son also does in the same way.
> —*JOHN 5:19*

All that the Father gives Me will come to Me, and the one who comes to Me I will certainly not cast out. For I have come down from heaven, not to do My own will, but the will of Him who sent Me. This is the will of Him who sent Me, that of all that He has given Me I lose nothing, but raise it up on the last day. For this is the will of My Father, that everyone who beholds the Son and believes in Him will have eternal life, and I Myself will raise him up on the last day."
—JOHN 6:37-40

Despite what I thought when I was a younger and more insecure man still searching for the approval of a father figure, this verse is not saying that Jesus did everything that the Father told Him to do and nothing without the Father telling Him to do it. Jesus did come to the earth to do the will of the Father, and He did execute that will perfectly, but not as a child led by the hand. He was a mature Son who had already submitted His character to the Father's discipline through the trials and difficulties of life.

> He's not looking to dictate our every move, because our obedience is not His end goal. The more mature we grow, the less clear and specific His instructions become.

The writer of Hebrews tells us that He "learned obedience from the things which He suffered" (Heb. 5:8). By the time Jesus started His public ministry, He was so intimately acquainted with the Father's nature that He could walk into any situation and intuitively know the Father's heart and general perspective. He was free of the illusion that there was any better, more effective, or more desirable way than alignment with the Father's nature. From that broad position of confidence, He was empowered to exercise unrestrained creativity because His initiative would naturally fit within the frame of the Father's will.

Of course one of the prerequisites for walking in *mature* sonship is understanding the general shape of the Father's plan for our lives. Each one of us is designed for a certain set of good works that accentuates a particular aspect of the Father's nature. Jesus knew why He was sent to earth. In the broadest possible terms, Christ came to earth to reveal the heart of the Father. He is the image of the invisible God, and as the only begotten Son, He was the only One who could perfectly and fully reveal *all* of the Father's nature. That is why He said, "For whatever the Father does, these things the Son also does in the same way." Within the general frame of that purpose, there were many good works that just naturally flowed out of the abundance of the Son's heart, and I expect there were also some tasks that the Father asked the Son to perform in a specific way at a specific time. In all cases, the Son was fully synchronized with the Father's will.

Think about the fact that Jesus fulfilled every Old Testament prophecy to perfection. His life is a fulfillment of all the law and the prophets on more levels than we can possibly comprehend. Every type, every shadow, every allusion, every overt prophecy, every "jot and tittle," from thousands of years worth of Old Testament writings all realized to perfection in the life of Christ. Now, do you think Jesus walked around consciously aware of every single prophetic fulfillment happening in His life in real-time? Perhaps. He is the living Word of God, so it's not impossible. But did He walk around making conscious decisions to process every facet of every detail of every variable that was happening to Him at every moment through the filter of some running commentary that He was receiving from the Father to perfectly fulfill a list of ancient prophecies? I don't think so. There's a simpler explanation that doesn't require a micromanaging God frenetically checking boxes on a task list of obedience—an explanation in which the Father is not a helicopter parent.

Jesus didn't need to *try* to fulfill the Old Testament prophecies. Those prophecies were about Him. They came from men and women who tapped into the spirit of prophecy, which is the testimony of Jesus (see Revelation 19:10). In various ways, they saw what He would do centuries and millennia before He did it; When His time came, He simply did what came naturally to Him as a mature Son seeking to emulate His Father, and the natural result was the fulfillment of Scripture. Our lives should be similar.

> For all who are being led by the Spirit of God, these are the
> sons of God.
> —*ROMANS 8:14*

Submission to God's will is less about following a list of orders than it is about longing for His nature, seeing His character, and reflecting His essence. If God gives explicit instructions, then obviously we should follow them, but those scenarios should be the exception rather than the rule. In my experience, when the Holy Spirit wants to influence my steps in a direction I wouldn't have naturally walked on my own, He leaves breadcrumbs—often hidden, frequently more subjective than I'd like—as invitations that still require the creative exercise of free will to follow. And I think that is what it really looks like for sons to be led by the Spirit of God.

So yes, by all means, we should desire to be completely and utterly submitted to our Creator. But ultimately, we submit to Him by doing what He designed us to do, which is to be like Him. And though that looks different for each person, the most fundamental expression of the Creator's nature is to creatively exercise our free will in selfless initiative that brings life and freedom to others.

FREE WILL PERFECTED

What does all of this have to do with the third stake of our frame? Again, it's all about free will. "Unless a grain of wheat falls into the earth and dies, it abides alone." Death is the necessary crucible for the perfection of human will. God did not create us as slaves, and He is certainly not trying to turn us into slaves now. God had to embrace sacrifice to create the idea of free will; then He had to become human to show what the perfect exercise of human will looks like; and then He had to embrace death as a human to close the impossible gap between human and divine character so that we could have a path to becoming suitable companions. A position that would allow us to exercise our gift of free will in ways that express God's nature and expand His authority throughout creation.

From our temporal human perspective, traumatized by the consequences of six thousand years worth of sin, it can be difficult to understand why God would choose something like death as the ultimate catalyst. If God designed the very fabric of the universe to support such massive risk, why didn't He better equip Adam and Eve right out of the gate to wield the responsibility of their free will? If the curse of death and the future of the human race rested on their ability to navigate a universe of choices with the grace and wisdom of the uncreated Creator, why did He create them in a state of innocent naïveté and then immediately present them with a test of the highest stakes? Was He setting them up to fail?

No, God wasn't setting Adam and Eve up to fail, nor did He want them to fail, but I suggest to you that perhaps *they had to fail.* There was no way for them *not* to fail. They were *destined* to fail simply because they were not God. They were made in His image but they did not possess His divine character and therefore could not possibly navigate a test of free will perfectly.

Stick with with me on this. If He was ever going to form a suitable companion, God had to give humanity the choice to either act like Him or not, even though He knew there was no way they could perfectly align their free will with His on their own. Why? Because they were not "born" with God's character.

Think about it: if God had created them from day one with the full database of experience, understanding, and wisdom necessary to make every choice from a position of perfect love rather than fear, selfishness, or any other lesser motivation whose origin was the void, then He would have been creating a pre-programmed robot. Yes, it would have removed the risk, but it would not have been the proper foundation for a suitable companion. And it would have been selfish on His part.

No, Adam and Eve had to start from zero in the character department. Zero is not evil, and it is much better than negative character, but it is an infinite distance from the righteousness of God's character. And since they were not God, Adam and Eve were destined to fall short in the exercise of their free will.

God always knew this was inevitable and that it would lead to the necessity of Christ's death. That was the plan all along. Christ's death was the inevitability factored into God's original choice to create on the canvas of the void. It was the only path that would allow Him to derive a suitable companion who was not only free but who also possessed the divine character to exercise that free will in perfect harmony with God.

That is why God's very first act of creation demonstrated the process of self-sacrifice that refines and perfects free will. In that one act, He established the principle of the seed and set the path for the future. It's not that He was experiencing death in that primordial moment, because death and darkness fled before His word. But by calling light from darkness He *was* writing the fundamental principle of new creation and embracing the necessity of Christ's eventual incarnation and death. In other words, the Word of God would need to experience death if He was to bear the fruit that would remedy God's aloneness. If you are familiar with C.S. Lewis's Chronicles of Narnia, you may recognize this principle as "the deeper magic from before the dawn of time."[2]

The incarnation and sacrifice of Christ were not some Plan B in response to mankind's sin. The Son of God was always going to have to fall into the earth and die. It was written into the fabric of the universe. There was no other way for God to derive a suitable, co-equal companion. A created thing could never be fully compatible with the otherness of the uncreated Creator. God's companion would have to be derived from His own side, formed from His own divine DNA, and pulled from His own sacrifice.

That means Adam was never the end goal; he was simply the raw material. Mankind was always destined to become the clay from which Jesus Christ would be formed as a human. We are the dust into which God eventually incarnated Himself as a human so that He could sacrifice Himself to become the seed of a brand new race of humans. When we first choose to accept Christ's death and resurrection on our behalf, we receive the imperishable seed of this new creation in our spirit. That seed is the free gift of His Spirit, the very DNA of the Living Word, and like all seeds, it is the prenatal version of what is to come—the promise of something much greater.

Again, it is all about choice. Free will is a pesky paradox, and that's why God concocted the entire universal drama of history—to perfect free will in His Bride. Free will is the most precious commodity given to us by God, but without His character we are hopelessly incapable of exercising it without destroying ourselves. And yet the potential it offers—the promise of becoming a suitable helper for the uncreated Creator—is so valuable that He was willing to allow us to tragically and utterly defile His gift in a way that would require His own death. His sacrifice not only redeems our disaster, but it also demonstrates the character traits that we must embrace to sanctify our own free will and make ourselves ready to become His Bride.

As we will see in future chapters, these character traits will never be more important than during the culminating years described in the book of Revelation. Just as Jesus learned obedience through the things that He suffered, the intense trials and tribulations at the end of the age are designed to shape the Body of Christ, like the hands of God performing those final, most glorious finishing touches while shaping Eve from Adam's rib. And like Jesus, obedience for the Body of Christ at that time will mean so much more than merely following orders.

> Adam was never the end goal; he was simply the raw material. Mankind was always destined to become the clay from which Jesus Christ would be formed as a human.

While the powers of darkness will be demanding absolute submission with unprecedented belligerence to create as many domesticated slaves and human robots as possible, the Spirit of Christ will be inviting a Bride to participate in her own divine forging process. He wants his Bride to become the liberated, courageous, creative, dangerous, and overcoming companion of the King. Depending on our responses, that divine forging process can either feel like the violent swings of a blacksmith or the tender leading of a dance partner.

As a partner, He is both a gentleman and a master instructor. He has already aced His own season of testing, so He understands that the process truly is like a dance, requiring both giving and receiving, resting and acting, waiting and motion, responding and initiating, pliability and backbone. He is adept at using the challenging rhythms of life to empower us with wisdom to synchronize with Him through all the steps.

CLOSING THE LOOP

And so we return to the thread of the seed as we round the fourth and final stake in our map. The seeds of the book of Revelation were planted in Genesis, and just as Eve was the closing act of creation before God's seventh-day rest, the final phases of the process He is using to fashion His Bride will be the culminating acts of history at the end of the age before the millennial reign of Christ. But, as we'll see when we get to the end of the book of Revelation, all of that is just the beginning of the story. After all, Adam and Eve were meant to come together for a purpose. They had a commission to accomplish: fill the earth and subdue it. So will it be with Christ and His Church, only their purpose extends beyond the natural boundaries of mankind's original commission, and it encompasses all of creation, both heaven and earth, spiritual and natural.

In that light, let's reread the passage associated with our fourth stake, where Paul closes the loop and ties the whole thing together:

> But now Christ has been raised from the dead, the first fruits of those who are asleep. For since by a man came death, by a man also came the resurrection of the dead. For as in Adam all die, so also in Christ all will be made alive. But each in his own order: **Christ the first fruits, after that those who are Christ's at His coming, then comes the end, when He hands over the kingdom to the God and Father, when He has abolished all rule and all authority and power.** For He must reign until He has put all His enemies under His feet. **The last enemy that will be abolished is death.** FOR HE HAS PUT ALL THINGS IN SUBJECTION UNDER HIS FEET. But when He says, "All things are put in subjection," it is evident that He is exempted who put all things in subjection to Him. **When all things are subjected to Him, then the Son Himself also will be subjected to the One who subjected all things to Him, so that God may be all in all.**
> —*1 CORINTHIANS 15:20-28*

Again, there is so much to digest here, but let's just focus on the progression. First, Christ became the first fruits of a new creation—also known as the last Adam (see 1 Corinthians 15:45)—during His earthly ministry. Next, His Bride, the Eve to His Adam, will be presented to Him at His second coming. Only after that can they together begin to fulfill the purpose of their union during the kingdom age of Christ's millennial reign. Adam and Eve failed in their commission to bring earth's ecology into alignment with the Garden of Eden. Christ and His Bride will succeed in bringing all things into alignment with the throne room of God, subjugating all heavenly and earthly authority and power to His Kingship.

The type of subjugation these verses are referring to isn't just about ruling over something. It's not about the domination of free will; it's first about removing the defilement, guilt, and shame of sin that separate creation from the Creator. And then it's about revealing the order and blessing of His principles so that all of creation can freely come into alignment with His divine character and nature.

Ephesians 1:10 describes this as "the summing up of all things in Christ, things in the heavens and things on the earth." It is the process of the King and His Bride being fruitful and multiplying, filling the heavens and the earth and subduing them. And just as the Bride learns obedience in subjugation to the King, becoming bone of His bone and flesh of His flesh as she learns to dance with the rhythms of His heart, the subjugation of all things during the kingdom age will follow the same pattern. Some with a willing heart will embrace the process, but those who choose the path of an enemy will be crushed underfoot. But in the end the entire universe will embrace Him and align with His divine nature.

Death is the final enemy that will be abolished at the very end of His millennial reign. Death is the essence of the void. Remember, the void was the first thing God formed as He stepped back to create a blank canvas for creation, and it will be the final thing abolished after all things have been summed up in Christ. After all, when the Bride has joined herself to Christ, and together they have completely multiplied His nature throughout creation, then death will have no more utility. And when He finally abolishes death and the void, then the entire heavens and earth will reflect the divine nature. Free will will be perfected, God's purpose will be fulfilled, all things will be elevated to congruence with His image, and God will be all in all. That is the crimson thread of God's Seed, and it forms a sublime frame through which the book of Revelation will release its most profound treasures.

While the powers of darkness will be demanding absolute submission with unprecedented belligerence to create as many domesticated slaves and human robots as possible, the Spirit of Christ will be inviting a Bride to participate in her own divine forging process.

CHAPTER 6

THE LEGEND - PART 1:
FRACTALS 101

or - "Haven't I seen this before?"

Now that the immensity of our map is properly framed, it's time to familiarize ourselves with its colors and markings so that they make sense later on when we encounter them in context. Think of these next few chapters as a legend that contains keys for unlocking deeper meaning on our journey. These aren't the only keys, but they are the ones we'll use early and most often.

I'm not suggesting that the Unveiling is complicated or reserved for the educated and sophisticated, but it *is* meant for the hungry and thirsty, for the desperate, for the persistent and unrelenting, for the insatiable lovers who won't be dissuaded by obstacles or mysteries or even the silences of God. Does that mean we must have all of these qualities before we embark? No! These qualities are essential, but they are imparted by the journey itself. So there *is* an entry requirement, but we meet it by setting our hearts on wanting to see Jesus, and then we grow from there. Now, let's go build that legend to help us better engage with His Unveiling.

PRINCIPLE PATTERNS

The keys of our legend are fun, mysterious, and often misunderstood. They are multicolored, multi-sided, and they unlock many doors. And while they may seem complex at first glance, they are as simple as a child's worldview. I'm not talking about hidden knowledge or mystical codes. The keys we are looking for unlock something much more useful than facts and information from the patterns and numbers of Revelation. They unlock transformative principles designed to grow us toward the ultimate goal.

Principles are fundamentally simple concepts that reflect the nature of the Word Himself, but the legend we build in these next few chapters to unlock those principles may at times seem challenging to understand, especially if these are new concepts for you. It

I'm not suggesting that the Unveiling is complicated or reserved for the educated and sophisticated, but it *is* meant for the hungry and thirsty, for the desperate, for the persistent and unrelenting, for the insatiable lovers who won't be dissuaded by obstacles or mysteries or even the silences of God.

doesn't help that the Western education system that many of us grew up with puts a premium on logic and empirical data *before* experience. Logic and data are important, but some things need to be *felt* in your spirit first, and then *experienced* with your soul before they can be grasped with the mind. Some truths require rumination, and rumination takes time. So please stick with me as we build out this legend. Give it time to marinate in your spirit if it doesn't immediately make sense in your mind. Your mind will eventually catch up with the logic, and the principles we encounter in the process will enlarge your ability to bask in the depth of God's plan and grow in awe of the amplitude of His love, rather than wasting time with fruitless debates about numerology.

Unlocking the numbers and patterns of the Unveiling starts with understanding the cyclical nature of the seed of God's Word. In a sense, all of history is nothing more than the lifecycle of this single seed. That's why we spent so much time in the last chapter unpacking the nature of the seed. But if we zoom in to specific periods of history, we can find the general pattern of the seed's lifecycle repeated in smaller ways, like microcosms of the whole. In this way, history is always repeating itself, as the seed of God's Word grows and matures and extends roots and branches in every direction. Certain branches and buds become visible at various points in time as they manifest attributes of the overall plant, but no single branch or bud is the fullness of the mature tree.

This also means that if we don't understand the endgame of the seed —or if we don't know what the mature plant looks like—we can easily mistake early stages of growth for the final state. Many have done this with the book of Revelation. They have found similarities between certain events in history and various prophecies in Revelation, and then wrongly assumed that those prophecies have therefore been fulfilled.

I have a different perspective. I believe the book of Revelation is always current in every time period, to every generation, not just because it tracks the growth of the original seed sown at the beginning, but because it is the Unveiling of Jesus that brings the seed to ultimate maturity. Remember, the book of Revelation is an invitation. Like a virtuous cycle, it is supposed to draw us in to see more of Jesus, which continually draws us closer to Him so that more of Him is revealed in us and through us. At some point, a generation of bondservants will fully heed its message and experience the ultimate fulfillment of God's Word. Until then, the seed continues to grow cyclically, manifesting in stronger and stronger ways throughout history, like dress rehearsals for the final performance.

Perceiving this cyclical nature of the seed is crucial for identifying and extracting life-giving principles from the patterns in Scripture. Some commentators refer to these biblical patterns as *fractals* because, like the fractals found in nature, they are divinely inspired, infinitely repeating, generally consistent at any level or context, and they reveal something profound about the nature of the Creator.

If the concept of a fractal feels abstract or strange to you, please feel free to think of a fractal as an elegant term for pattern. Why not just stick with the word *pattern* and avoid potential confusion or controversy? The answer is mostly semantics and personal preference. The idea of a pattern feels a bit flat and two-dimensional to me, while the idea of a fractal feels more textured and three-dimensional. Remember what I said about the difference between truth and principle? I see patterns as collections of truths (data and facts), while fractals are collections of principles intentionally organized by God to reveal aspects of His divine nature. Even so, I will sometimes use the terms interchangeably.

I encourage you to perform a simple internet search for "fractals in nature" to see how prevalent fractals are throughout every level of creation. These naturally occurring patterns have something to tell us about God, like fingerprints of His divine essence hidden in plain sight,

> The book of Revelation is always current in every time period, to every generation, not just because it tracks the growth of the original seed sown at the beginning, but because it is the Unveiling of Jesus that brings the seed to ultimate maturity.

inviting us to investigate and comprehend. If physical fractals can reveal the beauty of Jesus Christ, how much more can the fractals in God's Word?

Unpacking scriptural patterns to better understand God's character is an ancient yet underutilized method of biblical exegesis. Few have invested the time and discipline necessary to plumb the depths of these relatively uncharted waters. It's strange if you think about it. We naturally analyze the smallest details of a person's speech and behavior in search of patterns that might reveal their inner heart and motivation. Why do we so often fail to look as deeply into God's Word?

In face-to-face conversation, we observe facial expression, body language, tone, cadence, sequence, enunciation, and so many other variables in addition to just the words spoken. With the written word we must dig deeper, but given a large enough sample size, over a sufficient passage of time, across a wide range of circumstances, a person's character is similarly revealed in the pattern of their words. What words did they choose in that situation? Why did they use different language in this situation? What was going on when they painted with that analogy? Why did they repeat three times here, but seven times there? Such questions asked of God's Word can be a static search for more data points, or they can be a dynamic adventure to uncover the deepest motivations of His heart. It just depends on what we're looking for.

I only hope to scratch the surface of biblical fractals as we build out our map's legend in the next few chapters. Still, the general foundation for much of what I'm going to say about fractals can be traced to the pioneering work of other brave men and women who have already walked this path over years and decades. In some ways, I am standing on the shoulders of giants in this section, though I intend to apply these patterns and principles in some original and unique ways based on my study of the book of Revelation.

THE ORIGINAL FRACTAL

Let's start with the first fractal in Scripture, found in Genesis 1:1—In the beginning *God.* Everything starts with the One, and by showing us the One at the beginning, God was establishing a pattern. Yes, for our purposes, one is a pattern. And what does the fractal of one point to? Let's break it down from what we know of God at the beginning. I'll walk you through my logic here. When I think of God at the beginning, I think of the *start*, the *source*, the *all, completeness,* and of course, *alone-ness.* These are all aspects of the One derived from the first day of creation, and they speak to God's essence and deepest motivation for action.

The apostle John illuminated this fractal even further when He described God's essence and motivation with two of the most profound statements in Scripture that harken back to the One on the first day of creation:

> "God is light."— from 1 John 1:5
> "God is love."— from 1 John 4:16

Essence and motivation that lead to expression. We humans are motivated to act by various things that are not always congruent with the core desires of our spirit. Paul described this dynamic in Romans chapter 7 when he lamented, "Why do I do the very thing I don't want to do?" Not so with God. He is perfectly congruent in every way. His essence, motivation, and action are one.

What happened with God … the One? At a basic level, He initiated a process that would eventually lead to a companion derived from His essence—His Oneness—so that the two could willingly become One in unity. And then through that unity become fruitful and multiply, to fill the universe with His essence, and to subdue it. We could add or subtract details to build this out more, but I'm sure you get the idea. We see this pattern in Genesis 1:1, and again in Adam and Eve, in the parable of the sower, and of course with Jesus and the Church.

There are many other ways to language this fractal while emphasizing different facets of the One, but they should always revolve around the congruency between His essence, motivation, and action. For example, a simple description can be derived from the well-known principle of the seed: *the one (seed) is alone until it produces fruit after its own kind through a process of self-sacrifice.* This description emphasizes the process, catalyst, and result of a seed. A similar but more generic description could be something like: *the fractal of one separates into two equal and complimentary halves that multiply the essence of the original through intimacy.* Or we could form a less cumbersome statement that emphasizes God's motivation: *love compels the One to fashion a co-regent companion to extend His rule throughout the universe.* All three versions are enlightening in their way.

You may not have noticed at the time, but we relied heavily on the fractal of One to build the frame of our map in the last chapter. We started with the concept of the seed of the Word of God, stripped the concept down to its essential elements, and then applied it in various ways to the creation story, adding depth of texture to familiar information, while hopefully fanning the passion of our spirit. And that is the main goal of viewing Scripture through the lens of God's fractals.

Here is another example of the fractal of One that may be less obvious:

> "Hear, O Israel! The LORD is our God, **the LORD is one!** You shall love the LORD your God with all your heart and with all your soul and with all your might. These words, which I am commanding you today, shall be on your heart. You shall teach them diligently to your sons and shall talk of them when you sit in your house and when you walk by the way and when you lie down and when you rise up. You shall bind them as a sign on your hand and they shall be as frontals on your forehead. You shall write them on the doorposts of your house and on your gates.
> —*DEUTERONOMY 6:4-9*

The Lord is one! Common explanations for this proclamation include: There is only one God, Yahweh, the God of Israel. Or, the three members of the Trinity are one. Or, the Lord is to be first and primary in all things. These are all true and powerful statements, but what happens if we apply the fractal of One to this passage, leveraging the weight and texture of the scriptural pattern?

From that perspective, when God declares that He is one, in addition to everything else we commonly think about this verse, isn't He also purposefully drawing attention to His aloneness? And to His intention to remedy that situation through sacrifice? You know, just like a seed. And doesn't this verse also carry the distinct connotation of a God who longs for relationship? Who is alone but passionately engaged in the process of fashioning a Bride through whom He can extend His essence and motivation of light and love to the universe so that God (the One) may be all in all? And in this statement can't you hear Him longing for His covenant people to participate in the process? It is from that place that He commands, "You shall love the Lord your God with all your heart and with all your soul and with all your might." He wants the soil of our hearts to be soft and ready to receive the seed of the Word when He appears. Perhaps this is why Jesus called this verse "the great and foremost commandment" in Matthew 22:38. For those who have ears to hear, this verse is like a clarion call to the Bride to understand God's intention and to respond by making herself ready.

Before we move on, I want to leave you with a final example of the fractal of One that is particularly relevant to the Unveiling, only this time I'll provide the verse without commentary. Apply the pattern of One and see if it enhances your emotional connection with the verse:

> After these things I looked, and behold, a door standing open in heaven, and the first voice which I had heard, like the sound of a trumpet speaking with me, said, "Come up here, and I will show you what must take place after these things."
>
> Immediately I was in the Spirit; and behold, a throne was standing in heaven, and **One sitting on the throne**. And He who was sitting was like a jasper stone and a sardius in appearance; and there was a rainbow around the throne, like an emerald in appearance.
> —*REVELATION 4:1-3*

GIVING AND RECEIVING

Now let's take a brief look at another fractal to hone our pattern-building skills. The fractal of two naturally flows out of the fractal of one:

> In the beginning God created **the heavens and the earth**.
> —*GENESIS 1:1*

The first chapter of Genesis has numerous examples of this foundational fractal, and as you might expect, they all share and build upon a common theme. Heaven and earth, light and darkness, day and night, and of course male and female. In each case, the two parts are created through a process of separation. What else do these examples have in common?

If you distill each pair down to their most essential attributes, at the heart of this fractal is the expression of the giving and receiving nature of God. The exact syntax is less important than the idea itself since we're using contemporary language to describe abstract biblical principles. Alternate terminology, such as dominion and intimacy or work and rest, could also be used.

Each of these expressions of the fractal of two also aligns well with the male and female dynamic of the human body. The male body is primarily designed as an expression of the giving, the dominion, and the work aspects of God's nature. The female body is primarily designed as an expression of the receiving, the intimacy, and the rest aspects of God's nature.

Notice that I didn't say that men are designed for dominion while women are designed for intimacy. We are more than just physical bodies. Each of us are complex, multifaceted beings in the image of our Creator, and we are all designed to express some measure of both the male and female aspects of God's nature regardless of our physical template. The physical template we are born with is merely how God has chosen to visibly express the deep truths hidden in this aspect of His nature. And even our physical bodies are embedded with both examples of giving and receiving. It's just that on the whole, as a general template, the male body more exemplifies one side while the female body more exemplifies the other.

So women are also created for dominion, building, and giving, while men are also created for intimacy, resting, and receiving. Each of us moves through life in both modes, receiving and giving in our relationship with God and others. Sometimes we initiate on our own. Sometimes we wait and receive.

Arthur Burk of the Sapphire Leadership Group, a Christian research center that specializes in finding transformative principles in the patterns of Scripture, refers to this dynamic as a *dance* because of the skill and artistry required for us to synchronize with God's ebbs and flows. When is it appropriate to be still and wait on Him like a female Bride? When is it appropriate to move forward in faith to build His kingdom like a male son? Learning to dance with God is a never-ending process of trial and error, and it is one of the great honors He has bestowed upon mankind through the gift of free will. Giving and receiving. Dominion and intimacy. Building and being. Male and female. Keep this construct in the back of your mind as we move forward because it is integral to understanding the ebbs and flows of the Unveiling of Jesus Christ.

INCLUSIVE AND DISEMPOWERING

This is a good time to preemptively clarify some language that you'll find throughout this series. In later chapters, we will repeatedly refer to the concept of sonship. As I mentioned above, this term has nothing to do with physical gender. Sonship speaks of a particular aspect of our relationship and posture toward God and His creation, and it flows from the fractal of two. For this reason, when talking about sonship I am going to resist the temptation to use more inclusive language like "sons *and daughters.*"

I bring this up now to avoid confusion if you are verifying anything in this book along with your Bible. In recent years, some popular translations have updated their New Testament text to include more gender-inclusive terms, such as adding "and daughters," in places where the original Greek only says sons.

Ancient society was undoubtedly far more male-dominated than it is today. Viewed through our modern lens, ancient Jewish culture was particularly chauvinistic. God is not a male chauvinist, even if His people have been at times. I believe the modern movement toward female empowerment is a beautiful and necessary development that flows from God's heart to form a coequal partner, though the devil is doing his worst to twist and defile that movement to the detriment of both genders. The entire goal of the fractal of two—the purpose behind the division of male and female, evening and morning, Jew and Gentile, etc.—is to create the opportunity for unity through diversity, intimacy, and sacrifice, all of which are required for new life. In the end, all will be summed up in Jesus Christ, but to get there we need stronger and more liberated women who reflect every aspect of Christ's sonship in their spirit, soul, and body. We also need men who are sensitive enough to wait and listen and receive from Jesus Christ the Bridegroom, without being emasculated of the strength, initiative, and vigor of their sonship.

Having said that, it is perfectly appropriate for us to call ourselves sons and daughters of God based on our physical gender. We should celebrate and affirm God's design. Physical gender is part of that, though it is only one small aspect of who we are. It matters, and it colors many aspects of our personalities, but it is not the primary lens through which God views us (see Galatians 3:28). Neither should it be the primary lens through which we view ourselves or others.

We'll talk more about this later in the series when we unpack the resurrection, but consider that the purpose of physical gender is transcended when we receive spiritual bodies. Jesus taught that in the age to come, humans will be like angels in that they will not participate in marriage or procreation (see Matthew 22:30). Much of our life on earth revolves around our physical gender, but it is only a temporary construct pointing to deeper spiritual truths.

So when it comes to modifying Scripture to assuage our twenty-first-century sensibilities, let's be careful not to obfuscate the nature of Jesus Christ by missing the point of the God-breathed language. If His words were chosen for our teaching, rebuke, correction, and training in righteousness (see 2 Timothy 3:16), they are there for a reason. Let's honor God by leaning into His intentional use of specific gender imagery when the context indicates it matters. Doing otherwise is not only foolish, but it subtly insinuates some nefarious things about God's character. Deeper treasures are hidden in His choice of gender language—treasures revealing aspects of our design "in the image of God" that are eternal and transcend our physical gender. Understanding this eternal perspective will be equally important when we start unpacking the Church's female role as the Bride of Christ in book 2.

THE FRACTAL OF THREE

Back to fractals. One of the more easily accessible patterns in Scripture is the fractal of three. Many Christians understand and apply this fractal intuitively without even realizing it. The most obvious example is the Holy Trinity, the One who is three unique, distinct, harmonious, and inseparably intertwined persons: Father, Son, and Holy Spirit. If we were to unpack what we know about each member of the Trinity and then overlay that information onto other lists of three—like the spirit, soul, and body of a human, or the holy of holies, inner court, and outer court of the tabernacle—our understanding of each would be greatly enriched.

For a simple example, consider what the Tabernacle of Moses reveals about the internal nature of God. It was one tabernacle made up of three sections. The sections were not equal in size or function. It wasn't like a pie divided into three slices, but rather a section within a section within a section. Each section contributed to the overall purpose of the whole, but life flowed from the inside out to God's people, while God's people moved from the outside in for increasing levels of intimacy with God.

The Father corresponds to the holy of holies, the Son to the inner court, and the Holy Spirit to the outer court. From this perspective, we should view the Trinity as more than just three facets of God. In other words, the Godhead is not *only* three ways in which God has chosen to reveal Himself to us, or *just* three personalities of the One. The Father, Son, and Holy Spirit can also be understood as three sections of God. They are all linked, but they each have a different function, a different focus, and a different way of interacting with creation while working together for the ultimate purpose of establishing intimacy with mankind in a way that will end God's aloneness and propagate His nature.

I am only making general observations here, but this fractal still holds true if you zoom in on the details of each section of the tabernacle: the layout of the furniture, the measurements, the fabrics, the colors, and the materials all reveal deeper aspects of the Father, Son, and Holy Spirit within the context of the fractal of three.

There are many other fractals throughout Scripture, and each flows from the original fractal of One to create kaleidoscopic views into different aspects of God's nature and plan that unlock unique treasures on the journey of Christ's Unveiling. And each fractal is best used for understanding principles rather than forming theology out of data.

CHAPTER 7

THE LEGEND - PART 2:
THE ORIGIN OF SEVEN

or - "Beyond completion"

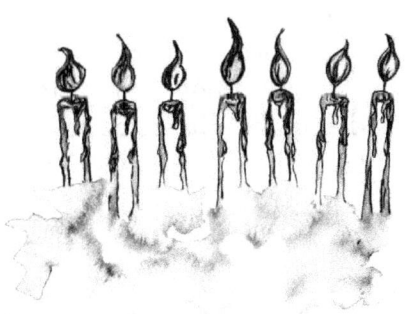

N ow we come to the fractal of seven. This one is my favorite because it unlocks so many unexpected, breathtaking layers within the Unveiling. In the first chapter of Revelation alone we see seven churches, seven golden lampstands, seven stars, and seven angels. Later we see seven spirits of God, seven eyes, seven lamps of fire, seven seals, seven trumpets, seven bowls, seven heads, seven mountains, and seven thunders. And those are just the obvious ones. There are so many sevens, and layers of sevens, you could almost say that the Revelation of Jesus Christ is built on the fractal of seven. And that's why it's not enough just to say that seven is the number of completion, or that seven is God's number—as if that means something useful for our journey.

There is an exhilarating and transformative reason for the sevens. Buckle up because this section might be a wild ride. As humans made in the image of God, the fractal of seven is woven into our very design, so don't worry if you find it both intuitive and unfathomable all at once— I often find myself standing somewhere in the tension between those two.

SEQUENTIAL STEPS FOR TRANSFORMATION

If the fractal of One explains God's desire to extend dominion through a co-regent companion, the fractal of seven reveals His method and process for creating that suitable companion. As with the seven days of creation, the order is especially important here. It represents a specific arrangement of seven aspects of God's essence revealed in His desired sequence. When the Master Artist paints Himself onto a blank canvas, every stroke is a curated revelation of His heart. And the revealing of that seven-fold essence is the very tool He uses to reproduce those attributes in His Bride and through His Bride into the rest of the universe. If that sounds like hyperbole, consider this basic principle of transformation:

> But we all, with unveiled face, beholding as in a mirror the glory of the Lord, are being transformed into the same image from glory to glory, just as from the Lord, the Spirit.
> —*2 CORINTHIANS 3:18*

This verse is familiar to many but often take it for granted. Yes, we know that we are transformed by the glory of the Lord. Yes, we know that our lives are supposed to go from "glory to glory," even if our day-to-day experience often falls so short of that lofty goal. But do we really understand the process that Paul is describing here?

We are transformed by seeing God's glory—that is, His essence—*as in a mirror*. A mirror is for looking at your own face, not someone else's. Likewise, we are not transformed by something external, or by striving to mimic something outside of ourselves. We are transformed by searching for, staring intently at, and unpacking the essence of God that is already in us through Jesus Christ.

If we are born again, He has already sown His essence into us. The more we fix our eyes on specifically identifying those aspects of Him that are already in us, the more the light of that glory shines through and transforms our spirit, soul, and body into His image. As we'll see in a moment, the fractal of seven acts as a prism to help us see the hidden beauty in God's light. That is why the fractal of seven features so prominently in the Unveiling.

The first time this fractal is seen in Scripture is with the seven days of creation, and as such, it is the clearest and

> When the Master Artist paints Himself onto a blank canvas, every stroke is a curated revelation of His heart.

richest portrayal. But before we go to Genesis, I want to focus on an example of the fractal of seven that predates even creation:

> John to the seven churches that are in Asia: Grace to you and peace, from Him who is and who was and who is to come, and from the **seven Spirits** who are before His throne,
> —*REVELATION 1:4*

> "To the angel of the church in Sardis write: He who has the **seven Spirits of God** and the seven stars, says this: 'I know your deeds, that you have a name that you are alive, but you are dead.
> —*REVELATION 3:1*

> Out of the throne come flashes of lightning and sounds and peals of thunder. And there were **seven lamps of fire** burning before the throne, which are the **seven Spirits of God**;
> —*REVELATION 4:5*

> And I saw between the throne (with the four living creatures) and the elders a Lamb standing, as if slain, having seven horns and **seven eyes, which are the seven Spirits of God**, sent out into all the earth.
> —*REVELATION 5:6*

These are just a few of the verses that refer to the seven Spirits of God. In two thousand years, the Church has developed a decent theology for understanding the Trinity, and many Christians rightly endeavor to know and experience relationships with all three members of the

Godhead, but how much focus has there been on the seven Spirits of God? I've heard some teachings but not many. Perhaps your mileage has varied. Either way, this is a topic that desperately needs unpacking, especially in light of the book of Revelation's reliance on the fractal of seven.

To that end, let's go back to John's introduction in Revelation, which paints an unambiguous picture of the seven spirits of God as synonymous with the Holy Spirit:

> John, to the seven churches in the province of Asia: Grace and peace to you from Him who is and was and is to come, and from the seven Spirits before His throne, and from Jesus Christ, the faithful witness, the firstborn from the dead, and the ruler of the kings of the earth.
> —*REVELATION 1:4-5*

Here John greets the seven churches in Asia with grace from the three members of the Holy Trinity, and in that greeting, the seven Spirits of God are seen in the role of the Holy Spirit. If you are not convinced by this single example, please just move forward with me as we explore the fractal of seven because I think the rest of this chapter will solidify the idea that the seven Spirits of God are an expression of the Holy Spirit, and therefore represent the origin of the pattern of seven.

LAMPS AND EYES

So what are the seven Spirits of God? In Revelation we see them as seven lamps of fire before the throne of God and as seven eyes of the Lamb that are sent out, or look out, into all the world. So they are lamps and eyes. It is no accident that these two concepts are linked together throughout Scripture. Let's start with the imagery of the lamps:

> Immediately I was in the Spirit; and behold, a throne was standing in heaven, and **One sitting on the throne**. And He who was sitting was like a jasper stone and a sardius in appearance, and there was a rainbow around the throne, like an emerald in appearance.

> Around the throne were twenty-four thrones; and upon the thrones I saw twenty-four elders sitting, clothed in white garments, and golden crowns on their heads.
>
> Out from the throne come flashes of lightning and sounds and peals of thunder. And there were **seven lamps of fire** burning before the throne, **which are the seven Spirits of God**.
> —*REVELATION 4:2-5*

God is One, but the light of His essence is expressed in multiple colors emanating like a rainbow from His throne. The seven lamps of fire burning before His throne personify those seven aspects of His light, and they illuminate creation with the knowledge of that sevenfold glory. I don't know whether the lamps are casting the seven aspects of God's light out into creation or casting that light toward the throne so that creation can see God's multifaceted glory, but the general point is the same.

Notice that Revelation makes no mention of *stands* in reference to the seven Spirits of God. They are seen as lamps of fire with no stands. In other words, within the context of this throne room scene, each lamp *is* fire—there are no devices or structures to contain, hold, or feed the fires. There isn't even any oil. They are self-sufficient, living fires of God's essence.

Elsewhere in Revelation, there are references to seven golden lampstands that represent seven churches, but with those lampstands, no mention is ever made of fire. So on the one hand we have fires with no stands, and on the other, we have stands with no fires. Sounds like two very separate things that are meant to become one, no? Put that on the shelf for now and we'll come back to it much later in our journey.

Now remember that the seven Spirits of God are pictured as lamps *and* eyes. This fascinating dichotomy is an expression of the fractal of two. Lamps give light. Eyes receive light. One without the other is useless, and both are functions of the seven Spirits of God. The imagery of the lamps is all about casting the light of God's essence in a way that creation can perceive it and be impacted by it. The imagery of the eyes is all about receiving light, and therefore illumination and sight. But if God is the source and giver of light, what is the role of His eyes? He doesn't need to receive light to give it. So what light do His eyes receive? Consider a few more verses:

> For the eyes of the LORD move to and fro throughout the earth that He may strongly support those whose heart is completely His.
> —2 CHRONICLES 16:9

> The LORD is in His holy temple; the LORD'S throne is in heaven; His eyes behold, His eyelids test the sons of men.
> —PSALM 11:4

> "But an hour is coming, and now is, when the true worshipers will worship the Father in spirit and truth; for such people the Father seeks to be His worshipers."
> —JOHN 4:23

The seven eyes of the Lord are looking for those whose hearts are singularly focused on Him because His heart is singularly focused on us. Remember, His goal is to fashion a suitable Bride, and it seems His seven eyes are ever looking, searching, staring intently at us, waiting for us to engage with Him so that He can pour more light into us, because His light is the essential element for building and transformation. It is a virtuous cycle in which He is both the source and the destination. Through that lens, consider the words of Jesus:

> "The eye is the lamp of the body; so then if your eye is clear, your whole body will be full of light. But if your eye is bad, your whole body will be full of darkness. If then the light that is in you is darkness, how great is the darkness!
> —MATTHEW 6:22-23

The eye is the lamp of the body. What a peculiar and fascinating statement! I've often heard this described as the eye gate, meaning that whatever we look at and focus on will enter our being and affect us either positively or negatively. It can include pictures, videos, books, and visual media of any kind. There is truth to the concept of the eye gate, but I don't think that is the main principle Jesus is highlighting here. What we allow to come into us from the outside has an impact, but there is another source of light that is far more important.

What is the source of that light? What does it mean for our eye to be clear, or for our eye to be bad? What causes our eye to fill us with either light or darkness? Let's build that out for a moment:

> The spirit of man is the lamp of the LORD, searching all
> the innermost parts of his being.
> —*PROVERBS 20:27*

Our human spirit *is* the lamp of the Lord. It is both derived from
and somehow connected to His Spirit. If you imagine your human spirit as a flame kept alight by the breath of God, then imagine that before
He sent your spirit into your body at the time of conception, He somehow dipped into the flame of *His* Spirit and extracted some for your
human spirit. The process in no way diminished His original flame, and
it resulted in an autonomous human spirit that is meant to be both separate and connected—entangled, if you will—to Him who is the source.

Now, if the lamp of the Lord is actually expressed in seven fires,
then it only makes sense that those attributes are also carried over to our
human spirit. We are, after all, made in His image. So our human spirit
also has seven portions of light, which are lesser expressions of the seven
aspects of God's glory—His essence and motivation. Like a lamp, we
shine forth some measure of each of those seven Spirits in a blend of
hues and intensities that is unique to every human. And just like the
seven spirits of the Lord, our human spirit has the dual roles of lamps
and eyes.

Okay, now back to that puzzling statement by Christ: the eye is the
lamp of the body. Notice that Jesus didn't say *your* eye is the lamp of
your body. He did say that if *your* eye is clear—or single as some translations render it—then *your* whole body will be full of light. But the original source of the light is not *our* lamp, it is *His*. His lamp shines in our
hearts as the source of the light of God's sevenfold essence, but the goal
of that inward shining is to entrain the seven flames of our own spirits
to His, so that His shining becomes our shining. The result should be
that He shines *out of* our hearts:

> For God, who said, "Light shall shine out of darkness," is
> the One who has shone in our hearts to give the Light of
> the knowledge of the glory of God in the face of Christ.
> —*2 CORINTHIANS 4:6*

Before Christ's work on the cross, every human spirit was separated
from the source of the light of God's glory in the same way that the nation of Israel was separated from the holy of holies by the temple veil.

The veil represented the shame of sin embedded in human flesh because of Adam's sin, and it is reinforced by every subsequent sin. Israel needed a temporary mediator in the form of the law of Moses just to see a reflection of God's glory so that their human spirits could have a level of illumination and connection to God. In other words, God's glory was both external and hidden behind a veil. But Christ's death and resurrection fixed both problems. His death tore down the veil through the sacrifice of His flesh, a savage demonstration of God's love which reconciled us to the Father by removing our shame. And His resurrection took that which was external and made it internal through the new birth. Now we have direct access to the fullness of the divine essence shining in the face of Jesus *within* us.

So God is the all-consuming, self-sustaining source. His Spirit is the lamp that gives unending light. Our spirits are also designed to give light, but we can only give what we have first received. The eyes of our spirit must first be focused on the face of Christ to receive that light. Perhaps that is what it means to have a clear eye. Whenever we see new aspects of God's essence shining in our hearts from the face of Christ, our spirit is enlightened, strengthened, and transformed by that knowledge, which causes the lamp of *our* human spirit to shine brighter and brighter throughout our being and through us into the world.

It is important to understand that God's Spirit does not shine directly out of us to the world. It shines *through* us. He is the source, but He has designed the process to include a transaction of light within us. We are not made to be robots or slaves. He puts His Spirit in us, but then it is our choice to focus the eyes of our spirit on Him so that His lamps can transform our lamps—and then our light, derived from His but filtered through our own unique design, fills our entire being and overflows to the rest of creation.

So when Jesus said, "The eye is the lamp of the body," He wasn't so much saying that we are illuminated or defiled by the external things that we look at. He was talking about an internal source of light that is meant to shine from our spirit into our soul and body and then out of us into the world. He reiterated

> Like a lamp, we shine forth some measure of each of those seven Spirits in a blend of hues and intensities that is unique to every human.

the same principle from a different perspective later on in the book of Matthew:

> It is not what enters into the mouth that defiles the man,
> but what proceeds out of the mouth, this defiles the man."
> —*MATTHEW 15:11*

Now take this concept of internal lamps and eyes and multiply it by seven because there are seven lamps and seven eyes in our spirit. Each of the seven portions of our spirit is made to receive the light from a particular aspect of God's essence to transform us, and then we are meant to shine *our* light into the world to transform creation. But it is all contingent upon the intentional practice and continued focus of each of the eyes of our spirit in seeking out the attributes of God revealed in the face of Christ.

To that end, consider Isaiah's classic prophecy describing the seven Spirits of God resting on the Messiah:

> The Spirit of the LORD will rest on Him, the spirit of wis-
> dom and understanding, the spirit of counsel and strength,
> the spirit of knowledge and the fear of the LORD.
> —*ISAIAH 11:2 NAS*

There is so much to extract from this verse. The sequence and pairing of the Spirits are fascinating and deeply significant, and the surrounding verses add rich context to the purpose of Christ's work, but in the interest of time, we will only focus on one thing: nomenclature. In this verse, we finally find language to begin identifying the different aspects of God's essence that are manifested in the seven Spirits of God:

1. The Spirit of the Lord
2. The Spirit of Wisdom
3. The Spirit of Understanding
4. The Spirit of Counsel
5. The Spirit of Might (or Strength)
6. The Spirit of Knowledge
7. The Spirit of the Fear of the Lord

Remember, these seven spirits give and receive the light of God's glory, the source of which is expressed as a rainbow around His throne. They take that which can only be seen in the holy of holies and cast it out wide to creation through us (the spirit of man is the lamp of the Lord). And as with the order of the seven days of the creation story, the order of the seven Spirits of God is important. It is an intentional sequence that represents the very process that God uses to bring His nature to bear on that which is outside of Himself. In other words, the order represents Christ's unction to form a suitable companion and to ultimately sum everything up in Himself. Even in the context of Isaiah 11, that is the purpose and power of the seven Spirits. And that process is the heart of the fractal of seven.

Take a moment to consider the nature of light. White light consists of the component colors of the rainbow that only become visible to the human eye when its various wavelengths are dispersed through a prism. I like to imagine that each color of the rainbow is an expression of the seven Spirits of God. The idea works whether you view the seven colors as white light plus the six colors of the classic color wheel (three primary and three secondary), or whether you hold to the traditional seven-color rainbow originally described by Sir Isaac Newton's prism experiments. I prefer the following model for various reasons that I won't get into here, though I rush to say that I have no solid evidence nor practical reason to be dogmatic about this:

1. Spirit of the Lord = unrefracted white light
2. Spirit of Wisdom = red
3. Spirit of Understanding = orange
4. Spirit of Counsel = yellow
5. Spirit of Might = green
6. Spirit of Knowledge = blue
7. Spirit of the Fear of the Lord = purple

In reality, the rainbow is an infinite spectrum of colors, each blending into the next in inexhaustible variations. The closer and clearer you look, the more variations you will see between colors. So too is the glory of God's essence and motivation shining from the face of Christ. God can't really be summed up in only seven attributes or colors, but since He has chosen to reveal Himself through that general lens, our goal should be greater than merely observing the surface white light. The closer and clearer we look, the more we'll see. There is a hidden beauty beyond the veil, and He has provided the fractal of seven as a prism to help us discover, receive, and experience His fullness. We were designed for nothing less.

This is a good spot to pause for a breath. If any of this still feels frustratingly esoteric, please stick with me. In the next chapter we will build out our understanding of the seven aspects of God's essence by comparing the seven Spirits of God to other prominent biblical examples of the fractal of seven. These more practical elements should help tie everything together, drive home the immense importance of the fractal of seven in a way that is useful to our journey, and build a larger framework for understanding the process of transformation contained in the book of Revelation.

God can't really be summed up in only seven attributes or colors, but since He has chosen to reveal Himself through that general lens, our goal should be greater than merely observing the surface white light.

CHAPTER 8

THE LEGEND - PART 3:
THE FRACTAL OF SEVEN

or - "What a prolific paintbrush!"

In the last chapter, we built a rudimentary but solid framework for understanding the seven Spirits of God, and we ended the chapter by identifying each of the seven Spirits according to Isaiah 11:

1. The Spirit of the Lord
2. The Spirit of Wisdom
3. The Spirit of Understanding
4. The Spirit of Counsel
5. The Spirit of Might
6. The Spirit of Knowledge
7. The Spirit of the Fear of the Lord

I like to think of these Spirits as the origin and foundation of the fractal of seven. So every time we see a list of seven somethings in Scripture, the pattern in some way ties back to the nature of the seven Spirits of God. The names listed in Isaiah 11 are indicative of their nature and the aspects of God's essence they reveal. In a moment we'll add detail and substance to that nature by looking at the seven days of creation. But first, we need to add one more layer of nomenclature to our vocabulary.

If the seven Spirits of God are the source that shines the seven aspects of God's light, how should we describe the seven eyes and flames of our human spirits? The names of the seven Spirits in Isaiah 11 are reserved for God. They are the living lamps that burn before His throne. They are the source. But our entire beings were designed as vessels to receive, synthesize, house, and redistribute ever-increasing measures of His manifold glory to the rest of creation. So how should we refer to the seven portions of our own spirit that play such a pivotal role in the process? The question is more than academic. Understanding the makeup of the seven portions of our spirit, and seeing how they relate to the seven aspects of God's essence, expands our capacity for intimacy with Him and provides a platform for seeing more of Jesus than we could otherwise.

To find the vocabulary we seek, we need to review a common Scripture from a non-traditional angle. Let's jump straight to the target and then zoom back out to see the context:

> E very time we see a list of seven some-things in Scripture, the pattern in some way ties back to the nature of the seven Spirits of God.

> For just as **we have many members in one body** and all the members do not have the same function, **so we, who are many, are one body in Christ**, and individually members one of another.
>
> Since we have gifts that differ according to the grace given to us, each of us is to exercise them accordingly: if **prophecy**, according to the proportion of his faith; if **service**, in his serving; or he who **teaches**, in his teaching; or he who **exhorts**, in his exhortation; he who **gives**, with liberality; he who **leads**, with diligence; he who shows **mercy**, with cheerfulness.
> —*ROMANS 12:4-8*

The most common application of this passage is that each of us is graced with a motivating design that fits into a spectrum of seven gifts. Just as our bodies are made of diverse systems working together in harmony, so too is the Body of Christ made of diverse members, each designed after the pattern of one of these seven gifts.

The seven gifts can also be viewed as different functions within the Body of Christ. They are often referred to as *redemptive gifts* because they represent the ways in which Christ works through His people to bring His redemption to bear on creation. Some translations use slightly different nomenclature, but we'll stick with the commonly accepted terminology adopted by many of those who have trail-blazed the redemptive gift teaching:

1. Prophet
2. Servant
3. Teacher
4. Exhorter
5. Giver
6. Ruler
7. Mercy

These seven gifts of grace are inherent from birth because they are part of our spiritual DNA. A leg doesn't strive to be a leg; it just is. A heart doesn't need a degree in blood pumping; the function is part of its nature. The pulmonary system doesn't require peer pressure to realize it prefers oxygen to carbon dioxide; it simply follows its design. Each function can grow stronger and more efficient with exercise and training, but it is designed and preprogrammed to flourish in its role. Sure, a leg can fulfill some of the functions of an arm in certain situations, but the role is (hopefully) temporary because the results are less than ideal for everyone involved. Likewise, each of our lives is designed to gravitate naturally toward the characteristics of one of these gifts, and it is somewhere within the pattern of that gift that we find our greatest fulfillment and connectivity to the rest of Christ's body, and our greatest efficacy in bringing His grace to bear on the world around us.

There is, however, a second application of this passage. After all, the verse compares the Body of Christ to an individual with many members. Likewise, the seven redemptive gifts also apply to the "members" of an individual human. Think of it as a macro and micro application of the fractal of seven.

In what way does each of us have "many members?" Yes, we have arms, legs, eyes, ears, a heart, a brain, etc., but we also have a human spirit with seven portions of light. And just as the seven Spirits of God are the names of the seven portions of light shining from the face of the glorified Christ, the seven redemptive gifts are the names of the seven portions of the human spirit that God has gifted to us—the very eyes and flames designed to receive and shine the spectrum of the light of God's essence within us.

So the prophet portion of our spirit is designed to receive most readily from the Spirit of the Lord; our servant portion from the Spirit of Wisdom; our teacher portion from the Spirit of Understanding; our exhorter portion from the Spirit of Counsel; our giver portion from the Spirit of Might; our ruler portion from the Spirit of Knowledge; and our mercy portion from the Spirit of the Fear of the Lord. In each case, the portions of our spirit are meant to receive His light and shine it into the rest of our being in practical ways that cause us to grow more and more into His image. We'll unpack that transformation process in a later chapter. For now, you only need to be aware of the connection.

THE CREATOR'S FINGERPRINTS

With that in mind, let's build out the fractal of seven—and learn more about the seven Spirits of God and the seven portions of our human spirit—by reframing the seven days of creation around the seven aspects of God's light. When Jesus created the universe, He used light as the foundational substance. He created light on the first day, and every subsequent day relied on the principles established during the creation of light. It's not a perfect analogy, but I like to think of the Word as the paintbrush and the light of the seven Spirits as the paint. Each day was a masterful stroke intended to unpack His essence in a specific sequence to establish the whole of creation.

Now, if the fractal of seven was the template used to design the *original* creation, it should come as no surprise that the Unveiling of Jesus will follow this same sevenfold expression of His essence to form His Bride into a suitable companion and fully establish the *new* creation.

The fractal of seven is the imprint of the seven Spirits of God and the very fingerprint of the Creator. The more we know what to look for, the better we can identify His handiwork, the more prepared we will be to cooperate with the power of His Unveiling, and the more quickly we will hasten His coming. To that end, let's review the seven days of creation to build out the general characteristics of the fractal of seven. For each day we'll unpack certain details about what was created and then we'll boil those details down to a simple statement of essence.

> The fractal of seven is the imprint of the seven Spirits of God and the very fingerprint of the Creator. The more we know what to look for, the better we can identify His handiwork.

DAY ONE: DESIGN UNLEASHED

On the first day, God expressed Himself as the Spirit of the Lord by releasing that which is closest to His nature: light. However, as we saw in our discussion of the frame, Genesis 1:1-2 describes the state of the heavens and earth *before* God spoke light. Nothing existed but a formless, shapeless, dimensionless void of darkness referred to as the deep or the waters.

Whatever is meant by "the waters," it certainly was not H_2O, since none of the fundamental principles that govern matter and energy yet existed. And it was over this orderless chaos that the Spirit of the Lord brooded, perhaps formulating the intricacies of His plan, imagining the impact that the divine principles of His Word would unleash upon the void.

When God said, "Let there be light," He was calling into existence much more than just the electromagnetic spectrum of radiation we refer to as light. For light to exist, there also had to be time, space, dimension, and all of the laws that govern the natural and spiritual realms. This includes every single known and undiscovered scientific, moral, and spiritual principle. All of these fundamental principles of design sprang out of the dimensionless darkness of "the waters" when God's Word called forth light, and they provided every necessary building block for the remaining days of creation.

After speaking light into existence, God also called light good and separated it from darkness, thus defining the concept of good and evil. Some people postulate that the creation of light also included the creation of certain classes of sentient spiritual beings, while others believe that these beings were created on subsequent days. I lean toward the latter because I see the first day as being all about fundamental building blocks and raw materials, but since both perspectives require significant speculation, I won't factor them into our discussion of the fractal of seven.

That was the data. What principles can be derived from the data? On day one we see light from darkness, order from chaos, the basic building blocks of heaven and earth, the fundamental principles that govern them both, and the concepts of good and evil. If these are the results of the Word of God expressing Himself as the first of the seven Spirits of God, what do they suggest about the nature of the Spirit of the Lord, and by extension, the prophet portion of our human spirit, which is a reflection of the Spirit of the Lord?

At the most basic level, the Spirit of the Lord identifies God's original design and then applies the appropriate principles of God's character to form the raw materials that will support His end goal. There is much more to be said about this first aspect of the divine nature, but this is enough to get us started. We will ride with this simple description for now and add detail in the next book as we encounter other instances of the fractal of seven on our journey through the book of Revelation.

> The Spirit of the Lord identifies God's original design and then applies the appropriate principles of God's character to form the raw materials that will support His end goal.

DAY TWO: SPACE TO THRIVE

On the second day, God fashioned the heavens using a mysterious and perplexing process enabled by the principles He created on the first day. He started by saying, "Let there be an expanse in the midst of the waters, and let it separate the waters from the waters." Remember, the waters at this point were still dimensionless chaos for which the Hebrew language had no better description. It is possible that the act of calling forth light also imbued the waters with the fundamental particles out of which everything else would eventually be formed, but either way, by the second day these waters were still not much more than a void. And it was in the midst of this chaos that God hammered out an expanse that divided the primordial waters into two classifications: the waters above the expanse and the waters below the expanse.

I find this division of waters fascinating because it likely has multiple meanings. On one level we can think of this as the dividing of the natural and spiritual. The waters above the expanse were the substance from which the spiritual realm would be derived, while the waters below the expanse were the substance from which the natural realm would be derived.

On a strictly physical level, the waters above the expanse were destined to be the particles that would form planets, stars, and other astral bodies on the fourth day. On another level, these waters can also be viewed as the actual H_2O water vapor held in the atmosphere, while the waters below the expanse were the waters out of which the planet Earth would be formed on the third day.

In any case, the main thrust of the second day was the creation of the expanse (some translations call it the firmament), which God named heaven.

> That hospitality— that divine desire and authority to work behind the scenes, using godly principles to build a platform and a safe space for others to thrive —that is the core of the Spirit of Wisdom reflected in the servant portion of our human spirit.

At the very least it included the atmosphere surrounding the Earth and probably all of the outer space we call the universe as well. In this way, the expanse provided separation, dimension, boundary, protection, cleansing, filtration, and a vast number of other essential elements for sustaining life on planet Earth. It may have also included the creation of the spiritual realm as a suitable habitation for spirit-based life.

We often take the invisible atmosphere and vastness of space for granted, but their precise design shows how God cares about the details of creating a hospitable, safe, and self-sustaining environment for us to thrive. And it is that hospitality—that divine desire and authority to work behind the scenes, using godly principles to build a platform and a safe space for others to thrive—that is the core of the Spirit of Wisdom reflected in the servant portion of our human spirit.

DAY THREE: SUBSTANCE UNPACKED

God's work on the third day was truly awe-inspiring. He spoke twice on that day. His first statement gathered the waters below the expanse into one place. I take this gathering to mean that God took the day-one principles and applied them to the dimensionless subatomic particles of the void to endow mass and gravity and all of the forces necessary for the formation of atoms, and for atoms to coalesce into molecules, and for molecules to form elements, and so on until the spherical planet earth was formed with its dry earth and seas.

The apostle Peter described it this way:

> For when they maintain this, it escapes their notice that by the word of God the heavens existed long ago and the earth was formed out of water and by water,
> —*2 PETER 3:5*

It is significant that the earth was formed out of water and by water. Remember that the primordial "waters" were divided on the second day, with some set aside for the spiritual realm and some set aside for the physical realm. Not only does this speak of the physical mechanics of how the land was formed from this primordial substance below the expanse, but it also suggests that there is a commonality between the spiritual and physical realms, as both were designed from the same original substance, and both are held together by the same principles of God's Word.

God's second statement on the third day was equally momentous and directly related to the first statement: He called forth vegetation from the newly formed earth, again building more complex systems from the initial day one principles, supported and protected by the day two environmental factors. We see a clear outworking of the principle of the seed on this day, though it is important to note that the principle of the seed was first instituted on the first day when God sowed Himself as the Word.

So the third step in the fractal of seven, which is the domain of the Spirit of Understanding and the teacher portion of the human spirit, is about taking that which is ethereal, raw, and conceptual, and converting it to practical, substantive resources that support life. It uses a deep understanding of God's character—and the principles that flow from that character—to bring the life of God to bear in new and exciting ways that are both the foundation (earth) and the food (vegetation) for more complex and glorious forms of life in the future.

> The third step in the fractal of seven ... is about taking that which is ethereal, raw, and conceptual, and converting it to practical, substantive resources that support life.

DAY FOUR: REALITY MADE VISIBLE

On the fourth day, the Word of God created the sun, moon, stars, and planets in that middle expanse called heaven. These heavenly bodies were designed to give light to the earth, and to govern day and night, and to separate light from darkness. They were also "for signs and for seasons and for days and years" (see Genesis 1:14).

There's a lot to digest here. How do we distill it all down to a salient point or two? Let's start with a song written by a shepherd who spent more time than most meditating on the Creator's work underneath the open sky:

> The heavens are telling of the glory of God;
> And their expanse is declaring the work of His hands.
> Day to day pours forth speech,
> And night to night reveals knowledge.
> —*PSALM 19:1-2*

This psalm of David perfectly captures the essence of the Spirit of Counsel and the exhorter portion of the human spirit as demonstrated on the fourth day. The creation of the sun, moon, and stars brought light and an understanding of time to the earth, but the underlying principle was all about making known the invisible attributes and purposes of God. Declaring the divine nature to creation. Shining heaven to earth.

In honor of the exhorter gift, which is exemplified by the line "day to day [they pour] forth speech," let's unpack this fourth step of the fractal of seven a bit more by adding additional detail.

Think about the creation of light on the first day. Whatever light came forth when the Word said, "Let there be light," may not have been within the electromagnetic spectrum of what we consider light, given that the fundamental particles that participate in the production of light had likely not yet been formed from the primordial "waters." Perhaps what came forth was a spiritual or even abstract light—the divine light of inspiration and the illumination of God's character and principles instigated by the self-sustaining fires of the seven spirits of God.

And even if the fundamental particles did exist as part of the waters at that time, and even if there was an explosion of natural light when He spoke the word into the void, there were no other living beings in existence at that time to see it. It was an expression of the divine essence that went unobserved.

My point is this: God had to create physical vessels capable of sustaining interaction with the fundamental forces of nature before light could directly impact the physical world. That's what the sun, moon, and stars were all about. They were there to harness His natural principles to produce light that would benefit the earth and its inhabitants.

Now apply that same idea to the spiritual realm. Not only did God populate the universe with the stars and planets in the physical heavens, but He created many varieties of spiritual beings to populate the spiritual heavens—probably on the fourth day as well. There is scriptural evidence to suggest that not all spiritual beings were created on the fourth day—it's possible that some came on earlier days, and maybe some came later. But at the risk of engaging in rampant speculation, I do believe the principalities and powers that the Apostle Paul often spoke of were created on the fourth day.

This is why the ancient prophets often spoke of celestial bodies as representative of spiritual beings. Stars are seen as angelic messengers, and various planets as powers and principalities that govern aspects of the heavenly realms. These ideas weren't just the pagan folklore of primitive societies—they were supported by the oracles of God throughout the Old and New Testaments. The fact that some of these spiritual powers fell from grace and began opposing God's plan is a discussion for another chapter. Their original design was to help mankind see certain attributes of God's divine character and aspects of His timing and purposes that we couldn't otherwise unpack from the earthly creation. It was a temporary tutorial assignment until Christ came to reveal all:

> To me, the very least of all saints, this grace was given, to preach to the Gentiles the unfathomable riches of Christ, and to enlighten all people as to what the plan of the mystery is which for ages has been hidden in God, who created all things; so that the multifaceted wisdom of God might now be made known through the church to the rulers and the authorities in the heavenly places.
> —*EPHESIANS 3:8-10*

So the heavens still declare the glory of the Lord, and we can still learn much by observing the design of the natural and spiritual worlds, but now that Christ has come we can finally understand the endgame. God has flipped the script. His intention all along was to declare the fullness of His divine nature *through* the Body of Christ to the rest of creation—including the celestial powers—and through that revelation to accomplish His ultimate purpose of extending His nature to all things.

And that is where we find the central role of the Spirit of Counsel. The Spirit of Counsel teaches the exhorter portion of our spirits, and the Body of Christ as a whole, how to see the divine nature in the face of Christ, and it teaches us to see reality through *that* light, and it empowers us to declare the light that we receive to others. Related to that, it also specializes in helping us see things as God sees them—in other words, as they really are—rather than as the world systems or powers and principalities in heavenly places want us to see them. And through that counsel, it helps us to synchronize with the times and seasons of God's kingdom.

> The Spirit of Counsel teaches the exhorter portion of our spirits, and the Body of Christ as a whole, how to see the divine nature in the face of Christ. ...

DAY FIVE: NURTURING AND STEWARDSHIP

On the fifth day, the Word of God called the first sentient life on earth into existence. This massive step forward in complexity included the "great sea monsters," and every other living creature that moves in the water, as well as every kind of winged bird. And for the first time, God blessed His creation with the command to "be fruitful and multiply."

So what are some of the characteristics of God's work on the fifth day that point to the essence of the Spirit of Might? A few key concepts that come to mind are life, reproduction, abundance, variety, choice, and even freedom of movement. All of these are fundamental to marine and avian life, but we need to dig deeper to find the pattern that points to the essence.

Recall that God made a point to bless His fifth-day creatures with the command, "Be fruitful and multiply." Why did He say this to the marine and avian life but not to the plants on the third day? I believe the essence of the Spirit of Might, and of the giver portion of the human spirit, is most easily seen in the answer to this question.

The first and most obvious step toward fruitful multiplication is reproduction. Although both asexual and sexual reproduction were introduced with plant life on the third day, it wasn't until fish and birds came along that sexual reproduction required direct interaction between male and female. Unlike the plant kingdom, birds (and most species of fish) reproduce through some form of intercourse.

The byproduct of reproduction through this type of basic physical intimacy is significant. Think about the random and detached nature of plant pollination. Couple this with the equally random mechanics of seed dispersal, and the result is a seed germination process that is completely separate and unassisted by the immobile "parent" plant. In other words, plants don't care for their young.

Not so with most of the animals created on the fifth day. God designed the sexual reproduction of marine and avian life to require an initial investment of basic physical intimacy, and the direct result is that one (and sometimes both) parents will guard their fertilized eggs with fierce loyalty and intense dedication.

Birds are especially known for exercising ingenuity with considerable time and resources to build nests for protection and warmth. Some fish engage in similar behavior. And even after the babies finally hatch, in many cases these same attentive parents continue investing significant energy to feed, protect, and train their young until the appropriate time of release. This is the first visible example in creation of the self-sacrificial, nurturing, protecting, provider heart of God, and it is one of the essential attributes that He recognized as good and then blessed to be multiplied on the fifth day.

That brings us to the essence of the Spirit of Might, and the aspect of God's character that is most clearly reflected in His work on the fifth day. When you boil it all down, it's about successful stewardship of resources, especially stewardship of the next generation. There are many other Godly attributes exemplified on the fifth day that relate to the Spirit of Might—attributes like abundance, variety, family, and community—but the ability to take the life of God in embryo form, successfully nurture it through the difficulties and dangers of life, and then release it back to God is the fundamental principle that supports them all. These attributes also perfectly describe the giver portion of our human spirit.

> When you boil it all down, [the essence of the Spirit of Might is] about successful stewardship of resources, especially stewardship of the next generation.

DAY SIX: KNOWLEDGE THAT LEADS TO FREEDOM

On the sixth day, God created the beasts of the field, the livestock, the creatures that crawl on the ground, and of course, man. You know the story. We spent the better part of a chapter looking at the creation of Adam and Eve as the raw material for the formation of God's suitable companion, and although those details are related to the essence of the sixth step of the fractal of seven, I don't want to rehash them here. Instead, we are going to approach the sixth day from a slightly different angle.

Have you ever wondered why God created humans on the same day as earthbound animals? I mean, we are the crown of God's creation, created in His image and likeness, the apple of His eye, the focus of His love and sacrifice. If we are so much more valuable to Him than elephants, goats, and ants, why didn't we get our own day?

At least part of the answer is so that God could highlight the similarities and differences between humans and the animal kingdom because at the heart of that contrast lies the nature of the Spirit of Knowledge. And although there are more obvious differences, the attribute I want to draw your attention to is mankind's *pursuit of knowledge*. If that phrase feels like an oversimplification that falls short of the other grand themes introduced on the sixth day, please allow me a moment to explain.

Knowledge means many things to many people. Ask a plumber, or a pianist, or a structural engineer, or a politician, or a cybersecurity analyst, or a banker, or a philosopher about knowledge and you'll likely get an answer that reflects the particular subset of data that they find most important. That is not a bad thing. The information that we find interesting is often a reflection of God's design, and we glorify our Creator when we pursue truth—scientific, moral, spiritual, or otherwise—to build toward the purpose for which He created us. Such pursuit of knowledge is noble, even if it wasn't intended to be the end goal:

> Now about food sacrificed to idols: We know that "We all possess knowledge." But knowledge puffs up while love builds up. Those who think they know something do not yet know as they ought to know. But whoever loves God is known by God.
> —*1 CORINTHIANS 8:1-3 NIV*

Obviously, Paul wasn't saying the pursuit of knowledge is wrong. He knew that Christ was the source and destination of all knowledge. He was saying that if anyone *thinks* they know something without that knowledge also enhancing their love of God, then they haven't looked deeply enough to gain a true understanding of the thing that they thought they were learning. If our knowledge doesn't lead us to experience and express the sacrificial love of God, then we have only accumulated empty data devoid of its true substance:

> that their hearts may be encouraged, having been knit together in love, and that they would attain to all the wealth that comes from the full assurance of understanding, result-

ing in a true knowledge of God's mystery, that is, Christ Himself, in whom are hidden all the treasures of wisdom and knowledge.
　　　—COLOSSIANS 2:2-3

It's not just religious and spiritual knowledge that is hidden in Christ. All the treasures of wisdom and knowledge are hidden in Him. That means the full value of every fact and truth and piece of data is only unpacked from His essence. Now, in that light, think about the very first recorded words that God ever spoke to humanity. He commanded them to subdue the earth itself and to rule over every living thing on the earth, and yet He didn't preprogram their brain with any of the necessary knowledge to succeed at such a monumental mission. He placed them in a vast sandbox of wild materials with no instructions other than a reference garden as a home base for training.

> If our knowledge doesn't lead us to experience and express the sacrificial love of God, then we have only accumulated empty data devoid of its true substance.

The earth was full of untamed, untapped potential. Mankind was called to observe the fingerprints of God in the garden, identify the specific attributes of God embedded in those fingerprints, and then derive principles from those attributes that they could apply in creative ways that extended the life and love and order of God throughout the rest of the earth.

No other creature was designed with the self-awareness, the drive, and the capacity to grow in their pursuit of the endless knowledge needed to cultivate all of the boundless diversity of creation. And God wasn't giving Adam and Eve a coloring book to measure how well they stayed within the lines, or a paint-by-numbers to replicate a specific color scheme. He was giving them a blank canvas with immense freedom to paint a picture of Divinity through the filter of their own creativity. And since creative freedom is one of the fundamental attributes of God, they were also meant to extend the same ethos into every system and structure they built in pursuit of their calling.

In other words, as mankind ruled over the plants and animals and earth, it was intended to be less about bending these things to human will and more about helping every aspect of natural creation find freedom, harmony, and fulfillment congruent with its design. It was meant to be a sacrificial kind of love that reflected God's original decision to limit Himself in creating free will.

This commission required significant wisdom and knowledge, and yet God intentionally created Adam and Eve with a deficit of both (and therefore a deficit of character) and then challenged them to learn how to be like Him. When He blessed them with their commission, He wasn't just asking them to fill their brains with information, facts, or even truths to make them effective rulers; He was inviting them to pursue the knowledge of God to prepare them for the next phase of their journey toward becoming suitable companions—which would of course also result in them becoming the most effective rulers.

In this way, mankind's original mandate involved a practical, dirty, messy, and wholly fulfilling process of trial and error to discover what worked and what didn't, and it was meant to prepare the earth and its inhabitants for the incarnation of Jesus Christ. That's where it was all leading. We often think of Christ's incarnation as a means to redeem humanity. It was that, but it was also so much more, and it would have been necessary regardless of our sin. It is difficult to speculate exactly how, but even if Adam had never sinned it was always God's plan for the Word to eventually take on human flesh, because it was only through death as a man that He could become the Firstborn of the new creation that united the heavenly and earthly realms into the one new Man that fully reflected the whole nature of the Godhead. Christ was ever and always the only path for mankind to fulfill their original commission before stepping into their ultimate purpose.

That is the essence of the Spirit of Knowledge and the main focus of the sixth step in the fractal of seven. The journey toward the Unveiling of Jesus Christ involves learning to see Christ in all things and then using that knowledge

As mankind ruled over the plants and animals and earth, it was intended to be less about bending these things to human will and more about helping every aspect of natural creation find freedom, harmony, and fulfillment congruent with its design.

to unleash the full value of His intention for creation. It is about experientially learning and applying the knowledge of God to extend His character throughout creation. The primary role of the ruler portion of our human spirit is to take this aspect of God's light and shine it into our spheres of influence. It is the penultimate step in the fractal and the final one to involve work.

DAY SEVEN: GOD'S PLAN FULFILLED

The seventh day is the simplest and shortest in terms of actual action, but it may be the most difficult day to unpack in terms of God's nature:

> And so the heavens and the earth were completed, and all their heavenly lights. By the seventh day God completed His work which He had done, and He rested on the seventh day from all His work which He had done.
>
> Then God blessed the seventh day and sanctified it, because on it He rested from all His work which God had created and made.
>
> This is the account of the heavens and the earth when they were created, in the day that the LORD God made earth and heaven.
> —*GENESIS 2:1-4*

The most obvious characteristic of the seventh day is rest. Not sleep but rest. Specifically, the Creator's rest from His work of creation. His rest was the satisfied rest of complete fulfillment. It was the rest of reflection after a job very well done. In a sense, the first six days work with longing toward the promise of the seventh day, but the seventh day looks back upon the previous six to savor the joy of the journey.

The seventh day was also the first time that God blessed and sanctified time itself. That means He set the seventh day aside as unique and holy and separate from the other days because on that day the nature of God was not merely reflected through actions or external objects. On the seventh day, God Himself directly expressed His deepest essence, His nature-at-rest, through His very presence and nothing else. He expressed Himself through a state of being rather than doing. On the seventh day, the I AM was simply the I AM.

The simple, unadulterated, absolutely overwhelming presence of God is the essence of the Spirit of the Fear of the Lord. Notice that the account of the seventh-day rest makes no mention of mankind. Adam had already been created, and possibly Eve as well, yet they did not interact with God on that day. Nor did any other created thing. I'm not saying that nothing else rested on the seventh day—perhaps everything rested in its own way—but the heart of the principle of the seventh day is all about God and God alone. It is about the expression of His holiness, His *otherness,* outside of creation.

One of the clearest examples of this reality is found in Moses' encounter with God at the burning bush when God first revealed Himself to mankind as I AM:

> Then the angel of the LORD appeared to him in a blazing fire from the midst of a bush; and he looked, and behold, **the bush was burning with fire, yet the bush was not being consumed**. So Moses said, "I must turn aside and see this marvelous sight, why the bush is not burning up!" When the LORD saw that he turned aside to look, God called to him from the midst of the bush and said, "Moses, Moses!" And he said, "Here I am." Then He said, **"Do not come near here**; remove your sandals from your feet, for the place on which you are standing is holy ground." And He said, "I am the God of your father—the God of Abraham, the God of Isaac, and the God of Jacob." Then Moses hid his face, **for he was afraid to look at God**.
> —*EXODUS 3:2-6*

> Then Moses said to God, "Behold, I am going to the sons of Israel, and I will say to them, 'The God of your fathers has sent me to you.' Now they may say to me, 'What is His name?' What shall I say to them?" And God said to Moses, "I AM WHO I AM"; and He said, "This is what you shall say to the sons of Israel: 'I AM has sent me to you.'"
> —*EXODUS 3:13-14*

Do you see the parallel with the seventh day? God appeared in the form of a burning bush that did not consume. It was a picture of the presence of God at rest, doing no work, using no resources, consuming no created fuel as He expressed Himself. And it was no accident that the uncreated Creator chose this form to first introduce Himself as I AM, highlighting His utterly unique, entirely indescribable self-sufficiency beyond and outside the canvas of creation. The deepest essence of I AM cannot be understood merely through His fingerprints—that is, from the imprint of His interactions with created things. We can only begin to know I AM through intimate encounters with His terrifying presence.

God told Moses not to come near the bush, but to remove his sandals where he stood from a distance. Removing his sandals was a sign of respect, but it was also an opportunity for Moses' feet to be as close to God as possible. I wonder if creation was similarly invited to observe the expression of God's rest from a safe distance on the original seventh day? Either way, the full, unmitigated expression of I AM is unapproachably reserved for God alone. Every created thing must stand at a distance. Even angelic beings like the cherubim and seraphim that are directly associated in Scripture with God's throne room stand at a distance, separate from the otherness of I AM.

And now we get to the point of the seventh day. Even from a distance, Moses was so terrified that he hid his face. Why does God express Himself like this to creation? Why did He dedicate the final day of His creative expression to resting apart, intentionally highlighting the depth of His otherness? And why does the Spirit of the Fear of the Lord instill such terror in the presence of His otherness? I'm not talking about the kind of presence we describe when we sense Him during prayer, worship, or fellowship with other believers. I'm not talking about the "wherever two or more are gathered in my name, I am there," kind of presence. I'm talking about the direct, unfiltered, manifest presence of God:

> While he was still speaking, a bright cloud overshadowed them, and behold, a voice from the cloud said, "This is My beloved Son, with whom I am well pleased; listen to Him!" When the disciples heard this, **they fell face down to the ground and were terrified**. And Jesus came to them and touched them and said, "Get up, and do not be afraid."
> —MATTHEW 17:5-7

and in the middle of the lampstands I saw one like a son of man, clothed in a robe reaching to the feet, and wrapped around the chest with a golden sash. His head and His hair were white like white wool, like snow; and His eyes were like a flame of fire. His feet were like burnished bronze when it has been heated to a glow in a furnace, and His voice was like the sound of many waters. In His right hand He held seven stars, and out of His mouth came a sharp two-edged sword; and His face was like the sun shining in its strength.

When I saw Him, I fell at His feet like a dead man. And He placed His right hand on me, saying, "Do not be afraid; I am the first and the last,
—*REVELATION 1:13-17*

Moses hid his face at the burning bush. The disciples fell on their faces on the mount of transfiguration. John fell like a dead man at the feet of the glorified Christ on the isle of Patmos. Many other similar examples exist throughout the Bible. This isn't an Old Testament versus New Testament thing, and it isn't some aspect of God that went away as a result of Christ's incarnation as a human baby.

As we'll see when we get into the book of Revelation, even the four living creatures and the twenty-four elders fall down in the presence of the Lamb who was slain when He takes the sealed scroll from the hand of the Father. Their response is overwhelming awe instead of fear, and we'll see why in a moment.

My point is that being anywhere near God's manifest presence is enough to reduce even the most mature saints to heaps of rubble and to elicit unrestrained acts of reverential worship from heavenly beings. But are any of these responses the ultimate goal of the Spirit of the Fear of the Lord, or are they just the most immediately obvious results?

> The deepest essence of I AM cannot be understood merely through His fingerprints—that is, from the imprint of His interactions with created things. We can only begin to know I AM through intimate encounters with His terrifying presence.

Remember the frame that we talked about in chapter four? What did we see as God's endgame?

> When all things are subjected to Him, then the Son Himself will also be subjected to the One who subjected all things to Him, **so that God may be all in all**.
> —*1 CORINTHIANS 15:28*

So that God may be all in all. No more separation. No more infinite divide. Not only will God no longer be alone, but ALL things will share in the fullness of His essence through Christ. That is the ultimate masterpiece that He is painting through the drama of creation, and the Spirit of the Fear of the Lord is the final color He will use to tie it all together.

On the one hand, the way God rested on the seventh day emphasized the impossible chasm between Him and the original creation, and on the other hand, it foreshadowed His intention for a new creation that would first spring from and then supersede the old as all things are summed up in Christ.

Until then, terror in the face of I AM is an understandable and wholly natural reaction, but only for those parts of our being that are not yet at rest with God in Christ.

> We have come to know and have believed the love which God has for us. God is love, and the one who remains in love remains in God, and God remains in him. By this, love is perfected with us, so that we may have confidence in the day of judgment; because as He is, we also are in this world. There is no fear in love, but perfect love drives out fear, because **fear involves punishment**, and the one who fears is not perfected in love.
> —*1 JOHN 4:16-18*

Fear and punishment are rooted in shame. Our natural fear of punishment in God's presence is a result of Adam rebelliously eating the fruit from the tree of knowledge of good and evil, which caused him to feel shame at the reality that he did not measure up to I AM. To be clear, even before Adam's fall, nothing in the original creation measured up to God's fullness, but there was absolutely no shame in that reality because that was how God designed the original creation. A created thing can never measure up to the uncreated Creator, nor does it need to.

But because of the fall, and because Adam and Eve reached for a shortcut they foolishly thought would close the gap between humanity and divinity, and because that shortcut gave them the knowledge of good and evil without the character to handle it, we are now trapped in the shame of our sin, forever wanting to measure up but utterly unable to do so. Now we all wrestle not only with sin but with thought processes and heart attitudes and deep areas of our soul that are afraid to see the face of God or to be in the presence of His otherness for fear of punishment. What a colossal conundrum perpetrated by that crafty serpent!

But Christ's death and resurrection offer the potential for a better way because Jesus has already measured up. All the fullness of the Godhead dwells in Him in bodily form, and He invites us to abide in Him —to reckon ourselves as one with the fullness of His essence. It is an invitation to enter the new reality of the new creation as a member of His Body. And in Christ the knowledge of good and evil and the tree of life exist in harmony with His divine character, and there is neither shame nor fear of punishment in His perfect love.

We don't achieve His righteousness, or accomplish His works, or measure up to His nature—we rest in them. His works are our works. His character is our character. His light is our light. The more we savor what we can see of His goodness in us and around us, and the more we stare intently into that mirror searching for His essence, the more we will start to take on His likeness in those areas, and the more light we will be able to see and savor. That is basic, fundamental Christianity, and yet allowing its reality to permeate every fiber of our spirit, soul, and body is a lifetime quest. And that is the work of the Spirit of the Fear of the Lord.

The Spirit of the Fear of the Lord is all about establishing the abiding presence of God in our lives, and its ultimate product is a perfected love that shines through the mercy portion of our human spirit to the world around us. As this seventh step of the fractal of seven has its work in our lives, we begin to become conduits of the presence of God to extend His rest wherever we go. There is a time and place for working, building, creating, and pursuing knowledge for our role in the expansion of the kingdom of Christ, but none of these are the purview of the mercy portion of our spirit. Mercy is about being. Being with Him in rest, savoring what He has done, and being transformed most deeply as all seven portions of our spirit are free to bask in the fullness of His unquenchable flames.

> We don't achieve His righteousness, or accomplish His works, or measure up to His nature—we rest in them.

Chapter 9

The Legend - Part 4: Bondservants

or - "So much more provision than I ever imagined! "

Before we continue our discussion of fractals, let's take a short detour to talk about bondservants. The book of Revelation was written to bondservants, so it would behoove us to understand the term and learn how to become one before we try to apply fractals to Revelation.

The term *bondservant* is only found in some translations of the Bible. Others simply render it as *slave* or *servant*. Regardless of which word your Bible uses, it's the context of the word that really matters. I like the nuance of bondservant because it highlights the difference between being a slave of God versus being a slave to sin. And once again, the difference revolves around free will. Consider the following verses:

> No longer do I call you slaves, for the slave does not know
> what his master is doing; but I have called you friends, for

> all things that I have heard from My Father I have made
> known to you.
> —*JOHN 15:15*

> Because you are sons, God has sent forth the Spirit of His
> Son into our hearts, crying, "Abba! Father!" Therefore you
> are no longer a slave, but a son; and if a son, then an heir
> through God.
> —*GALATIANS 4:6-7*

These are just a couple of examples of how our relationship with God is continually reframed as higher and deeper than slaves. We are sons of God. We are the Bride of Christ. We are friends and heirs. And yet so often the writers of the New Testament specifically called themselves slaves of God (or sometimes bondservants). Why?

I believe the answer goes back to God's ordinance on slavery in the Old Testament. Although the word bondservant doesn't appear in the text, perhaps it is the perfect English term to summarize the concept described in those verses. And as we'll see in the next chapter, the Exodus description of bondservants ties directly back to Paul's discussion of the seven redemptive gifts in Romans chapter 12.

MY OWN POSSESSION

Allow me a moment to set the stage. The context begins in Exodus 19 where God is about to make an astounding offer to the people of Israel:

> Now then, if you will indeed obey My voice and keep My
> covenant, then you shall be My own possession among all
> the peoples, for all the earth is Mine; and you shall be to
> Me a kingdom of priests and a holy nation.' These are the
> words that you shall speak to the sons of Israel."
> —*EXODUS 19:5-6*

My own possession. Not a tribe of priests; a *kingdom* of priests. This suggests that the Levitical priesthood was not God's original design. He didn't intend to have a subset of His people involved in "full-time ministry" while the rest of the nation pursued lesser things. His highest purpose was not to separate the sacred and the secular. He wanted the entire nation of Israel to be holy priests who could minister directly to Him, experience His presence, and bring the knowledge of His glory to the world in the context of their own vocations and extended communities. After stating this intention, He commanded Moses to consecrate the people and have them wash their garments and abstain from sexual relations while they prepared to meet God on the third day to receive His covenant offer directly. In other words, God was asking Israel to view themselves as His possession, and He gave them two days to align their entire being with that reality. As we'll see in the next chapter, it was the old covenant version of Paul's exhortation in Romans chapter 12:

> Therefore I urge you, brethren, by the mercies of God, to present your bodies a living and holy sacrifice, acceptable to God, which is your spiritual service of worship.
> —*ROMANS 12:1*

This was a literal offer to Israel, who is the natural seed of Abraham, but it is also a prophetic shadow of the offer that Jesus makes to His Church, who is the spiritual seed of Abraham. Christ's work on the cross has consecrated us. Now we are in the "two-day" period of preparation before Christ's return. During this time our goal should be to learn how to present our bodies as a living and holy sacrifice to Him. Such an action is about so much more than just our body. It is about the joyful alignment of our spirit, soul, and body with His nature. To willingly present our bodies involves accepting the reality of His design for our being, and it requires the volition of our spirit and the acceptance of our soul to consummate the action. To present our bodies as a living sacrifice is the first step in allowing our spirit to take the reins of our life in following the Spirit of God rather than allowing our body and soul to continue steering the ship toward the desires of our flesh.

Now skip forward to Exodus 20. God descended on Mount Sinai with thunder and lightning and trumpets and smoke, introducing Himself as "I am the LORD your God, who brought you out of the land of Egypt, *out of the house of slavery.*" He then spoke the Ten Commandments directly to the people. He was offering them relationship and access to their original birthright and calling, which was to work *with* Him to shine His light into the world. Yes, He came to take possession of that which He already owned, but He wasn't calling them back into another form of slavery. He was calling them to something much higher.

Unfortunately, Israel wasn't ready. The people were afraid. The shaking and fire and smoke and trumpets that God sent to Mount Sinai were meant to instill the fear of the Lord, but as we saw in the last chapter, the fear of the Lord is ultimately intended to drive away the mindsets that keep us separate from Him—it isn't meant to drive *us* away.

The fear of the Lord is all about the presence of the Lord. It means that He has drawn near to be with us because He loves us enough to invest His energy into transforming us until we are one

> To present our bodies as a living sacrifice is the first step in allowing our spirit to take the reins of our life in following the Spirit of God rather than allowing our body and soul to continue steering the ship toward the desires of our flesh.

with I AM. It *is* a terrifying thing for the parts of our being that are not yet at rest in Him, but He comes in this posture to drive away every other fear that we have until the only fear remaining is the idea of ever *not* being in His presence.

> When all the people witnessed the thunder and lightning, the sounding of the ram's horn, and the mountain enveloped in smoke, they trembled and stood at a distance. "Speak to us yourself and we will listen," they said to Moses. "But do not let God speak to us, or we will die."
> —*EXODUS 20:18-19*

Israel's reaction to God's posture revealed the depth of their nation's wounded soul. They were delivered out of Egypt, but they still had the mindset of slaves. They viewed God as a taskmaster who wanted to take but never give. They didn't trust Him and couldn't hear His heart. They experienced the overwhelming display of God's power through the filter of an abused slave, and they saw nothing but a terrible reminder of judgment and wrath. They couldn't hear the offer inherent in His presence, nor see the unlimited security and resources His display of power represented. Centuries of Egyptian slavery had immersed them in an identity of powerlessness and poverty they were not ready to surrender.

As a result, they missed out on the fullness of God's plan by responding in fear and asking Moses to be their mediator and buffer.

God was not surprised. It was all part of the plan. He knew they were not ready, and He was prepared to meet them where they were. They were still slaves at heart, so God withdrew to a safe distance in accordance with Israel's self-imposed limits, willing to play the long game in the quest for their hearts. And it was in this new diminished reality after Israel had shrunk back, that God gave them the ordinances of the Mosaic law beginning in Exodus 21.

THE FIRST ORDINANCE

The very first ordinance wasn't about the tabernacle, the tithe, or even sacrifices and offerings. No, it was all about slavery. This was no coincidence. God was saying something profound to Israel. They had chosen a lesser path, so God gave them laws that were appropriate for slaves—laws that would treat them like children until Christ came to reveal the mature path 1,500 years later. And the very first ordinance of this law was exquisitely crafted to drive home the difference between the relationship He was offering and the type of slavery that still ruled their minds:

> "Now these are the ordinances which you are to set before them:
> "If you buy a Hebrew slave, he shall serve for six years; but on the seventh he shall go out as a free man without payment.
> —*EXODUS 21:1-2*

Hebrew slaves were to serve for six years and then be set free in the seventh year. On the surface this ordinance was all about outlawing perpetual slavery in Israel, ensuring that Israelites would never be born into slavery and viewed as the possession of another human. To be clear, the type of slavery allowed within this ordinance was more of an indentured servitude for paying off debts or working one's way out of poverty. God loves free will and despises slavery, but apparently, this was an acceptable compromise in an unjust world full of fallen humans with the freedom to violate His nature in ways that led to the existence of slavery.

Ultimately this ordinance also represented a much deeper truth that cut to the heart of Israel's wounds. To understand where I am going, think of this ordinance as a parable in which the nation of Israel themselves were the slaves. God had just brought Israel—or *bought* them—out of Egypt, but they quickly made it clear that they were still slaves at heart and unready for freedom. So God gave them a system for working out their slave mindsets in indentured servitude while learning something of His heart from His written law for a period of time. At the end of that period, He

> They were delivered out of Egypt, but they still had the mindset of slaves. They viewed God as a taskmaster who wanted to take but never give. They didn't trust Him and couldn't hear His heart.

would offer to release them from their debt into the mature freedom of Christ. But would Israel learn the right lessons from the law that God intended as a temporary tutor, or would they double down on their slavery and remain in bondage, unable to comprehend His full offer?

On the one hand, the Israelites were happy to be freed from Egypt, but they wanted nothing to do with the process that would set their whole being free to unite with God and become everything they were designed to be. They saw themselves as separate from Him, and they desired to stay that way. They had embraced the illusion of the possibility of having their own possessions, their own way, their own identity apart from Him. On the surface that may sound like freedom, but it is a tragic mindset of slavery. God already owns the whole earth. He already owns us. True freedom begins with surrendering to that reality and embracing the glorious purposes for which He designed us.

So in this parable, the "freedom" of separation at the end of the sixth year was a lesser option that God was offering Israel, and He still offers it to us today. In His ultimate goal to form a Bride, He doesn't force His will over ours. Even after we are born again and set free from sin and death, He still allows us to serve Him out of a sense of requirement, or fear, or even to build silos around what we will offer to Him and what we won't. Like slaves who perform their work for their own benefit, always with an eye toward the time of their freedom, we can choose this legitimate, if shortsighted, path. But He offers a more excellent way, as described in the second half of God's ordinance on slavery:

> But if the slave plainly says, 'I love my master, my wife and
> my children; I will not go out as a free man,' then his mas-
> ter shall bring him to God, then he shall bring him to the
> door or the doorpost. And his master shall pierce his ear
> with an awl; and he shall serve him permanently.
> —EXODUS 21:5-6

So in some cases, a slave would come to love their master and their master's household so deeply during their six years of service that they would choose a life of serving instead of freedom. This slave would then go through a ceremony in which their ear would be nailed to the door or doorframe of the master's house signifying that they were forever bonded to the master's household. They became His possession forever. It was a voluntary commitment made out of love, but it was a permanent transaction.

Imagine the sacrifice! Imagine the level of trust involved in this decision! In reality, these slaves had come to recognize what the others could not—they were already free! During their six years of slavery, they had come to clearly see and truly understand their master's heart of love. Everything they needed, everything they wanted, their entire identity could only be found in connection to their master, and his resources were beyond anything they could access on their own. They were freer serving him than they were pursuing an illusion of separation. And beyond that, they understood that the bonding worked in both directions. The master was also committed to caring for the slave as he would a member of his own household. And for these reasons, the master could fully trust the bondservant to be faithful with his resources. This is the essence of a bondservant, and it is a beautiful picture of the difference between the letter of the old covenant and the spirit of the new covenant.

It is hard to envision any slave volunteering to remain a slave forever in this world. Human masters are flawed and limited, and slavery has undoubtedly been one of the worst evils in history. God never designed humans to lord it over other humans. But when God is the master, every situation works together for our good, every trial is an opportunity, every difficulty is crafted to strengthen and legitimize, and all things work in accordance with the master's will to extend the rule of His household, of which we are a part.

The path of the bondservant represented God's original invitation to Israel on Mount Sinai in Exodus 20, and it is the holy, acceptable, and spiritual act of worship He desires from us today. Only a bondservant will be able to see provision and resources for building God's kingdom amid the shaking and fire and smoke that transpire throughout the book of Revelation. Only bondservants are sufficiently free from a mindset of

God already owns the whole earth. He already owns us. True freedom begins with surrendering to that reality and embracing the glorious purposes for which He designed us.

fear and unprofitable slavery to recognize the offer of Christ's Unveiling. Only bondservants are properly positioned for the transformation that is to come. The book of Revelation is written for bondservants.

A SEQUENCE OF POSTURES

How does the posture of bondservant fit with our other positions in Christ? One way to look at it is through the fractal of three. In our relationship with the Holy Spirit, we move from indentured slaves to bondservants. In our relationship with Jesus, we are His betrothed and will eventually be His wife. And in our relationship with Father, we are on a continuum from children to mature sons.

These aren't strict silos. There is overlap. We can interact with each member of the Trinity from each of these positions, and each posture feeds into the other. We learn much about sonship from Jesus; the Holy Spirit is the quintessential friend of the Bridegroom who helps prepare the Bride; and the Father who owns all things is a loving master. The roles of the Godhead are separated by dotted lines, not bold boxes, and so are the different aspects of our relationship with Him.

Even within the main three, He remains our King, our friend, our counselor, our helper, and many others. But the main three especially tie our design to the triune essence of the designer. For that reason, it is important not to think of these positions in a hierarchy. It is not better to be a Bride than a son, nor a son than a bondservant. All three are necessary, glorious, and eternal. God is three in One, and we will always relate to Him in these three main ways.

Having said that, our lives are meant to follow the general biblical pattern of the tabernacle. We are made to approach God from the outside in, moving from outer court to inner court to holy of holies. But it doesn't stop there. We are then meant to take the glory of God that we experience behind the veil back out in reverse order from holy of holies to inner court to outer court, and finally to the rest of the outside world. So the journey inward is primarily about aligning the eyes of our spirit to see, receive, and respond to the light of God, which for us is a female disposition. The journey back out is primarily about initiative and giving and creating and building with the light of God we have received, and that is a male disposition. Remember the eyes and flames?

I hasten to say that the moment we accept Christ's death and resurrection on our behalf, we have everything we need in Jesus. His work has already torn the veil and made the way for us to enter into transformational relationships with each member of the Trinity, but there remains a process for us to learn how to access the treasures of those relationships. And that process follows a general sequence as Jesus ushers us through the tabernacle.

I don't mean to suggest that we all follow the same growth sequence in our relationship with God. Our journeys are often nonlinear. For instance, we can be a bondservant in some areas of our lives while still having a slave mindset in others. Depending on our past experiences and current circumstances, He may present Himself first as Father for a season before drawing us into a bondservant or bridal posture. But on balance, over time, the general flow of life is meant to follow the sequence of the tabernacle, and this holds even more true during the ultimate unfolding of Christ's Unveiling, which is an intentional, concentrated sequence designed for maximum efficacy.

In book 2 we'll see this process begin to unfold in dramatic detail when we dive into the book of Revelation, but at a general level, it is quite simple. We move from slave to bondservant in the outer court as we experience the primary ministry of the Holy Spirit. That prepares us to enter the inner court as newly betrothed lovers. In the inner court, we experience the dominion and power of Jesus Christ, which moves us from anticipating virgins to a married Bride who has become one flesh with the Bridegroom. We then enter the holy of holies with the attitude of wild-eyed lovers enraptured by our Bridegroom.

That is an amazing place to be, but it is not the end. In the holy of holies we transition from primarily receiving to primarily giving as we experience the heart of the Father. We don't stop being bondservants and Brides, but standing in the full light of Him who is the source, receiving from the One who determines our essence, we see the fullness of who we are in relation to the Godhead, one another, and creation. In that place, we are made ready to participate with the Son of God in building the kingdom as His fully suited companion.

I n our relationship with the Holy Spirit, we move from indentured slaves to bondservants. In our relationship with Jesus, we are His betrothed and will eventually be His wife. And in our relationship with Father, we are on a continuum from children to mature sons.

CHAPTER 10

THE LEGEND - PART 5:
MEMBER METAMORPHOSIS

or - "Why should I care about any of this?"

N ow that we know something about bondservants, we can use that information to understand how God applies the fractal of seven for transformation. In previous chapters, we discussed fractals in an abstract context. Now it's time to apply our legend in a more practical way to the path ahead. In other words, we need to answer the most important question in this entire discussion of fractals: So what? Or put another way, how does this help us? After all, what good are even the highest quality tools if you don't know how to use them?

Remember the verse in Romans 12 that lists the seven redemptive gifts from which we derived the names of the seven portions of our human spirit that correspond to the seven Spirits of God?

> Since we have gifts that differ according to the grace given
> to us, each of us is to exercise them accordingly: if
> **prophecy**, according to the proportion of his faith; if

service, in his serving; or he who **teaches**, in his teaching; or he who **exhorts**, in his exhortation; he who **gives**, with liberality; he who **leads**, with diligence; he who shows **mercy**, with cheerfulness.
—*Romans 12:6-8*

This passage contains an excellent example of how Christ uses the principles contained in the fractal of seven to transform the Body of Christ, but to see the process we need to take a step back to gain some contextual perspective. We won't read it all here, but the context of the redemptive gift discussion begins way back in Romans 9. Let's look at just a few of the key points from those chapters:

I am telling the truth in Christ, I am not lying, my conscience testifies with me in the Holy Spirit, that I have great sorrow and unceasing grief in my heart. For I could wish that I myself were accursed, separated from Christ for the sake of my brethren, my kinsmen according to the flesh, who are Israelites, to whom belongs the adoption as sons, and the glory and the covenants and the giving of the Law and the temple service and the promises, whose are the fathers, and from whom is the Christ according to the flesh, who is over all, God blessed forever. Amen.
—*ROMANS 9:1-5*

Notice Paul's intensity: "I could wish that I myself were cursed and cut off from Christ for the sake of my brothers." That is some passionate language, and it is a fervor that is carried through to Romans 12. You see, Paul had a unique insight into God's hidden cosmic plan for creation, which he often referred to as the mystery of Christ. This revelation was likely derived from his experience of being caught up to the third heaven as described in 2 Corinthians 12 and enhanced by his brilliant education in the Mosaic law and Old Testament theology as a young Pharisee under the tutelage of the renowned Gamaliel.

Whatever the source of his understanding, Paul spent the next three chapters of Romans weaving a panoramic masterpiece about God's plan for both Israel and the Gentile church. Beginning with the nation of Israel's original calling, he explained their current rejection of Christ, their temporary estrangement from the promises of God, the resulting extension of salvation to the Gentiles, and finally the promise of Israel's future redemption at the end of the age.

In the middle of this exquisite discourse, Paul used the analogy of an olive tree to illustrate God's plan. In one sense, the olive tree represents the promises originally given to Abraham, but ultimately the olive tree is a picture of the Body of Christ. Jesus is the root of the tree. Israel are the natural branches that grew from the tree. When Israel rejected Christ they were broken off from the tree, and then the Gentile church was grafted in as wild olive branches:

> For if [Israel's] rejection be the reconciliation of the world, what will their acceptance be but life from the dead? And if the first piece of dough be holy, the lump is also; and if the root be holy, the branches are too. But if some of the branches were broken off, and you, being a wild olive, were grafted in among them and become partaker with them of the rich root of the olive tree, do not be arrogant toward the branches; but if you are arrogant, remember that it is not you who supports the root, but the root supports you.
> —*ROMANS 11:15-18*

This olive tree analogy perfectly aligns with the seed nature of the Word of God, and it is the context of the seven redemptive gifts discussion in Romans 12, which is all about the redemption, growth, unity, and ultimate perfection of the Body of Christ, both Jew and Gentile together. To drive that home, Paul summed up God's plan with the following statement before launching into Romans 12:

> For I do not want you, brethren, to be uninformed of this mystery—so that you will not be wise in your own estimation—**that a partial hardening has happened to Israel until the fullness of the Gentiles has come in**; and so all Israel will be saved; just as it is written,
> "THE DELIVERER WILL COME FROM ZION,
> HE WILL REMOVE UNGODLINESS FROM JACOB."
> "THIS IS MY COVENANT WITH THEM,
> WHEN I TAKE AWAY THEIR SINS."
> From the standpoint of the gospel they are enemies for your sake, but from the standpoint of God's choice they are beloved for the sake of the fathers; **for the gifts and the**

> **calling of God are irrevocable.** For just as you once were disobedient to God, but now have been shown mercy because of their disobedience, so these also now have been disobedient, **that because of the mercy shown to you they also may now be shown mercy. For God has shut up all in disobedience so that He may show mercy to all.**
> —*ROMANS 11:25-32*

Walk through this with me. God has a plan for the perfection of the Body of Christ. The olive tree will not be whole until the natural branches are grafted back in. The Body of Christ will not be perfected until Israel and the Gentiles are united as one new man (see Ephesians 2:15). Right now, even more so than in Paul's time, the Body of Christ is missing an essential element, and we are lesser for it. That is not to say that we, the Gentile Church, cannot fulfill our purpose in these times without the nation of Israel, but our callings are intimately linked.

The Gentile Church only came into existence because of Israel's disobedience. But now Israel as a nation will not turn to Jesus until "the fullness of the Gentiles has come in." The "fullness of the Gentiles" means much more than just a number. The Gentile Church must reach full maturity, fully manifesting the nature of Christ to the degree that the wild branches can before the rest of the natural branches are grafted back in. In God's plan, the Church is called to so gloriously shine the undiluted light of God that she moves the nation of Israel to jealousy and draws them to Christ (see Romans 10:19; 11:13-14).

Paul goes so far as to say that Israel's acceptance back into the Body of Christ will be "life from the dead." That's not just poetic language for Israel coming back to life in some abstract or figurative way. "Life from the dead" is talking about the first resurrection. That's right, the event that some people refer to as the rapture, or our gathering together to Christ, is tied directly to Israel's acceptance of Jesus! That is why Paul was so passionate about this subject. More than passionate, in fact. It almost seems like he had an ax to grind with the Gentile Church. "Do not be arrogant," he insisted. It is as if he was pleading, "This isn't just about you!"

He was an apostle to the Gentile Church, and he understood that the maturation of the Gentile Church would trigger the redemption of Israel, which would trigger the final perfection of Christ's Bride. But he also knew Israel's history, and he understood that Israel's rejection of Christ was rooted in the very same mindset of slavery that they displayed when they shrunk back from God's offer at Mount Sinai. Against that backdrop, Paul launched into Romans 12, essentially starting where Exodus 20 left off … with another invitation to become bondservants:

> **Therefore I urge you, brethren**, by the mercies of God, to present your bodies a living and holy sacrifice, acceptable to God, which is your spiritual service of worship. And do not be conformed to this world, but be transformed by the renewing of your mind, so that you may prove what the will of God is, that which is good and acceptable and perfect.
> —*ROMANS 12:1-2*

Can you hear Paul exhorting the young Gentile Church not to make the same mistakes Israel made at the beginning? Israel's small-mindedness became a self-imposed glass ceiling. But God's plan is so much greater. If we will embrace His offer, even though there is no way we can fully understand it; if we will trust Him like those ready to make a bondservant commitment; if we will offer our spirit, soul, and body to Him, only then do we position ourselves to *begin* the process of transformation offered through Christ's Unveiling.

Notice that one of the results of embracing the process is that we will prove God's will. We'll unpack what that means for us in a moment, but in the greater context of the book of Romans, one thing we already know is that the Gentile Church is destined to manifest aspects of God's ultimate plan for a companion in such a profound way that Israel will be moved to jealousy. Our transformation process itself will testify to Israel: *This is what Yahweh was offering to you! This is what your nation was born for! This is what your trials and tribulations and disciplines and tumultuous past were all about!*

> In God's plan, the Church is called to so gloriously shine the undiluted light of God that she moves the nation of Israel to jealousy and draws them to Christ

That in itself is inspiring, but Paul didn't stop there. Like a wise master builder preparing an appropriate foundation to support the eventual full glory of the owner's house, Paul had seen the blueprints, and it made him passionate about preparing the Church to become everything Christ intended. He clearly understood the actual process required to move from slaves to bondservants, from engaged to married, from children to sons, because he proceeded to describe the primary tool that would be used in the work. And it all revolved around the fractal of seven and the redemptive gifts. Now let's reread those verses, this time looking for process rather than just nomenclature:

> For through the grace given to me I say to everyone among you not to think more highly of himself than he ought to think; but to **think so as to have sound judgment**, as God has allotted to each a measure of faith. **For just as we have many members in one body and all the members do not have the same function, so we, who are many, are one body in Christ, and individually members one of another.**
>
> Since we have gifts that differ according to the grace given to us, each of us is to exercise them accordingly: if **prophecy**, according to the proportion of his faith; if **service**, in his serving; or he who **teaches**, in his teaching; or he who **exhorts**, in his exhortation; he who **gives**, with liberality; he who **leads**, with diligence; he who shows **mercy**, with cheerfulness.
> —*ROMANS 12:3-8*

Remember, the context is Paul's exhortation to embrace a bondservant commitment, which initiates transformation through the renewing of our minds. But then he drilled down on what is required for our minds to be renewed to understand God's will. It starts with accurately discerning the gifts given to us, first individually, and then corporately.

In a corporate context, we need to understand our redemptive gift to fit correctly into the universal Body of Christ, and all seven gifts need to be fully functioning for the Body of Christ to be whole. But the corporate Body cannot grow to maturity unless the individual members are also growing in their own arenas. So it is equally vital that we each understand the design of our own members, and that those members come to maturity for us to be whole as individuals.

That means each portion of our human spirit must grow in its capacity to receive the light that shines in the face of Christ. We need to "think so as to have sound judgment" about the seven portions of our spirit receiving light from the seven Spirits of God. In other words, it's not enough to just look for the surface white light of God's glory. We grow the most as we learn to unpack the spectrum of God's light, and He has provided the fractal of seven to help us identify and understand the attributes of each color.

God has a way of doing some of that whether or not we are consciously aware of the process—but the book of Revelation invites us to become active participants in the most exciting stages. The fractal of seven is the basic process of transformation that Jesus will use throughout Revelation as He takes us individually and corporately through a maturation process that follows the pattern of the tabernacle. Each phase will be like a seven-step process in which He progressively reveals another aspect of Himself to the seven portions of our spirit. The journey from slave to bondservant requires these seven steps, and then the journey from betrothed to bride requires another application of the seven steps, as does the transformation from child to mature son. Each of the three main parts of our being must see and experience the full spectrum of the light of God's glory to become like Him in that area. And just as Paul alluded to in Romans chapter 12, the process in Revelation applies on both an individual and corporate level.

As with Israel at Sinai, it all starts with the invitation from God to present our bodies as a living sacrifice. That is the entry point to the process of Christ's Unveiling. And as with Israel, we must see this invitation for what it is. It is not a command to embrace more slavery. It is not a mandate to try harder, to give more, or to achieve some level of holiness by "crucifying our flesh." Forcing our flesh to abstain from evil through the exercise of our soul is

> We need to "think so as to have sound judgment" about the seven portions of our spirit receiving light from the seven Spirits of God. In other words, it's not enough to just look for the surface white light of God's glory.

not wrong—and sometimes it is all we know how to offer—but no amount of mental gymnastics or religious teeth-gritting will produce the life of Christ in us. I know this from personal, painful, repetitive, and mostly unfruitful effort.

The spiritual and acceptable bondservant posture requires that our human spirit has first heard His invitation and then responded by stepping forward to take the lead. Our human spirit is uniquely designed to recognize spiritual provision that our soul and body would otherwise miss on their own. When we give our spirit permission to engage in the process, our spirit begins to take the reins, our soul begins to surrender the driver's seat, and our bodies can then fall in line. It is the opposite dynamic to what we see in the world:

> For all that is in the world, the **lust of the flesh** and the **lust of the eyes** and the **boastful pride of life**, is not from the Father, but is from the world. The world is passing away, and also its lusts; but the one who does the will of God lives forever.
> —1 JOHN 2:16-17

The world is in bondage to its base desires. For many, the body runs the show as it follows after its lusts, the soul is drawn toward and eventually overwhelmed with the body's urges, and the spirit, which has not turned to the face of Christ, is either consumed with empty darkness or utterly powerless. I refer to this as the nature of the beast. It is the end result of a slave mindset. The closer we get to the end of the age the more obvious this dynamic will be.

But the process of His Unveiling starts with an invitation to leave behind the mindset of slavery that keeps us in bondage to such elementary principles of this world. That doesn't mean that we must conquer sin before we begin. That is a result, but not the prerequisite or even the goal. Remember, a slave can't recognize the full value of the assets available to them from the master because they see themselves as separate, so they fall back on their own minuscule resources. That's why we must start by embracing the mindset of a bondservant who desires to be a good steward of every good gift we have received. Fractals can be a key to help us identify and understand those resources.

That is one of the main themes of the book of Revelation. It is a detailed, step-by-step, prophetic chronicle of the bondservant's transformation process as they behold new facets of Christ never before imagined and respond with growth that utterly eclipses the kingdom of darkness.

Hang in there if any of this still sounds esoteric or nebulous. We'll continue leveraging fractals throughout this book to help solidify these concepts in your mind, though much of our work with the fractal of seven will begin in book 2. You'll get plenty of practice when you need it most.

The fractal of seven is the basic process of transformation that Jesus will use throughout Revelation as He takes us individually and corporately through a maturation process that follows the pattern of the tabernacle. Each phase will be like a seven-step process in which He progressively reveals another aspect of Himself to the seven portions of our spirit.

CHAPTER 11

SCALE AND TIMING - PART 1:
NATURAL BRANCHES, NATURAL TIMELINE

or - "Do you mean that literally?"

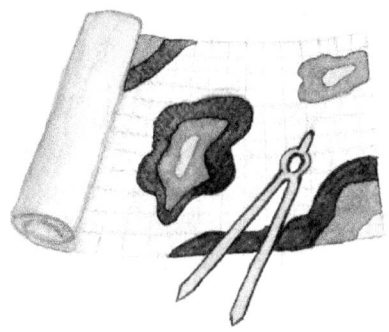

M ost maps are marked with a scale and some type of coordinate system for calculating distance and time from one point to another. One inch equals a thousand miles, or something like that. The scale on our map is not quite that straightforward, but since you're still with me after the fractal discussion, I think you'll find this scale concept elementary.

I'm using terms like scale and distance figuratively here, but they are helpful constructs for thinking about the timing of the book of Revelation. One of the most controversial aspects of any discussion about Revelation is timing. When will it start? How long will it last? Within those questions are a thousand subcategories of arguments about the sequence and duration of specific events. On the one hand, I would like to avoid this topic because I've seen these arguments distract from the transformational power of the Unveiling, but on the other hand, God intentionally planted many time-related markers throughout His Word relating to His Unveiling. If He went through the trouble of adding a coordinate system to His map, we would be foolish to ignore it.

So let's investigate some of the verses that provide a grid for understanding the timing of the Unveiling. We'll focus mainly on the book of Daniel in this chapter, but we'll hold our theories loosely, and we'll err on the side of principle rather than fact. I'm most interested in deriving a general sequence rather than putting dates or boxes around events. Remember that the seed nature of the Word of God can wreak havoc on our dogmatic interpretations of prophecy. In the end, predicting the timing and chronology of events may be the least important part of the book of Revelation.

I'm not saying that timing is unimportant, but whatever way we think things are going to unfold is bound to fall far short of reality. I struggle to think of a single biblical prophecy that unfolded exactly the way Israel or the first-century church expected. In hindsight, the fulfillment makes perfect sense, but even the plainest prophecies often confound the wise with multiple levels of meaning within meaning (think three-dimensional fractal versus two-dimensional pattern). For that reason, we'll spend our energy trying to find Jesus in the prophecy rather than worrying about particulars that are out of our control. That is the difference between a bondservant mindset and a slave mindset. Said another way, slaves need every detail spelled out, while sons thrive on mystery. Let's approach this topic like sons looking for inspiration to take initiative rather than slaves looking for security in knowledge.

THE FINAL WINDOW OF TIME

One of the most common theories about the end times is that they include a seven-year tribulation period that closes out this age and ushers in a new age called the millennial reign of Christ. There are variations within this basic premise, as well as alternate viewpoints that see the book of Revelation as largely metaphorical, or allegorical, in the sense that there is no literal seven-year culmination period, or that the entire church age has been an expression of the millennial reign of Christ. I'm not going to address all of those arguments here. I don't particularly care for the "tribulation period" label, which I have yet to find anywhere in Scripture, but I will present evidence that supports something of a literal seven-year period culminating in a literal one-thousand-year reign of Christ on earth.

Having said that, I think you'll find my perspective on the seven-year period to be quite different than most. I will leave room for variations, and as with all prophecy, I fully expect that there are multiple layers and levels within levels of symbolism, and metaphorical interpretations that can also have merit without diminishing the ultimate fulfillment.

You may not agree with a literal timeline, and I'm okay with that. We all see in part and know in part, and

Remember that the seed nature of the Word of God can wreak havoc on our dogmatic interpretations of prophecy. In the end, predicting the timing and chronology of events may be the least important part of the book of Revelation.

for that reason, my viewpoint is subject to change, though I currently believe it provides an effective grid for understanding and eventually experiencing the full transformational power of Christ's Unveiling. And it is to that end that we will investigate this subject.

The entire concept of the final seven-year period is mainly rooted in a prophecy from the book of Daniel. This topic is incredibly complex and nuanced, which is partly why it has so many interpretations. It draws on multiple prophecies throughout the book of Daniel that span thousands of years and require extensive historical context to weave together. Perhaps that's a study for a future book. My goal in this chapter is to give you the nickel version of the tour without dragging you through ten miles of jungle terrain along the way. If you like the jungle or are curious about the indigenous plants and the makeup of the soil, I encourage you to revisit this topic on your own. Perhaps the highlights you see here will be enough to keep you going in the right direction if you decide on a self-guided tour later. Or, perhaps you'll find a different trail altogether.

Let's start with some quick context. When Daniel was a young man some 2,500 years ago, the kingdom of Babylon attacked Jerusalem and led many of the inhabitants of Judea into captivity. From then on, Daniel lived in Babylon under the rule of various pagan kings and kingdoms. He lived most of his life dispersed from his home country, but he never lost his great passion to see Jerusalem restored to God, and Israel restored as a nation—an ethos similar in some ways to the apostle Paul's experience. With that lens, we come to Daniel chapter 9:

> In the first year of Darius the son of Ahasuerus, of Median descent, who was made king over the kingdom of the Chaldeans—in the first year of his reign, I, Daniel, observed in the books the number of the years which was revealed as the word of the LORD to Jeremiah the prophet for the completion of the desolation of Jerusalem, namely, seventy years. So I gave my attention to the LORD God to seek Him by prayer and supplications, with fasting, sackcloth and ashes.
> —DANIEL 9:1-3

The year was circa 538 BC, about nine hundred years after Mount Sinai, and nearly seventy years after the start of Israel's Babylonian captivity. Darius the Mede had just become the new king of the Babylonian empire when Daniel discovered that Israel's captivity was originally prophesied to end after seventy years (see Jeremiah 25:11; 29:10). The time was near, so Daniel dove into a period of intense intercession.

Beyond just asking for the release of Israel from captivity and the restoration of Jerusalem, I believe Daniel was praying for Israel to finally enter the fullness of her calling. At this point in his life, Daniel was an old man who had already seen the rise and fall of kings and kingdoms, and through it all, he had experienced miraculous deliverances and mind-blowing spiritual experiences that gave him an utterly unique perspective on earthly and heavenly affairs. He had seen many great and terrible prophetic visions of the time of the end, and though he may not have initially understood everything, he must have gathered that God's plan went far beyond just restoring Israel to her homeland. He had prophetically observed the ultimate establishment of the kingdom of God over the entire earth with the glorified Christ as King. So when Daniel interceded for Israel, he was bringing all of that experience and expectation to the table. And in that place, a revelation came to him from the angel Gabriel:

> And he gave me instruction and talked with me, and said, "O Daniel, I have now come forth to give you insight and

understanding. At the beginning of your supplications the command was issued, and I have come to tell you, for you are highly esteemed; so give heed to the message and gain understanding of the vision.

Seventy weeks have been decreed for your people and your holy city, to finish the transgression, to make an end of sin, to make atonement for iniquity, to bring in everlasting righteousness, to seal up vision and prophecy, and to anoint the most holy place.
—*DANIEL 9:22-24*

So let's get this straight. Daniel fasts and intercedes for God to end the seventy-year judgment against Israel, and then Gabriel shows up with a message about seventy *weeks* and *more* judgment. What?! So the seventy-year Babylonian captivity wasn't the end of God's discipline for Israel?

ISRAEL'S ORIGINAL REBELLION

To track what is going on here, we need to first understand the reason God chose the original seventy-year judgment in the first place. And to do that, we need to take a temporary detour away from the book of Daniel and away from our discussion of scale and timing. As far as detours go, this one may feel initially unnecessary and unrelated to our destination, but it contains important context for this chapter and beyond. I just want you to know that in advance in case you start to feel like we're getting lost. Let's get started:

And those who had escaped from the sword he carried away to Babylon; and they were servants to him and to his sons until the rule of the kingdom of Persia, to fulfill the word of the LORD by the mouth of Jeremiah, **until the land had enjoyed her Sabbaths**. All the days of its desolation it kept Sabbath until seventy years were complete.
—*2 CHRONICLES 36:20-21*

How strange. In sending the people of Judea into captivity for seventy years, God was giving the land a chance to experience seventy years' worth of Sabbath rest. This is an unfamiliar concept for many Christians, but it is immensely important to God:

> The LORD then spoke to Moses at Mount Sinai, saying: "Speak to the sons of Israel and say to them, 'When you come into the land which I shall give you, then the land shall have a sabbath to the LORD. Six years you shall sow your field, and six years you shall prune your vineyard and gather its crop, **but during the seventh year the land shall have a sabbath rest**, a sabbath to the LORD; you shall not sow your field nor prune your vineyard.
> —LEVITICUS 25:1-4

Here we go again with the fractal of seven. It's not just for God and humans; it's for land too. More on that in a minute. First, notice that God cares deeply about the health of land. A simple concordance search for every occurrence of the word "land" in Scripture reveals His extraordinary passion for land. Especially—though not exclusively—the land of Israel. Over and over again He calls the land of Israel His possession. Not just the people, but also the land specifically. And above it all is the city of Jerusalem on Mount Zion, the apple of God's eye. Some would say that God's preoccupation with the land of Jerusalem is simply a prophetic picture of His love for the Bride of Christ (and we'll see how true that is in a later chapter), but there is also far more to it than that. I don't pretend to fully understand the dynamic, but physical land is clearly important to the Creator, and He has a peculiar focus on the land of Israel.

I suspect that at least part of the reason God cares so much about land goes back to the third day of creation when He bonded matter together with His very word, drew the earth out of the waters, established its foundations, set its boundaries, and then went one step further by drawing life out of that matter to form seed-bearing plants and vegetation out of the earth. Matter itself is held together by His word at a subatomic level. That endows the earth with an immense deposit of God's life and essence that allows plants to do what they do, but it may also contribute to an interchange between the natural and spiritual realms in ways we don't yet understand.

Think about a physical seed. For all of our modern advances, scientists have yet to create a machine that comes close to matching the simple efficiency, effectiveness, and sustainability of a seed. A single acorn produces a towering oak tree from nothing more than soil, water, sunlight, and air, without significantly diminishing the resources around it. The life-producing power of a seed is nothing short of miraculous.

That is why the apostle Paul used the picture of a seed to describe the process of our physical bodies putting on immortality at the first resurrection (1 Corinthians 15). We are sown a natural body and raised a spiritual body. The spiritual body is somehow derived in part from the physical—that is how a seed works. And this is not just true of the human body. In the end, all of creation will become new. First cleansed, then healed, and eventually transformed. Heaven and earth will be summed up in Christ. At the end of Christ's millennial reign the physical and the spiritual realms will merge as heaven and earth take their next step into unity in Christ, which will make for a more suitable habitat for the Lamb and His wife. We'll talk more about that in later books in this series, but my point is that even now physical land has an embryonic component of God's life that is precious to Him and should be invaluable to us.

I don't know why, but it seems that some land has more—or at least more obvious—deposits of God's life than others. Scripture suggests as much. Perhaps you've experienced this dynamic yourself. Have you ever been to a particular mountain, stream, or coastline that just sings to you? A specific area of land where you feel closer to God, where you can't help but sense an aspect of His heart, or are reminded of a facet of His character? Those aren't just latent memories or the product of your imagination. Your spirit is sensing the particular deposit of God's life in that part of the earth, and just being in that place strengthens your connection to the Creator. Since God's essence is expressed in seven portions, it is no stretch to expect that different areas of land can have different deposits of that sevenfold essence, and that each is meant to draw the different portions of our spirit toward Him in different ways. These are spiritual treasures from which we are meant to partake. And based on the testimony of Scripture and the preponderance of human history, Jerusalem is particularly (though not exclusively) wealthy in that department.

Now back to Leviticus 25. Remember the seven-year cycle for slaves to choose "freedom" or become bondservants? Well, it seems there is a sister principle that applies to land. In both cases, the seven-year cycle was ultimately about rest. Becoming a bondservant is a form of rest from our striving, because we are surrendering to the reality that He is the owner and we are forever His stewards. And those who embraced the path of bondservant in Israel found themselves resting in a very natural way as they obeyed the master in allowing the land to have its own seventh-year rest. No sowing or pruning was to be done in the seventh year. That means the very first year of a newly initiated bondservant was one of exceptional emotional and physical rest.

It was no accident that these two rest cycles aligned. As the bondservants rested, the land rested, and because the land rested, the bondservants were able to rest. It was God's design for this to benefit the people and the land of Israel on so many levels. Think about what would happen if no slaves ever chose to become bondservants. The newly freed slaves would have no reserves for the future and would be under immense pressure to sow and prune their own land during the very year the land was supposed to rest. And over time the owners would be under increasing pressure to have their dwindling staff work the land during the seventh year to make up for lost productivity. I suspect this dynamic played a major role in Israel's rebellion. Whenever the people refused to let the land rest on the sabbath years, they also missed out on the spiritual deposits of God's life in the land. And by rebelling against God, they were also defiling the land. It was a terrible cycle that continually compounded into more missed opportunities to grow in intimacy with God, less thankfulness and resting in His provision, and more striving over time.

> At the end of Christ's millennial reign the physical and the spiritual realms will merge as heaven and earth take their next step into unity in Christ, which will make for a more suitable habitat for the Lamb and His wife.

PERVERTED PRINCIPLES, DEFILED LAND

Just to be clear, I am not saying that Israel's seventy-year Babylonian captivity was God's judgment for failing to observe the land's sabbath rest cycle. God ultimately separated Israel from their land because they committed detestable acts of idolatry that defiled the Temple, the city of Jerusalem, and the land of Israel in general:

> "I brought you into the fruitful land to eat its fruit and its good things. But you came and defiled My land, and My inheritance you made an abomination.
> —*JEREMIAH 2:7*

Notice that the full weight of Israel's defilement did not happen overnight—it was a steady accumulation from the moment they settled into the promised land and began "playing the harlot" with pagan gods many centuries before the Babylonian captivity. From the time of the Judges through the time of Kings, Israel continued their incremental cycle of idolatry followed by judgment, followed by repentance, followed by deeper idolatry. Eventually, the cup of their sin overflowed and God poured out His wrath through Babylon.

So what was the proverbial straw that broke the camel's back? How exactly did Israel defile the land so deeply that God was forced to remove the people and purge the land with fire? What specific acts made God's inheritance an abomination? Jeremiah explained it in detail:

> Therefore thus says the LORD, "Behold, I am about to give this city into the hand of the Chaldeans and into the hand of Nebuchadnezzar king of Babylon, and he will take it.
>
> "The Chaldeans who are fighting against this city will enter and set this city on fire and burn it, with the houses where people have offered incense to Baal on their roofs and poured out drink offerings to other gods to provoke Me to anger.
>
> "Indeed the sons of Israel and the sons of Judah have been doing only evil in My sight from their youth; for the sons of Israel have been only provoking Me to anger by the work of their hands," declares the LORD.
>
> "Indeed this city has been to Me a provocation of My anger and My wrath from the day that they built it, even to this day, so that it should be removed from before My face, because of all the evil of the sons of Israel and the sons of Judah which they have done to provoke Me to anger—they,

their kings, their leaders, their priests, their prophets, the men of Judah and the inhabitants of Jerusalem.

"They have turned their back to Me and not their face; though I taught them, teaching again and again, they would not listen and receive instruction. **But they put their detestable things in the house which is called by My name, to defile it**. They built the high places of Baal that are in the valley of Ben-hinnom **to cause their sons and their daughters to pass through the fire to Molech**, which I had not commanded them nor had it entered My mind that they should do this abomination, to cause Judah to sin.
—*JEREMIAH 32:28-35*

There is a general reference to brazen and shameless idol worship on rooftops, but the main judgment seems to be directed at two particular practices: setting up idols in the temple of God, and participating in child sacrifice. I do not want to distract from our current discussion of land—after all, we are already on a detour from building out the scale and timing of our map—but I need to take a quick moment to reframe these two practices around the concept of humanism. It will be a quick diversion for something we don't necessarily need to know right now, but it will pay dividends later on in our journey through the book of Revelation.

My simple definition of humanism is any attempt to replace God with mankind. There are many forms of humanism, but in my mind, they can all be divided into two basic categories: religious humanism and secular humanism. Religious humanism is usually the subtler of the two forms, as it uses deception to take God's place and redefine the divine, while secular humanism overtly opposes God and His divine character.

From that perspective, the abomination of setting up an idol in God's temple is the ultimate expression of religious humanism. It is the same root principle on display in mankind's original rebellion in the Garden of Eden. It is an attempt to grasp for God's divinity rather than resting in His plan to share the entirety of Himself with us. We do the same whenever we rely on religion, or religious institutions, or religious knowledge, or any other ostensibly spiritual endeavor to legitimize ourselves. But whenever we stare at an idol of our own making rather than our Maker, we neither see nor are transformed by the divine principles of God's character. That is often the very reason we place idols in God's temple (our hearts) to begin with—we desire imaginary "freedom" rather than trusting His kind intentions. The result is always devolution and slavery, and it causes us to defile everything we touch.

On the other hand, child sacrifice (causing their children to pass through the fire to Molech) is the ultimate abomination that flows from the secular side of humanism, and it is the downstream result of religious humanism. It makes sense that the longer we stare at an idol, the less like God we become. So in humanity's colossal misunderstanding of God's heart, and in our resulting attempts to be free from His design by setting up idols to replace Him, we have somehow even perverted the concept of His sacrificial love. Remember, the sacrifice of God's Son was written into the fabric of the universe, but in God's case the sacrifice was the ultimate act of selfless love, and it was the deepest, most abiding expression of His character.

God was willing to self-sacrifice to elevate the universe and unite it with His Son, but secular humanism perpetrates child sacrifice for self-gratification, comfort, convenience, and self-advancement. The most obvious form of contemporary child sacrifice is abortion, but it also includes child sex trafficking, and any other detestable perversion that steals, kills, or destroys the most innocent and vulnerable of humanity for selfish gain. Please understand that I am not sitting in judgment over every instance of abortion, nor do I intend to deal out shame, but it must be said that intentionally destroying innocence for personal gain is an affront to God's character, and it is an abomination that defiles us and the physical matter around us.

Okay, so Israel played the harlot with these abominations and incurred God's wrath in the form of Babylonian captivity. It was no coincidence that God chose Babylon as the captor. Babylon was the spiritual head of all world systems at the time, and although the physical kingdom of Babylon is long gone, its spiritual system still thrives today. We'll talk more about this later, but the Babylonian system is built on humanism, and it is the root of the authority that Satan has leveraged to rule from the spiritual shadows to this day. In Jeremiah's day, it was the natural destination for a rebellious Hebrew nation under discipline for embracing the slavery of humanism.

It's not that God desired for His people to live under such perverse oppression, but sometimes when a child is continually rebellious after ignoring every warning and rejecting every mercy, a parent's only recourse is to allow them to suffer the consequences of their actions. Temporarily expelling Israel from their land into Babylonian captivity was the most appropriate method of instruction. The remorseless perpetrators of the abominations would die off, the collective psyche of the nation would absorb some difficult lessons as an entirely new generation grew up in Babylon, and the land of Israel would enjoy a sabbath rest to recuperate from the defilement.

Okay, now you can take everything I just mentioned about abominations, humanism, and the Babylonian system and stick it on the shelf in the back of your mind. These embryonic concepts will provide some useful context for our discussion of scale and timing in the book of Daniel, but their main value will manifest later in our journey through the book of Revelation. The focus of our journey will ever and always be the transformational glory of Christ's Unveiling rather than the works of the enemy, but we will find expressions of that glory while observing the way His enemies are overcome.

STEWARDSHIP SQUANDERED

Back to the subject of land so that we can finish this detour. We've seen that the land of Israel was defiled and needed a sabbath rest. Now imagine what could have been if Israel had simply obeyed God's land-related commands when they first entered the promised land. What would have happened if Israel had properly stewarded the land that God gave them and availed themselves of His provision in the ways He intended? If they had observed the ordinance about the land's sabbath cycle, wouldn't the land that flowed with milk and honey have nurtured them spiritually as well as physically?

The sabbath rest for the land was designed as a buffer against Israel's propensity to forget her God, a shield against the creeping religious and secular humanism of the surrounding world systems. If they cared for the land, it would care for them. Even during those years when God was seemingly silent and distant—when there were no prophets or miracles or external manifestations of His glory—the land was meant to be an active reminder of His goodness and a constant source of revelation about His character. The mountaintop where Abraham's faith pleased God, the land where Jacob dreamed of a ladder to heaven, the valley where he wrestled with God, the parting of the Jordan River, the slaying of Goliath, the many battles and miraculous deliverances: these and countless other divine encounters were part of the DNA of the land, and it still had so much more to tell about the Creator in general, and the coming Messiah in particular. What would have happened if Israel steward-ed these immense treasures rather than acting like slaves afflicted with perpetu-al poverty?

Think about the immensity of the treasure that Israel abdicated. Warning: this will require some arithmetic. When God finally disciplined the people with seventy years of captivity and purged their defiled structures, the land of Jerusalem and the surrounding region of Judea were able to enjoy seventy years of Sabbath rest. Given the seven-year sabbath cycle command that the land was to be worked for six years and then rested for one year, we can conclude that God was providing the land seventy *cycles* worth of rest in one giant dose. In other words, seventy years of rest covered seventy missed sabbath cycles worth of rest. If you are following the math, seventy sabbath cycles are equivalent to 490 years (70 x 7). That suggests that from the time they entered the promised land to the beginning of their Babylonian captivity, Israel neglected the land's sabbath cycle for 490 years.

> Sometimes when a child is continually rebellious after ignoring every warning and rejecting every mercy, a parent's only recourse is to allow them to suffer the consequences of their actions.

We don't know precisely what was going on in Israel when this rebellion started because the Bible doesn't associate exact dates to most of the events during that period of Israel's history, but counting 490 years backward from the start of the Babylonian captivity would land somewhere around the end of the time of the Judges and the beginning of the rule of King Saul.

This is a fascinating possibility considering that the book of Judges specifically mentions that the *land* of Israel experienced rest during the years that some of the more successful judges ruled Israel after delivering them from their neighboring oppressors. It would make sense if Israel's insistence on having a human king to make them more like the neighboring world systems coincided with a greater embrace of humanism and a neglect of the spiritual treasures in their land. This is all speculation, but my main point is that Israel wasted 490 years worth of opportunity to learn more about God's heart through His fingerprints on their land. That's 490 years of rebellion. Remember that number, and the reason for that number, when we return to Daniel's prophecy of the seventy weeks in the next chapter.

Before we move on, consider the following passage in light of God's discipline and long-suffering forgiveness. Perhaps Jesus had Israel's 490-year rebellion in the back of His mind when He answered Peter here:

> Then Peter came and said to Him, "Lord, how often shall my brother sin against me and I forgive him? Up to seven times?" Jesus said to him, "I do not say to you, up to seven times, **but up to seventy times seven.**
> —*MATTHEW 18:21-22*

CHAPTER 12

SCALE AND TIMING - PART 2:
SEVENTY TIMES SEVEN

or - "That's a lot of forgiveness!"

With that detour complete, we now know something of why God sent Israel into captivity in the first place, and we are better positioned to understand His response to Daniel's intercession for Israel's freedom:

> **"Seventy weeks** have been decreed for **your people and your holy city**, to finish the transgression, to make an end of sin, to make atonement for iniquity, to bring in everlasting righteousness, to seal up vision and prophecy, and to anoint the Most Holy Place.
> —*DANIEL 9:24*

Notice this prophecy is for the people *and* the land. Both must work together to bring about God's purpose. The Hebrew word translated *weeks* here literally means *sevens* or *sevened*. What Gabriel probably said was, "Seventy sevens have been decreed. ..." Most scholars agree that the term *weeks* in this context refers to a period of seven years (i.e., a week of years), which makes sense considering this entire drama is wrapped around the seven-year sabbath rest cycle for the land. "Seventy weeks" literally means seventy sets of seven-year periods, which equals a total of 490 years decreed for the people and the land. Are you tracking? This prophecy was not about the previous 490 years of rebellion that led to Israel's captivity—it was about another period of 490 years still to come.

So let's reframe the prophecy. In answer to Daniel's intercession about the restoration of Israel, God responded with a significantly larger perspective. It's as if the Creator was saying, "Okay, the seventy years are up, but there's so much more going on than you know. The land is cleansed and rested and ready to give its treasures to the people again, so I'm about to reunite them. But this is just the first step in a grander process designed to bring the *people* to rest. They disobeyed for seventy sabbath cycles because of their slave mindset, so I'm giving them seventy more sabbath cycles to learn how to choose the rest of a bondservant. And they're going to need every second of it. The root of their rebellion runs deep and has yet to be dealt with, so they will continue to shun my treasures and reject my gift. Greater defilement and destruction are still to come, but once the full measure of their sin has manifested, I will lay the ax to the root, and open their eyes to my plan, and only then will they finally choose to enter my rest."

I know that was clunky and that I took significant liberties, but I do think that is essentially what God was saying. To put it more succinctly, He was setting aside seventy sets of seven-year periods that were specifically designed to perfect Israel as she interacted with the land of God's possession, and specifically with the city of Jerusalem, to bring forth the Messiah in the right time and place. And as we'll see in a moment, Israel's perfection will only come through tribulation.

SEVEN OBJECTIVES

Before we look at the structure of the seventy-weeks prophecy, let's take a moment to unpack its purpose. Gabriel said that during this period seven specific objectives would be accomplished through the people and land of Israel. So right off the bat, we should be viewing the seventy weeks through the fractal of seven, meaning that the seven objectives can be seen as seven progressive, sequential steps meant to reproduce the sevenfold essence of God to perfect Israel as part of His suitable companion.

Gabriel described the objectives of the seventy weeks as follows:

1. Finish the transgression
2. Make an end of sin
3. Make atonement for iniquity
4. Bring in everlasting righteousness
5. Seal up the vision
6. [Seal up] prophecy
7. Anoint the most Holy Place

A study of each of these seven points could fill volumes. In many ways, these seven objectives are a picture of God's entire work of redemption through Jesus Christ. There are multiple ways to look at each objective, and there are likely multiple levels on which each will be fulfilled in Israel, the Body of Christ, and all of creation. Having said that, any spiritual or symbolic significance cannot negate the fact that there must also be a literal, practical way in which they apply, through Christ, to the people and land of Israel. If you are inclined to disagree, just remember Paul's passionately unambiguous discourse in the book of Romans. If Israel are the natural branches, shouldn't we expect a very natural and literal process that grafts them back into the olive tree? One that also fully reconciles Israel to the life of God deposited in her land?

From that perspective, we can also frame these seven objectives as seven steps for reconciling Israel to her original birthright. In the vernacular of Romans 12, this is God's prescription for Israel to present the seven aspects of Her corporate body as a living sacrifice, holy and acceptable to God.

Please note that the prophecy does not mention the Gentile Church because, at the time of Daniel's vision, the mystery of the Church had not yet been revealed. But as we saw in the book of Romans, the destinies of the natural and wild branches are indivisible. The Gentile Church will play a major role in Israel's healing, especially in the second half of the prophecy's final week. Having said that, in this chapter, we are going to focus almost exclusively on the nation of Israel. At times you may wonder what any of this has to do with the Church or with us as individuals. Be patient. The best way to build a practical and useful grid for understanding the timing and sequencing of the book of Revelation is to view Daniel's seventy-week prophecy from Israel's perspective. Our focus will begin shifting to the Church's role in the Unveiling in the next few chapters, but first, we need to gather data points related to the natural branches. Now back to the seven objectives:

OBJECTIVE 1: FINISH THE TRANSGRESSION

Transgression is willful rebellion against God's principles. What was Israel's original rebellion that still needed to be finished during the seventy weeks? In the context of Daniel chapter 9, was it their idolatrous and murderous abominations that defiled the land and precipitated their captivity in the first place? Perhaps, but those abominations were the fruit of their rebellion, not the root.

Israel's transgression started much earlier. Their first national rebellion was at Mount Sinai when they corporately shrank back from God's offer to be His possession, His kingdom of priests, and His holy nation. They were abused slaves so terrified of punishment that they couldn't perceive the goodness of God's design, so in that moment, they embraced a subtle form of religious humanism in an attempt to maintain their illusion of freedom: "Moses, you become our idol. You stand between us and God. We'll stand back here where we can safely maintain our separation and autonomy."

If you recall our discussion of the seven days of creation, the first step of the fractal of seven was the expression of God's original design. Likewise, this first objective of Israel's seventy-week prophecy is all about dealing with their original rejection of God's design, and with their attempts to redefine His design around their own slave mindset. God intends to heal the root of that rebellion to prepare them for sonship. But first, they must *finish* the transgression, and that implies more rebellion in the future, possibly culminating in one last, desperate embrace of the abominations of humanism when its ultimate manifestation arises at the end. The repercussions of that decision will be so ruinous for the nation of Israel that she will finally be shaken free from her spirit of slavery just in time to embrace the returning King, whose merciful intention is to graft them back into His body. More on that later.

OBJECTIVE 2: MAKE AN END OF SIN

Whereas transgression is willful rebellion against God's principles, sin is simply falling short of God's principles, even when done in ignorance, immaturity, ambivalence, or through some other weakness.

In what way is Israel destined to make an end of sin? On the one hand, this could be a reference to Christ's work on the cross, which, at the time of the prophecy, was destined to be instigated by Israel's leadership hundreds of years later. When Christ died, the old nature and its sin also died for all those who choose to rest in Him. From that perspective Israel would be committing the ultimate sin of ignorance, while also inadvertently facilitating an end of sin by instigating Christ's crucifixion. That could be a legitimate fulfillment of the prophecy—each of the prophecy's seven objectives ultimately revolve around Christ—but right now we are focusing on a more practical fulfillment that specifically illuminates God's plan for the natural branches.

Think about the Levitical priesthood. They had two primary roles: to minister to God and to minister to the other eleven tribes. The priesthood stood between God and the people to help Israel manage their sin problem enough to maintain some semblance of a relationship with a holy God. It wasn't God's original design, but it was all the nation could handle.

Now think about Israel's original calling. They were to be a kingdom of priests and a holy nation. The entire nation was to become intimately acquainted with God's nature and to share that nature with the nations of the world. A kingdom of priests wouldn't need to be so focused on managing the sin of their own nation; the horizontal aspect of their ministry could be outwardly focused on the rest of the world. Such was the calling of a bondservant nation.

As a holy nation, Israel was designed to cooperate with the Spirit of Wisdom to positively impact the overall spiritual and moral atmosphere of the world by disseminating a general level of God's light. Christ was the only one who could end the root of mankind's sin and elevate humanity to the fullness of God's intention, but Israel was supposed to help prepare the way for His incarnation.

In the fullness of time, Christ came into the world through Israel, even though Israel failed to willingly cooperate in the process. What would world history have looked like if Israel had fully embraced their calling to prepare His path rather than embracing the world systems of humanism? We may never know on this side of eternity, but according to the second objective of the seventy-week prophecy, we can be assured that Israel will eventually grasp their calling before the end. They didn't intentionally prepare the world for Christ's first coming, but they most certainly will come around just in time to be a powerful witness to the entire world of God's faithfulness right before His second coming. And like the principles seen during the second day of creation, Israel's testimony at the very

> As a holy nation, Israel was designed to cooperate with the Spirit of Wisdom to positively impact the overall spiritual and moral atmosphere of the world by disseminating a general level of God's light.

end of the age will contribute to a faith-filled atmosphere on the earth that will be vital to supporting the work of God's people in bringing healing to the nations during the millennial reign of Christ.

OBJECTIVE 3: MAKE ATONEMENT FOR INIQUITY

Iniquity means twisting, or something twisted. It is the warping, or perversion, of the principles that reflect God's character. Iniquity is what happens inside of us when our hearts are focused on an idol, and it is the opposite of the power of Christ's Unveiling. Jesus illustrated this principle beautifully in the Sermon on the Mount after explaining that the eye is the lamp of the body:

> But if your eye is bad, your whole body will be full of darkness. So if the light that is in you is darkness, how great is the darkness!
> —*MATTHEW 6:23*

A common progression (or digression in this case) is that sin leads to transgression which leads to iniquity, which leads to more sin, transgression, and iniquity in a downward spiral of devolution, which eventually produces abomination and then destruction. We can see this cycle at work on an individual and cultural level throughout world history.

Every culture is designed by God to reflect different aspects of His nature, and every nation falls short of that mark to various degrees and in various ways, either through ignorance or rebellion, which eventually leads to iniquitous defilement over time. Part of Israel's original calling as a kingdom of priests was to cooperate with the Spirit of Understanding to help other nations identify and unpack their own unique treasures by intentionally, incrementally, and practically teaching them God's divine principles. It's not that Israel was meant to tell other countries who they were supposed to be or how they were supposed to conduct their business—the intention wasn't to conform other nations to Israel—but Israel was designed to help release other nations into their own unique representation of God's unfathomably diverse glory by simply shining the light of His character.

Israel's sin, rebellion, and iniquity caused her to shun this aspect of her birthright, but Daniel's seventy-week prophecy describes God's plan for restoration. In the law of Moses, atonement for iniquity required sacrifice. Jesus Christ provided the perfect and final atonement, but as Israel chose self-righteousness while instigating His crucifixion and rejecting the value of His sacrifice, they are now experiencing a commensurate measure of God's judgment that will not be complete until the end of the seventy-week prophecy when the natural branches are grafted back into the tree that represents the Body of Christ. And only when the Body of Christ is finally whole and completely joined to the Head will she be released as the tree of life to bring healing to the nations.

Israel's seventy weeks are about taking responsibility and atoning for her iniquity, which will prepare her to participate in the healing of other nations, and the untwisting of millennia worth of iniquity that has clouded the world's perception of God's character.

> Part of Israel's original calling as a kingdom of priests was to cooperate with the Spirit of Understanding to help other nations identify and unpack their own unique treasures by intentionally, incrementally, and practically teaching them God's divine principles.

OBJECTIVE 4: BRING IN EVERLASTING RIGHTEOUSNESS

The first three objectives were about healing the negatives. Rebellion, sin, and iniquity are the veils that attempt to keep mankind from seeing Christ. Bringing in everlasting righteousness is about the transformation that begins as those veils are removed.

Ever since they shrank back from their full birthright on Mount Sinai, Israel has seen righteousness through the lens of an incomplete and sometimes warped view of the law of Moses. The law of Moses *is* righteous. It is God-breathed and accurately represents His standard of righteousness, but the greatest treasures of the law are hidden in the principles of God's character that they reveal. In other words, the spirit of the law versus the letter of the law. The letter of the law was given as a tutor to an immature and rebellious nation of wounded slaves to sustain them until Christ came to demonstrate true sonship in the spirit of the law. When the national veil that keeps Israel from seeing Christ is finally removed, the physical earth itself will be shaken and purified by her incomparable capacity to see God's glory and to understand the depth of the righteousness of His character hidden in the principles of the law.

Another way to think about Israel's role in "bringing in everlasting righteousness" is described in David's magnificent song about the coming King in Psalm 24. Please take your time and read the whole thing, imagining this as the corporate testimony of Israel after she turns to Jesus. As you read, remember the fourth day of creation when God placed the sun, moon, and stars in the sky to illuminate the earth and to mark the seasons and days and years, because this Psalm describes Israel cooperating with the Spirit of Council to express those same divine principles.

As the natural branches, Israel has a special corporate calling to impact the natural realm, cleanse the physical land, declare the times and seasons of God, bring the natural realm into alignment

> When the national veil that keeps Israel from seeing Christ is finally removed, the physical earth itself will be shaken and purified by her incomparable capacity to see God's glory and to understand the depth of the righteousness of His character hidden in the principles of the law.

with those seasons, and prepare the earth to receive the everlasting right-eousness of the King. The spiritual realm is a different matter. Transfor-mation of the spiritual realm is largely the purview and responsibility of the wild branches of the Gentile Church, but we'll talk about that later:

> The earth is the LORD'S, and all it contains,
> The world, and those who dwell in it.
> For He has founded it upon the seas
> And established it upon the rivers.
> Who may ascend into the hill of the LORD?
> And who may stand in His holy place?
> He who has clean hands and a pure heart,
> Who has not lifted up his soul to falsehood
> And has not sworn deceitfully.
> He shall receive a blessing from the LORD
> And righteousness from the God of his salvation.
> This is the generation of those who seek Him,
> Who seek Your face—even Jacob. Selah
> Lift up your heads, O gates,
> And be lifted up, O ancient doors,
> That the King of glory may come in!
> Who is the King of glory?
> The LORD strong and mighty,
> The LORD mighty in battle.
> Lift up your heads, O gates,
> And lift them up, O ancient doors,
> That the King of glory may come in!
> Who is this King of glory?
> The LORD of hosts,
> He is the King of glory. Selah
> —PSALM 24

OBJECTIVE 5: SEAL UP VISION

The "vision" could mean a lot of things, but I take it as a general refer-ence to the vision of the heavenly tabernacle that Moses had on Mount Sinai. This vision became the template for the physical tabernacle of Moses and the foundation for the entire form and structure of the Jew-ish religion, including the very law itself.

To seal up typically means to close, to hide from view, or to keep something from being understood. So in one sense, this alludes to the current partial hardening that keeps Israel from seeing how the entire law points to Jesus Christ. This is a fascinating juxtaposition of ideas considering that the book of Revelation is about unsealing, unveiling, and unleashing. From that perspective, sealing up the vision also has an element of finality and completion. Think about a grave being sealed after the body is laid to rest. That chapter of existence is over, having run its full course, never to be seen again. So too will the law of Moses have run its full course for Israel when her eyes are finally opened to understand the true purpose of the law as a temporary mentor leading them to Christ.

To seal up has another meaning that is even more impactful in this context. When a king writes a law, establishes a command, or enters into a covenant, it becomes official when sealed by the royal signet ring. On the one hand, the law of Moses will have run its course for Israel when they embrace Christ, but at the same time, the principles of God's heart behind that law—the spirit of the law—will be established on the earth with Christ's return. And closely related to that, the new Jerusalem that comes down out of heaven—the very city that Abraham was searching for, and the very mystery behind Moses's original vision—will also be established in reality. To seal up the vision is ultimately about the marriage ceremony of the Lamb and His Bride, but we'll come back to that concept later.

OBJECTIVE 6: SEAL UP PROPHECY

I doubt Gabriel had a specific prophecy in mind, but rather he was referring to prophecy in general, especially the words of the Old Testament prophets.

The "prophecy" is closely related to the "vision," which is why they are linked in the text when Gabriels says, "To seal up vision *and* prophecy." Together the vision and prophecy are a reference to the spirit of the law and the prophets, or the principles behind the letter of the law and the words of the prophets. Both are testimonies of Jesus:

> Philip found Nathanael and said to him, "We have found Him of whom Moses in the Law and also the Prophets wrote—Jesus of Nazareth, the son of Joseph."
> —*JOHN 1:45*

> But now apart from the Law the righteousness of God has
> been manifested, being witnessed by the Law and the
> Prophets, even the righteousness of God through faith in
> Jesus Christ for all those who believe; for there is no distinc-
> tion;
>
> —ROMANS 3:21-22

The "vision" (and therefore the law) was essentially a representation
of God's plan to form a suitable companion. As the fifth step in the
fractal of seven, it is the work of the Spirit of Might, and it aligns with
the redemptive gift of giver. The tabernacle was a picture of His Bride,
and the law a veiled expression of His plan to perfect Her in love. But
the "prophecy" (the summation of the Old Testament prophets) was a
testimony of the coming King and His intention to expand His kingdom until all of heaven and earth are summed up in Him. Said another
way, the "prophecy" is about the knowledge of the glory of the Lord filling the earth as the waters cover the sea. In the sequence of the seven
objectives of Israel's seventy weeks, it coincides with the redemptive gift
of ruler, and it echos the role of the Spirit of Knowledge to bring everything into alignment with the King. The Bride will be the first and most
crucial step of that plan because only through the Bride can Christ be
fruitful and multiply, but the "prophecy" is fundamentally focused on
the process that God uses to become all in all through the reception of
His divine principles.

The essence of prophecy is perfectly summarized toward the end of
the book of Revelation:

> Then he said to me, "Write, 'Blessed are those who are in-
> vited to the marriage supper of the Lamb.'" And he said to
> me, "These are true words of God." Then I fell at his feet
> to worship him. But he said to me, "Do not do that; I am a
> fellow servant of yours and your brethren who hold the
> testimony of Jesus; worship God. **For the testimony of
> Jesus is the spirit of prophecy**."
>
> And I saw heaven opened, and behold, a white horse,
> and He who sat on it is called Faithful and True, and in
> righteousness He judges and wages war. His eyes are a
> flame of fire, and on His head are many diadems; and He

> has a name written on Him which no one knows except Himself. He is clothed with a robe dipped in blood, and His name is called The Word of God. And the armies which are in heaven, clothed in fine linen, white and clean, were following Him on white horses. From His mouth comes a sharp sword, so that with it He may strike down the nations, and He will rule them with a rod of iron; and He treads the wine press of the fierce wrath of God, the Almighty. And on His robe and on His thigh He has a name written, "KING OF KINGS, AND LORD OF LORDS."
> —*REVELATION 19:9-16*

After hearing that the testimony of Jesus *is* the spirit of prophecy, John immediately witnessed the fulfillment of everything that the Old Testament prophets declared. In other words, the "prophecy" will be sealed up when Christ returns as the warrior Bridegroom King.

As for Israel, she is presently estranged from the spirit of the law and the prophets, but in the closing years of the seventy-week time period, the faithful remnant of Israel will have their own "Emmaus Road" experience during which the Unveiling of Jesus will gradually unseal the entire law and the prophets so that they can finally see how their entire history was to bring forth Christ and His purposes:

> And He said to them, "O foolish men and slow of heart to believe in all that the prophets have spoken! "Was it not necessary for the Christ to suffer these things and to enter into His glory?" Then beginning with Moses and with all the prophets, He explained to them the things concerning Himself in all the Scriptures.
> —*LUKE 24:25-27*

OBJECTIVE 7: ANOINT THE MOST HOLY PLACE

Some translations say, "To anoint the most Holy." The imagery is that of the Levitical priesthood ceremonially consecrating the tabernacle and its utensils for service in preparation for God's presence to inhabit the holy of holies. It also conjures the picture of Samual anointing a young David. In either case, this is all about welcoming the holy presence of the King of Kings as He finally arrives on earth.

This seventh step aligns with the work of the Spirit of Fear of the Lord, and it will finally usher Israel into the sabbath rest of unity with I AM, as described in one of David's songs of ascent:

> Behold, how good and how pleasant it is
> For brothers to dwell together in unity!
> It is like the precious oil upon the head,
> Coming down upon the beard,
> Even Aaron's beard,
> Coming down upon the edge of his robes.
> It is like the dew of Hermon
> Coming down upon the mountains of Zion;
> For there the LORD commanded the blessing—life forever.
> —PSALM 133

As the natural branches, the nation of Israel—or at least the faithful remnant of Israel who have maintained a connection, however tenuous, to the faith of their fathers and the promise of a Messiah—have a role to play in welcoming Christ and His newly wedded Bride to earth, and in the welcoming, to be united back into the olive tree.

NOT YET PERFECTED

With that general summary of the seven objectives in hand, take a step back and look at the seventy-weeks prophecy as a whole. What conclusions can we draw that will help us understand the timing and sequence of end-times events? First, has Israel completed any of these objectives? Not likely. Is Israel already grafted back into Christ? Certainly not. Has Israel already been perfected? The answer is obvious. Although the provision for her perfection was established through Christ's work on the cross, most of Israel is currently estranged from Christ, and therefore unable to fulfill her destiny.

As with the Gentile Church, Israel has yet to fulfill her purpose in God's plan for creation, and that means her

> As with the Gentile Church, Israel has yet to fulfill her purpose in God's plan for creation, and that means her seventy-week period cannot possibly have finished yet.

seventy-week period cannot possibly have finished yet. Why does that matter? And why did I take so much time expounding on the purpose of the seventy-weeks prophecy just to conclude that the period is not yet over? All of this is merely the starting point for understanding the rest of the prophecy and its relationship to the Unveiling of Christ. Now let's see what *else* Gabriel prophesied …

CHAPTER 13

SCALE AND TIMING - PART 3: THE HOURGLASS

or - "Is the clock ticking?"

After announcing the sevenfold purpose of Israel's seventy weeks, Gabriel continued by describing a sequence of events that would provide contextual markers for understanding the timing and duration of the prophecy. Remember the thick jungle foliage I warned about? That's where we are now. This next part can get complicated, but don't worry—we'll simplify as much as possible, stick to the highlights, and move quickly toward our goal. If you enjoy the beauty of complexity, I encourage you to use these cliff notes as the starting point for your own investigation.

As we go through the seventy-weeks prophecy, remember the context: Israel's Babylonian captivity was divine discipline for 490 years worth of rebellion, idol worship, and the pagan practice of child sacrifice, all of which left the people and land of Israel utterly defiled. God called a timeout by removing the people from the land just long enough for the rebellious generation to die out while the land enjoyed a season of rest and recuperation. This was vital because the people of Israel and the land of Israel were designed to bless each other in a symbiotic relationship. The seventy-year captivity was like a reset button. It returned the people and the land back to the spiritual state they were in when Israel first entered the promised land with Joshua.

The Babylonian captivity wasn't designed to deal with the root issue of Israel's spirit of slavery, and it certainly wasn't the full measure of discipline that Israel would need to endure to enter mature sonship as a nation, but it did return them to zero and give them a chance to start building toward their destiny again. And that's where the seventy-weeks prophecy begins. Let's jump in. Note that I'm using the Revised Standard Version for these verses because I find it clarifies a few key points that are more ambiguous in some other translations:

> 25) "Know therefore and understand that from the going forth of the word to restore and build Jerusalem to the coming of an anointed one, a prince, there shall be **seven weeks**. Then for **sixty-two weeks** it shall be built again with squares and moat, but in a troubled time.
>
> 26) And after the sixty-two weeks, an anointed one shall be cut off, and shall have nothing; and the people of the prince who is to come shall destroy the city and the sanctuary. Its end shall come with a flood, and to the end there shall be war; desolations are decreed.
>
> 27) And he shall make a strong covenant with many for **one week**; and for half of a week he shall cause sacrifice and offering to cease; and upon the wing of abominations shall come one who makes desolate, until the decreed end is poured out on the desolator."
> —DANIEL 9:25-27 RSV

Rather than telling Daniel exactly when the seventy weeks would start and end, Gabriel gave contextual clues that could only be understood as the actual events began to unfold. He listed a few earmark events that would occur during the 490-year period and specified when, relative to the rest of the seventy weeks, each event would take place. In this way, he separated the seventy-week period into three distinct sections: seven weeks, sixty-two weeks, and one week. Added together, these three sections combine for a total of seventy weeks. In terms of years, the sections equal a period of 49 years, a period of 434 years, and a period of 7 years, all of which add up to 490 years.

I should point out that the final week, the last seven-year period, is peculiar in its construction. Gabriel said the final week begins with a covenant with many, but then he drew specific attention to the middle of the week. This middle of the seventieth week is immensely important, but not for the reason that many people think. More on this shortly.

Hang in there if your eyes are glazing over from all these numbers. There is a simple point here, and it doesn't require any more math. The reason God divided the seventy weeks into multiple sections is that the prophecy was meant to span a period much longer than 490 years from start to finish, and the timeline would start and stop based on whether or not Israel was actively drawing life from her land and moving toward her purpose. And that means the sections of the prophecy would neither occur contiguously nor uninterrupted.

Think of the seventy-week prophecy as an hourglass. When God started the hourglass, the seventy weeks would start counting down. After the first seven weeks (forty-nine years), God would turn the hourglass on its side to pause the countdown for an unspecified amount of time. When He started the hourglass again, the seventy weeks would tick down for another sixty-two weeks (434 years) and stop again for a pause that would last an unspecified amount of time before He started the hourglass for the final week (seven-year) countdown. But then in the middle of the seventieth week, the hourglass would again stop for a final pause of undefined length before finally starting again for the last 3.5 years of history:

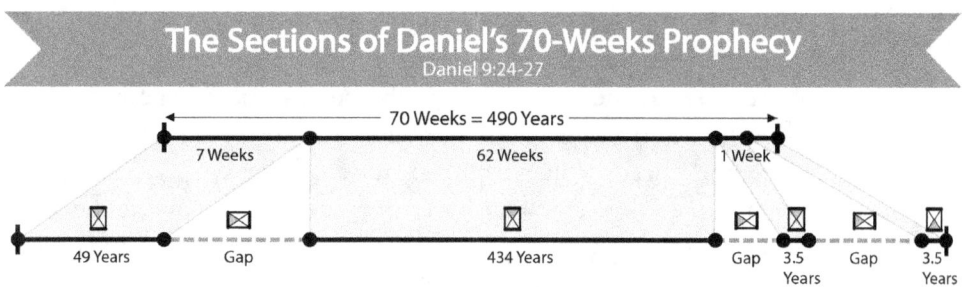

The Sections of Daniel's 70-Weeks Prophecy
Daniel 9:24-27

Although a detailed discussion of the first two sections (the first sixty-nine weeks) is beyond the scope of this book, I'll add a few possible dates and supporting historical context to the timeline in a moment.

The exact dates are less consequential than the general mechanics involved in the flow from one section to the other. I'm less concerned about precisely when the seven weeks started or when the sixty-two weeks stopped than I am with understanding why and how they lead to the final week of the prophecy. I'm not saying that information is unimportant, but I haven't taken the time to study exactly what the pattern of the first sixty-nine weeks might suggest about Christ's Unveiling. I suspect there are jewels to be found in that study. If you decide to go down that path, I'd love to hear what you find.

> The reason God divided the seventy weeks into multiple sections is that the prophecy was meant to span a period much longer than 490 years from start to finish.

Either way, there is enough ambiguity in the original prophecy to allow for minor variations to the timeline. Just remember that Israel has not yet accomplished the stated objectives of her seventy-week period, so whether or not you agree with the dates I'm about to suggest, we should at least agree that the seventieth week cannot have already ended.

Notice that I did not say the seventieth week itself has not already begun. That's because I believe that it started a long time ago and that we are currently in the middle of the seventieth week, nestled somewhere in the gap between the first and second halves of the seventieth week. Don't worry, I'll explain exactly what I mean by that in the next chapter.

One more word about the gaps before we move on. The built-in gaps of unspecified length allowed God to provide a detailed prophecy about Israel's future all the way up through the end of the age without actually telling us when the end would come. The gaps also allowed for human choice and the ever-important exercise of free will. Remember Peter's words about looking for and hastening the coming of the day of the Lord? There is some combination of factors that need to be in place in both the Church and Israel before the final 3.5 years begins. Only the Father knows that heavenly calculation, but I believe our choices are the main variables. Sure, there are other factors: geopolitical events, Satan's plans, the advancing of the beast's agenda, and other dark powers play a role, but none of these determine when the hourglass starts for the final time as much as the Body of Christ's response to the Bridegroom's invitation.

As we'll see in a moment, the division of the seventy weeks into multiple sections was not arbitrary. It all revolved around the land of Israel in general and the city of Jerusalem in particular. The clock would only tick when Israel was drawing life from the spiritual and natural treasures in her land and progressing toward her calling. The clock would stop when they were not. That is what the seventy weeks were designed for, and that is why I am going to suggest that the clock for the seventy weeks started for the first time when God first announced through Jeremiah that Jerusalem's desolation was only temporary and that its ultimate restoration would come at the hands of the Messiah.

Without getting into all the specific dates and complex timeline of everything that was going on in Jerusalem at that time, when Jeremiah declared God's promise of restoration, a measure of life started flowing to the people

> The built-in gaps of unspecified length allowed God to provide a detailed prophecy about Israel's future all the way up through the end of the age without actually telling us when the end would come.

again in the form of hope: Hope in God's mercy, hope that they would be reunited with the land, but most importantly, hope in the coming Messiah, who was prophesied to be born in the land of Israel and to rule from Jerusalem. That hope gave them something to hold on to while they were in Babylon, even if they weren't physically back in the land yet. Read a few excerpts from Jeremiah's words to see what I mean:

> "Now therefore thus says the LORD God of Israel concerning this city of which you say, 'It is given into the hand of the king of Babylon by sword, by famine and by pestilence.'
>
> "Behold, I will gather them out of all the lands to which I have driven them in My anger, in My wrath and in great indignation; and I will bring them back to this place and make them dwell in safety.

"They shall be My people, and I will be their God; and I will give them one heart and one way, that they may fear Me always, for their own good and for the good of their children after them.

"I will make an **everlasting covenant** with them that I will not turn away from them, to do them good; and **I will put the fear of Me in their hearts** so that they will not turn away from Me.

"I will rejoice over them to do them good and **will faithfully plant them in this land with all My heart and with all My soul**.

"For thus says the LORD, 'Just as I brought all this great disaster on this people, so I am going to bring on them all the good that I am promising them.
—*JEREMIAH 32:36-42*

While they are coming to fight with the Chaldeans and to fill them with the corpses of men whom I have slain in My anger and in My wrath, and I have hidden My face from this city because of all their wickedness:

'Behold, I will bring to it health and healing, and I will heal them; and **I will reveal to them an abundance of peace and truth.**

'I will restore the fortunes of Judah and the fortunes of Israel and will rebuild them as they were at first.

'I will **cleanse them from all their iniquity** by which they have sinned against Me, and I will **pardon all their iniquities** by which they have sinned against Me and by which they have transgressed against Me.

'It will be to Me a name of joy, praise and glory before all the nations of the earth which will hear of all the good that I do for them, and they will fear and tremble because of all the good and all the peace that I make for it.'
—*JEREMIAH 33:5-9*

'Behold, days are coming,' declares the LORD, 'when I will fulfill the good word which I have spoken concerning the house of Israel and the house of Judah. 'In those days and at that time **I will cause a righteous Branch of David**

to spring forth; and **He shall execute justice and righteousness on the earth**. 'In those days Judah will be saved and **Jerusalem will dwell in safety**; and this is the name by which she will be called: the LORD is our righteousness.'
—*JEREMIAH 33:14-16*

We could go on and on from the words of Jeremiah and other prophets, but you get the picture. These prophecies reached far beyond Israel's return from her seventy-year Babylonian captivity and any subsequent work to rebuild the temple and city of Jerusalem. These were promises of ultimate restoration, and the remnant of Israel being planted securely in their land was a key ingredient that needed to be in place before the Messiah could come forth. In hindsight, we now also understand that these are key ingredients before Israel can see the Unveiled Christ and thereby enter into the rest of their calling.

Jeremiah's prophecies were the context in which Daniel received the seventy-week visitation, and they were the frame in which the seventy weeks were meant to fit. So it makes sense that this "going forth of the word to restore and rebuild Jerusalem" would trigger the beginning of the seventy weeks, and that every other aspect of the seventy weeks would revolve around Jerusalem's ultimate restoration, which in turn revolves around Jesus.

With that in mind, here are some potential dates for the first sixty-nine weeks of the timeline to help us prepare for a deeper discussion of the final one-week period that culminates the entire prophecy:

The 70 Weeks Allotted for Israel's Perfection
Daniel 9:24-27

587 B.C. (Israel's 70 Weeks Begin)
> Promise of future Jerusalem restoration (Jeremiah 32)
> Promise of future Messianic covenant

70th Week Begins
> Stong covenant with many

2nd Half of 70th Week Begins
> Arrival of the "desolator"

444 ~ 440 B.C. (62-Week Period Begins)
> Nehemiah begins rebuilding Jerusalem

7 Weeks		62 Weeks		1/2 Week		1/2 Week
49 Years	Gap	434 Years	Gap	3.5 Years	Gap	3.5 Years

538 B.C. (7-Week Period Ends)
> Daniel receives 70-Weeks prophecy
> Cyrus decrees end of Jewish captivity
536 B.C.
> Foundations of second temple laid
> 70-year captivity officially ends

6 ~ 3 B.C. (62-Week Period Ends)
> Birth of Jesus Christ

1st Half of 70th Week Ends
> End to sacrifice and offering

End of 70th Week
> Israel accepts Christ
> "Strong covenant" fully made
> 70-Weeks prophecy complete
> The "desolator" is destroyed

The seventy-week hourglass started with Jeremiah's prophetic word (timeline point #1), and that messianic hope carried the people for the next forty-nine years through the end of their captivity when Cyrus, the King of Persia who conquered Babylon, allowed the Jews to return to their homeland to rebuild their temple (timeline point #2). Note that God Himself called Cyrus "my anointed one" in Isaiah 45.

When the first group of Jews returned to Jerusalem after Cyrus's decree, they only got as far as laying the temple foundation before abandoning the work in favor of rebuilding their own houses and properties. They let fear of the surrounding nations and desire for comfort cause them to forsake their calling—in other words the old slave mindset was back. That's when the seventy-week hourglass stopped:

> Know therefore and understand that from the going forth
> of the word to restore and build Jerusalem to the coming of
> an anointed one, a prince, there shall be seven weeks.
> —*FROM DANIEL 9:25 RSV*

Eventually, God sent prophets like Haggai and Zechariah to rekindle the work, but it wasn't until Nehemiah arrived in Jerusalem some ninety years later and called the people to repentance that the rebuilding and repopulating of the actual city of Jerusalem began (timeline point #3). With the people back in their land and finally engaging with the city of Jerusalem, the hourglass started again and the sixty-two weeks section commenced:

> Then for sixty-two weeks it shall be built again with squares
> and moat, but in a troubled time.
> —*FROM DANIEL 9:25 RSV*

The hourglass continued to run for the next 434 years. As the city of Jerusalem and the population of Israel grew, so too did their desperation for the Messiah. During that time, Israel faced many troubles as world empires rose and fell around them. Persia, Greece, and Rome each had their turn as the dominant power, and each persecuted Israel in various ways. And even though various kings and emperors invaded Jerusalem over the years—some even desecrating the rebuilt temple and performing abominable acts in the holy of holies—the hourglass of Israel's seventy-week prophecy continued to run as long as the people remained in their land, in possession of Jerusalem, with the hope of the messianic prophesies still working in their hearts.

Somewhere between six and three BC, or sixty-two sevens after Nehemiah rebuilt the walls of Jerusalem, the hope of Israel finally appeared when Jesus was born in Bethlehem. On the surface, it may seem that the birth of the Messiah only received a passing note in Israel's seventy-week prophecy, but in reality, the entire prophecy revolves around Him. When Christ appeared, the hourglass stopped (timeline point #4). This was Israel's chance. Her entire history had been building toward this moment. Would she embrace the gift of God? Would she recognize the fulfillment of all the law and the prophets that now graced her land in the form of human flesh? All of creation leaned in with breathless anticipation to see how Israel would respond.

You know the rest of the story. Just as Daniel prophesied, Israel missed the day of her visitation. It was as if they were back at the base of Mount Sinai, and again they chose to shrink back from the fullness of God's offer. They were still slaves at heart, unwilling to surrender their identity to the One who offered Himself in exchange for their everything. Notice the language used by Gabriel:

> And after the sixty-two weeks, an anointed one shall be cut
> off, and shall have nothing;
> —*FROM DANIEL 9:26 RSV*

In one sense being "cut off" could be a simple reference to Christ's crucifixion. Christ is the anointed one, the Messiah. I don't discount that perspective, but I think the meaning is much deeper. I see this as another reference to the olive tree. Remember that Christ is the root of the olive tree, and Israel is His natural branches. So when the leadership of Jerusalem offered Messiah up to Pontius Pilot and the people declared, "His blood shall be upon us and our children," perhaps they were, in their minds, cutting this man off from their nation. From Israel's perspective, they were cutting off a false messiah. But Jesus is the source of all life. He is the root. In reality, they were in that moment cutting themselves off from the root.

The cutting off of Israel from the root would eventually have dire consequences for the people and the land—especially the city of Jerusalem—but God had one more task for each before sending judgment. The first sixty-nine weeks had brought forth Jesus in the fullness of time, and He was able to draw natural and spiritual resources from the people and the land of Israel during His earthly ministry. But it was equally important that His Body—the early Church—was also born and nurtured in the same land, among the same people, experiencing the same oppositions. These treasures became a part of the Church's DNA. But once that nurturing period was over—once the young Church was established through persecution and the wild branches of the Gentiles grafted into the root—the next phase of Israel's seventy-week timeline was ready to begin:

> and the people of the prince who is to come shall destroy
> the city and the sanctuary. Its end shall come with a flood,
> and to the end there shall be war; desolations are decreed.
> —*FROM DANIEL 9:26 RSV*

In the year 70 AD the city of Jerusalem and its temple were utterly destroyed by Roman armies. "The prince who is to come" is a reference to the supernatural creature that ruled over the spiritual atmosphere of Ancient Rome, as well as a reference to the human ruler who will exemplify that creature's authority on earth at the end of the age. We'll spend some time unpacking that topic in a future chapter. That evil spirit has big plans, but he deserves little more than a passing mention in the grand scheme of Christ's Unveiling. In the end, he is nothing more than another tool in God's hand to perfect His Bride. But none of that is the point right now. For the moment, just note that it was the *people* of the prince that destroyed Jerusalem in 70 AD and not the prince himself.

It is also important to understand that the destruction that began with a specific event in 70 AD has continued in a general sense until now. After 70 AD the nation of Israel was dispersed and Jerusalem remained in an almost constant state of either desolation, war, or both. It wasn't until 1967 AD that the city of Jerusalem finally came back into possession of the partially restored nation of Israel.

> From Israel's perspective, they were cutting off a false messiah. But Jesus is the source of all life. He is the root. In reality, they were in that moment cutting themselves off from the root.

I would argue that Jerusalem is still under some level of desolation today. The city itself is mostly occupied by Israel, but the temple is still in ruins, having never been rebuilt after 70 AD, and Israel is hardly free to possess the city as she would like. The international community is constantly pressuring Israel to divide Jerusalem in half to accommodate the demands of Muslim leaders, and the area as a whole is under constant threat of war and terrorism. More importantly, Israel is still cut off from her Messiah.

The current spiritual and geopolitical climate of Israel still fits into the general timeframe described by Gabriel's statement: "The people of the prince who is to come shall destroy the city and the sanctuary. Its end shall come with a flood, and to the end there shall be war; desolations are decreed." And that leads us to the most practical questions of the chapter: Where are we now? And what of the seventieth week? I'm glad you asked ...

CHAPTER 14

THE SEVENTIETH WEEK - PART 1:
THE STRONG COVENANT

or - "Who is He?"

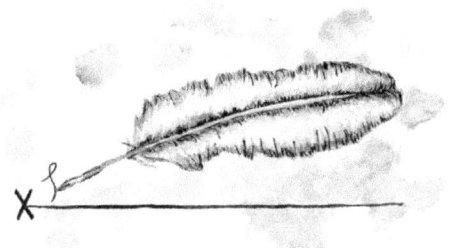

I like to think of the first sixty-nine weeks as setting the stage, introducing the characters, and moving them into position, but the most exciting drama is reserved for the final week. The seventieth week contains all of the necessary elements for Israel to finish the transgression, make an end to sin, make atonement for iniquity, bring in everlasting righteousness, seal up the vision and prophecy, and anoint the most Holy Place.

The seventieth week is typically considered to be the final seven-year period of history. Maybe that perspective carries a kernel of truth, but I'd like to present an alternate viewpoint that I believe fits much more naturally into the overall canvas of God's Word, and better compliments the masterpiece of Christ's Unveiling.

Up until this point, we've viewed the Seventy Weeks prophecy as an exclusively Jewish affair. There was a good reason for that. The prophecy was specifically decreed for the people and land of Israel to fulfill their birthright as a nation. And for the first sixty-nine weeks Israel was "the only game in town" when it came to God's covenanted people. But now that we're focusing on the seventieth week, it is time to introduce some additional layers.

We started with the natural branches because most of the concepts we'll find in the book of Revelation originated in the Old Testament, and many of the spiritual dynamics active on the earth at the end of the age will mirror the dynamics that were active at the end of the sixty-ninth week when Jesus was born. Israel and the Church will experience the Unveiling of Jesus in drastically different ways, but their paths are meant to intermingle and impact one another during that time. As we shall see, the very pressures that drive Israel toward ultimate rebellion will draw the Church into ultimate maturity during the seventieth week.

PIVOTAL IDENTITY

With all of that in mind, let's begin building our seventieth-week outline:

> And he shall make a strong covenant with many for one week; and for half of a week he shall cause sacrifice and offering to cease; and upon the wing of abominations shall come one who makes desolate, until the decreed end is poured out on the desolator."
> —*DANIEL 9:27 RSV*

Two main interpretations of this verse hinge on the identity of "he." The most common teaching is that "he" refers to the prince who is to come since it was his people who destroyed the city and the sanctuary in the previous verse. But there is a better way to understand Israel's seventieth week, and it starts with identifying "he" as the Messiah. If you've studied the seventieth week of Daniel, you may have already heard or considered that idea. It is a less common viewpoint that I dismissed early on in my study because I couldn't make sense of it with the rest of Scripture. But it turns out that I was simply holding the map wrong. Once I started looking at things from the perspective of principles, or more specifically, looking for the pattern of Christ's life, it all began to fit together with the simple inevitability of a jigsaw puzzle.

Let's take a small step back to get a better view of the events surrounding the seventieth week before tying it back to Jesus:

> 26) And after the sixty-two weeks, an anointed one shall be cut off, and shall have nothing; and the people of the prince who is to come shall destroy the city and the sanctuary. Its end shall come with a flood, and to the end there shall be war; desolations are decreed.
> 27) And he shall make a strong covenant with many for one week; and for half of a week he shall cause sacrifice and offering to cease; and upon the wing of abominations shall come one who makes desolate, until the decreed end is poured out on the desolator."
> —*DANIEL 9:26-27 RSV*

Remember, Christ's birth happened at the end of the sixty-ninth week. Then the nation of Israel—or Christ, depending on how you look at it—was cut off thirty-three years later when Jewish leadership rejected Jesus. Some forty years after that a period of desolation began when the city of Jerusalem and the Temple were destroyed by Roman armies. But notice what Gabriel said about the period of destruction, **"To the end** there shall be war; desolations are decreed.*"* Follow my logic here: If the period of destruction runs all the way **to the end**, then that means it must include the final seventieth week. In other words, the destruction doesn't come to an end *before* the seventieth week begins. The book of Revelation corroborates that the period of destruction and desolation happens throughout the second half of the seventieth week. And if there is overlap, that means the seventieth week begins either sometime during or even before the period of destruction, since it doesn't begin after.

Why is that important? Otherwise, one might assume that the seventieth week described in verse 27 must take place *after* everything described in verse 26. But that is not the case. I suggest to you that the seventieth week started the moment Jesus Christ came out of the baptismal water and the Father declared, "This is My beloved Son in whom I am well pleased." That is when the hourglass of the seventieth week started, and it continued running until the feast of Passover a few years later when Israel made a deal with Rome to have the Messiah crucified. All of this happened in the background of verse 26 *before* the people of the prince destroyed the city and the sanctuary.

Before we move on, let's address one central question that helps tie everything together. How long was Christ's earthly ministry? The Bible doesn't give a direct answer, but contextual and historical clues strongly suggest that the time between His baptism and His crucifixion was 3.5 years. That is a commonly accepted belief among many scholars based upon deductive reasoning from compelling biblical and extra-biblical evidence. Without getting into the technical details, the evidence suggests that both His birth and His baptism

> I suggest to you that the seventieth week started the moment Jesus Christ came out of the baptismal water and the Father declared, "This is My beloved Son in whom I am well pleased."

thirty years later took place in the seventh month of the Jewish calendar during Israel's fall feast season. From the Gospel of John we can deduce that, after His baptism, Jesus visited Jerusalem three distinct times for the spring feast of Passover before His fourth and final Passover visit at the time of His crucifixion. That makes it 3.5 years in total.

To be fair, not all scholars agree with the 3.5-year ministry argument. Some place more weight on the Synoptic Gospels (Matthew, Mark, and Luke), which mention only one trip to Jerusalem at the very end of Christ's ministry, and they therefore postulate that His ministry lasted only about one year. But the Synoptic Gospels do not preclude additional Jerusalem trips just because they only mention Christ's final visit, and many theologians point out that while the other gospel writers tended to arrange events by theme at the expense of accurate order, John seemingly placed a higher premium on organizing events into chronological order. Therefore, John's gospel is most instructive for accurately reconstructing Christ's steps when overlayed with the details of the other gospel accounts.

So we are going with the idea that Jesus' ministry was 3.5 years long. We can't be dogmatic about this since Scripture doesn't explicitly declare it to be true, but as we move forward you'll find just how well the 3.5-year ministry fits with the sum of what Scripture does say.

Okay, back to Daniel chapter 9. When verse 27 says, "And he shall make a strong covenant with many for one week," it is talking about the work that Christ started during His ministry on earth, beginning with

His baptism. We'll see the significance of the one-week (seven-year) duration in a moment.

The strong covenant is the new covenant, which is for all peoples and nations and tribes and tongues. Jesus demonstrated His worthiness to be the High Priest and mediator of the new covenant during His entire ministry, and then He initiated the covenant with His death and resurrection at the end of His ministry.

Gabriel then said that "for half a week he shall cause sacrifice and offering to cease." Please don't mistake this statement to mean that Jesus caused sacrifice and offering to cease for *only* 3.5 years. He abolished the need for sacrifice and offering for sins for all of eternity. So it's not talking about the length of time that these would be ceased, but rather the length of time it would take for Him to cause the ceasing. "For half a week" is a reference to the 3.5-year ministry of Christ, which culminated in the perfect, finished, once-for-all sacrifice of the Lamb of God. We rightly think of His death and resurrection as the initiation of the covenant, but His entire time of ministry was about preparing the perfect sacrifice. That means it took the entire first half of the seventieth week for Jesus to "cause sacrifice and offering to cease."

Likewise, when it says, "He shall make a strong covenant ... for one week," that doesn't mean the covenant is only a seven-year covenant. The new covenant is eternal. However, the full

Contextual and historical clues strongly suggest that the time between His baptism and His crucifixion was 3.5 years.

application of the covenant will take one week—seven years in the Daniel 9 timeline—to be completely applied. The seventieth week is all about the application of the new covenant.

SITTING AND WAITING

By the middle of the week, Christ's work was finished, perfectly accomplished on the cross. So why does it say that He made a strong covenant with the many "for one week"? What is the purpose of the week? If He only worked for 3.5 years, what could be left that still needs to be accomplished during the second half of the seventieth week? The writer of Hebrews explains it beautifully:

> Every priest stands daily ministering and offering time after time the same sacrifices, which can never take away sins; but He, having offered one sacrifice for sins for all time, SAT DOWN AT THE RIGHT HAND OF GOD waiting from that time onward UNTIL HIS ENEMIES BE MADE A FOOTSTOOL FOR HIS FEET.
> —HEBREWS 10:11-13

In this one passage, we find a summary of the entire seventieth week. The first half of the week was all about the work of Jesus, our High Priest. When He completed His work, He sat down and began a period of waiting. That waiting period is the final gap in the series of gaps we saw throughout Daniel's seventy-week prophecy—it is an indeterminate length of time between the end of the first half and the beginning of the second half of the seventieth week during which the hourglass of the prophecy is paused. I believe we are currently somewhere in the midst of that pause, waiting for the second half to start.

During this time, Jesus is waiting until His enemies are made a footstool for His feet. What a fascinating statement! According to the apostle Paul in Colossians 2:15, Jesus has already overcome the heavenly principalities and powers, and He has already disarmed His enemies and made a public spectacle of their powerlessness. So what is He waiting for? In what sense do His enemies still need to be made a footstool for His feet?

The answer to that question is precisely what the second half of the seventieth week is all about. The first half was designed for Jesus Christ, the Head of the Body, to overcome all the power of the enemy. The second half will be designed for us, the Body of Christ, to finally appropriate the grace He has provided through the new covenant to follow in His footsteps to actually, literally, and practically overcome all the power of the enemy at the end of the age. That is the testimony of the book of Revelation, and that is what we will see when the power of Christ's Unveiling is working in us and through us. Let's update our seventy-week timeline in that light:

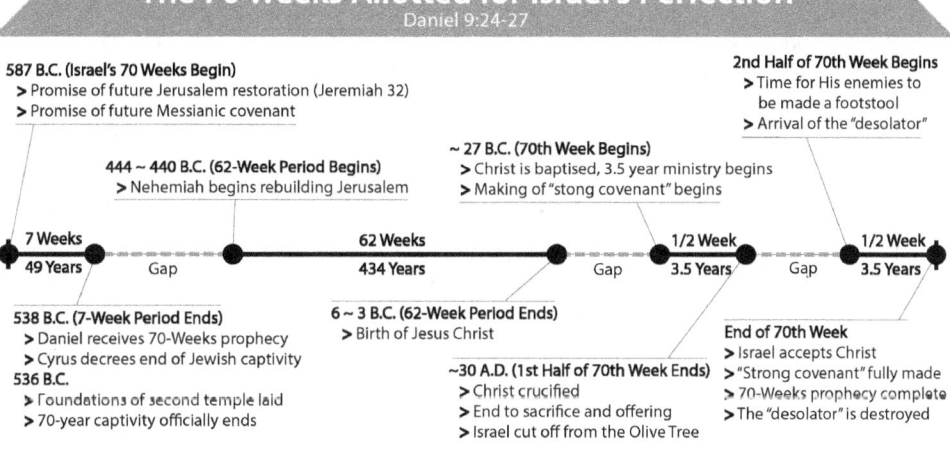

The 70 Weeks Allotted for Israel's Perfection
Daniel 9:24-27

587 B.C. (Israel's 70 Weeks Begin)
> Promise of future Jerusalem restoration (Jeremiah 32)
> Promise of future Messianic covenant

2nd Half of 70th Week Begins
> Time for His enemies to be made a footstool
> Arrival of the "desolator"

444 ~ 440 B.C. (62-Week Period Begins)
> Nehemiah begins rebuilding Jerusalem

~ 27 B.C. (70th Week Begins)
> Christ is baptised, 3.5 year ministry begins
> Making of "stong covenant" begins

7 Weeks — 49 Years | Gap | 62 Weeks — 434 Years | Gap | 3.5 Years — 1/2 Week | Gap | 1/2 Week — 3.5 Years

538 B.C. (7-Week Period Ends)
> Daniel receives 70-Weeks prophecy
> Cyrus decrees end of Jewish captivity
536 B.C.
> Foundations of second temple laid
> 70-year captivity officially ends

6 ~ 3 B.C. (62-Week Period Ends)
> Birth of Jesus Christ

~30 A.D. (1st Half of 70th Week Ends)
> Christ crucified
> End to sacrifice and offering
> Israel cut off from the Olive Tree

End of 70th Week
> Israel accepts Christ
> "Strong covenant" fully made
> 70-Weeks prophecy complete
> The "desolator" is destroyed

So Jesus is the template, and His ministry is the pattern that will best inform our understanding of the final 3.5 years of history during the second half of the seventieth week. We'll spend significant time unpacking that concept in the coming chapters, but before we go there, we need to take another step back to see the rest of what Gabriel said about the second half of the seventieth week:

> And he shall make a strong covenant with many for one week; and for half of a week he shall cause sacrifice and offering to cease; **and upon the wing of abominations shall come one who makes desolate, until the decreed end is poured out on the desolator."**
> —DANIEL 9:27 RSV

Notice that the entire week revolves around Christ's new covenant, yet the second half apparently doesn't commence until the coming of "one who makes desolate." This desolator was referred to in verse 26 as "the prince who is to come." Remember that it was his people who began destroying the city and the sanctuary after Israel was cut off from Christ. That period of destruction began around 70 AD and continues even today. But the final destruction and desolation will not begin until the actual arrival of the prince at the start of the second half of the seventieth week. At that time the prince will perform the ultimate act of desecration and rebellion by setting up an idol of himself in the holy of holies. That abomination will stand in the temple for the remaining 3.5 years of the seventieth week until the prince is utterly destroyed by Christ's appearance.

A ROSE BY ANY OTHER NAME

The second half of the seventieth week is referred to in various ways throughout Scripture. In some places, it is called "1,260 days," in others "42 months," or even "a time, times, and a half of a time," but in every case the writer is referring to the final 3.5 years of this age. Here is each reference in order:

> He will speak out against the Most High and wear down the saints of the Highest One, and he will intend to make alterations in times and in law; and they will be given into his hand for **a time, times, and half a time**.
> —*DANIEL 7:25*

> I heard the man dressed in linen, who was above the waters of the river, as he raised his right hand and his left toward heaven, and swore by Him who lives forever that it would be for **a time, times, and half a time**; and as soon as they finish shattering the power of the holy people, all these events will be completed.
> —*DANIEL 12:7*

> From the time that the regular sacrifice is abolished and the abomination of desolation is set up, there will be **1,290 days**. Blessed is he who waits, and comes to the **1,335 days**.
> —*DANIEL 12:11-12 (we'll discuss these extra thirty and seventy-five days later)*

> Leave out the court which is outside the temple and do not measure it, for it has been given to the nations; and they will tread under foot the holy city for **forty-two months**.
> —*REVELATION 11:2*

And I will grant authority to my two witnesses, and they will prophesy for **twelve hundred and sixty days**, clothed in sackcloth."
—*REVELATION 11:3*

Then the woman fled into the wilderness where she had a place prepared by God, so that there she would be nourished for **one thousand two hundred and sixty days**.
—*REVELATION 12:6*

There was given to him a mouth speaking arrogant words and blasphemies, and authority to act for **forty-two months** was given to him.
—*REVELATION 13:5*

Again, the "he" that many of these verses mention is "the prince who is to come," as seen in Daniel 9:26. Some people call him the antichrist. We also see him in Scripture as the man of lawlessness, the son of perdition, the beast that comes up out of the sea, the boastful horn, and sundry other names. Throughout Scripture his coming is associated with the activity of Satan at the time of the end:

Children, it is the last hour; and just as you heard that antichrist is coming, even now many antichrists have appeared; from this we know that it is the last hour.
—*1 JOHN 2:18*

As we'll see in the next chapter, the apostles learned directly from Jesus that the physical coming of the antichrist was a marker of the end of the age, but they also understood that the spirit of antichrist was already at work on the earth even before the first century. They had seen the work of this spirit in their time, and they interpreted the increasing rise of many antichrists as a sign that they were in the last hours, or as other writers called it, the last days. The last days began at the start of the seventieth week when Jesus began His ministry. Many antichrists have appeared on the scene since that time. Obvious examples could include Judas Iscariot, the Roman General Titus who destroyed the temple in 70 AD, and Adolph Hitler. History is replete with many subtler examples as well. These men were influenced by the spirit of antichrist, though none fulfilled the final manifestation that will come at the end of the age. Likewise, although we are in the last days even now, the end does not start in earnest until the second half of the seventieth week begins.

With all of that in mind, the final 3.5 years sound quite terrible on the surface. Fortunately, there is so much more going on *underneath* the surface when it comes to the Unveiling of Christ. Only by viewing this period through the context of His Unveiling can we discern its truly glorious nature.

> Jesus is the template, and His ministry is the pattern that will best inform our understanding of the final 3.5 years of history during the second half of the seventieth week.

It may not be obvious just yet, but the antichrist does not set the timing or agenda for end-times events. As we shall see in the book of Revelation, there will be a far greater heavenly drama unfolding at that time—a divine romance in which Jesus Christ is the director and star. All other subplots only facilitate His Unveiling. Just as the timing of the first sixty-nine weeks revolved around the preparation and coming of Messiah, and just as He initiated the first half of the seventieth week by His baptism in the Jordan River, Christ Himself will initiate the second half of the seventieth week after the Body of Christ has submitted to a similar baptism. But I'm getting ahead of myself. My point is that despite what all of the verses about 1,260 days and forty-two months suggest when read without context, the main purpose of the second half of the seventieth week has nothing to do with the power and authority of the antichrist. Yes, the antichrist will have a measure of both, but don't forget this simple truth:

> By this you know the Spirit of God: every spirit that confesses that Jesus Christ has come in the flesh is from God; and every spirit that does not confess Jesus is not from God; **this is the spirit of the antichrist**, of which you have heard that it is coming, and now it is already in the world. **You are from God, little children, and have overcome them; because greater is He who is in you than he who is in the world**.
> —*1 JOHN 4:2-4*

"Greater is He who is in you than he who is in the world." Don't miss the context. It's all about overcoming, and John intentionally frames the test in relation to the spirit of antichrist. "You are from God, little children, and have overcome them." Never will this be more true than during the second half of the seventieth week, because the antichrist is merely a blunt instrument allowed by God to create opportunities for the Body of Christ to learn how to overcome.

If you're struggling to reconcile John's statement with all of those other verses we just read describing the power and authority of the antichrist during the final 3.5 years, you are not alone. This puzzle has resulted in the propagation of far too many escapist and defeatist theologies. Some say that the Church is raptured before the antichrist rises to power. Others say the Church is present but dominated and martyred on a massive scale before Christ returns. But escaping is not overcoming, and neither is being dominated. How do we resolve this conundrum? What does it look like for followers of Christ to overcome amid persecution? Before we turn to the words of Jesus for more clarity, consider the following verse as a preview of coming attractions for the bondservants of God alive during the second half of the seventieth week:

> But Jews came from Antioch and Iconium, and having won over the crowds, they stoned Paul and dragged him out of the city, **supposing him to be dead**. But while the disciples stood around him, **he got up and entered the city**. The next day he went away with Barnabas to Derbe. After they had preached the gospel to that city and had made many disciples, they returned to Lystra and to Iconium and to Antioch, strengthening the souls of the disciples, encouraging them to continue in the faith, and saying, "**Through many tribulations we must enter the kingdom of God.**"
> —*ACTS 14:19-22*

Paul was courageous and entirely undeterred in the face of severe persecution, and as a result, he received miraculous protection. Despite the enemy's best efforts, nothing could stop the advancing message of the kingdom of God, and the greatest tribulations only served to enhance Paul's experience and testimony of that kingdom. So will it be for the Church at the end of the age. And so may it be with us today.

The first half was designed for Jesus Christ, the Head of the Body, to overcome all the power of the enemy. The second half will be designed for us, the Body of Christ, to finally appropriate the grace He has provided through the new covenant to follow in His footsteps to actually, literally, and practically overcome all the power of the enemy at the end of the age.

CHAPTER 15

THE SEVENTIETH WEEK - PART 2:
SIGNS OF HIS COMING

or - "Did you feel that?!"

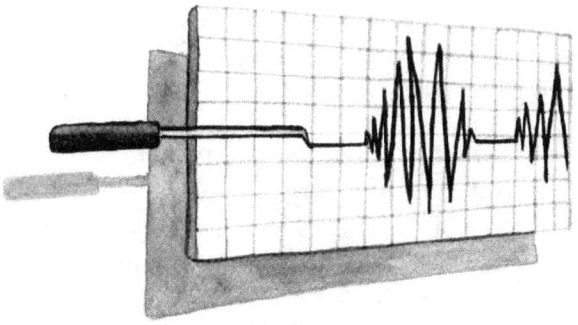

Jesus described the seventieth week in an astonishing panoramic overview of the end times that ties directly into the flow of Daniel's seventy-week prophecy. To set the stage, it was shortly after His triumphal entry into Jerusalem, and about two days before His crucifixion during the feast of Passover. Remember, by that time the seventieth week had already begun, and Jesus was nearing the end of His ministry (and therefore the end of the first half of the seventieth week). He had just publicly excoriated the scribes and Pharisees, seven times condemning their hypocrisy and empty religion and greed, ending with a savage proclamation against their spiritual harlotry that echos through the ages:

> "Jerusalem, Jerusalem, who kills the prophets and stones those who are sent to her! How often I wanted to gather your children together, the way a hen gathers her chicks

under her wings, and you were unwilling. Behold, **your house is being left to you desolate!** For I say to you, from now on you will not see Me until you say, 'BLESSED IS HE WHO COMES IN THE NAME OF THE LORD!'"
—*MATTHEW 23:37-39*

Jesus came out from the temple and was going away when His disciples came up to point out the temple buildings to Him. And He said to them, "Do you not see all these things? Truly I say to you, **not one stone here will be left upon another, which will not be torn down.**"

As He was sitting on the Mount of Olives, the disciples came to Him privately, saying, **"Tell us, when will these things happen, and what will be the sign of Your coming, and of the end of the age?"**
—*MATTHEW 24:1-3*

The subtext here is delicious. Right after pronouncing a curse upon the city of Jerusalem and the sanctuary, Jesus left the temple and ascended the nearby Mount of Olives. In that place—the very mountain where the Old Testament prophet Zechariah prophesied that Christ would return at the battle of Armageddon to set up His kingdom—the disciples came to Him with questions about His return.

They had observed His pronouncement against the city, and they likely equated the destruction He had just described with Daniel's seventy-week prophecy. Perhaps they understood that they were living in the seventieth week. If so, they were correct, though they still did not grasp the true purpose for His first coming, nor did they know there would be a gap of time before the second half of the seventieth week began. Perhaps they assumed that the temple destruction was imminent and that the second half of the seventieth week was soon to commence. In any event, they certainly did not yet understand that Jesus had to die to fulfill the prophecy of Passover, which is why they asked, "When will these things happen [the destruction of Jerusalem and the temple], and what will be the sign of Your coming, and of the end of the age?" In their minds, Jerusalem's destruction would lead directly to the end of the age when Messiah would come in power to set up His kingdom.

It was in that context that Jesus launched into His famous Olivet Discourse, adding detail to Daniel's prophecy and correcting many of

His disciples' misconceptions. Let's step through a portion of His response to add another layer to our outline of the seventieth week. We'll stay very high level for now, though we'll return to these verses later in this series when we're ready to mine for deeper treasures:

> And Jesus answered and said to them, "See to it that no one misleads you. For many will come in My name, saying, 'I am the Christ,' and will mislead many. And you will be hearing of wars and rumors of wars. See that you are not frightened, for those things must take place, but that is not yet the end. For nation will rise against nation, and kingdom against kingdom, and in various places there will be famines and earthquakes. But all these things are merely the beginning of birth pangs.
> —*MATTHEW 24:4-8*

Remember that the disciples' first question was essentially, "When will Jerusalem and the temple be destroyed?" The angel Gabriel had described that event to Daniel as more of a *period* of destruction, desolation, and war that would start after the anointed one was cut off and last to the end, and Christ's response expounded upon that reality with a sequence of four characteristics that further defined the period of destruction:

1. Many will be misled from the true Christ
2. Wars and rumors of wars
3. In various places there will be famines
4. [In various places there will be] earthquakes

These four markers generally describe the gap between the first and second halves of the seventieth week. There have been false Christs, wars, famines, and earthquakes throughout the last two thousand years, and those difficulties will increase in frequency and intensity the closer we get to the end. That is why Jesus called these four markers "the beginning of birth pangs," or birth *pains* in other translations. Birth pains are the result of contractions. They are indications of a coming birth, and they are essential in preparing the mother's body for the birth.

Notice that Jesus did not call these four markers contractions. He likened them to the pains associated with contractions, but not the contractions themselves. This is a very important distinction that will make more sense when we get to the book of Revelation and see the *actual* contractions that cause these pains. I'm not just parsing words to sound clever. Perspective is everything when it comes to the Unveiling. So we'll wait until the next book to unpack these four markers.

For now, let's just say that the last two thousand years' worth of difficulties can be viewed as the pains associated with early contractions. The earliest contractions are known as Braxton Hicks contractions, which are basically just practice contractions, or false labor, that God designed to help the mother prepare physically and emotionally for the rigors of labor. These types of contractions are valuable, though they do nothing to impact the mother's cervix nor position the baby for the birth. Some Braxton Hicks can be intense enough to fool a new mom into thinking she is entering real labor before the actual time. So too have some previous generations of Christians believed that Christ's return was imminent based on the trials and tribulations of their day.

Eventually, Braxton Hicks contractions do give way to the real thing. In this metaphor, the real labor, and therefore the associated real labor pains, will begin just before the beginning of the second half of the seventieth week. In other words, false Christs, wars, famines, and earthquakes will increase in frequency and intensity the closer we get to the end, but during the final generation, they will truly begin in earnest as we approach the last 3.5-year period. That generation will eventually see the ultimate manifestation of a false Christ misleading many, followed by the most intense ethnic conflict and wars, famines, and earthquakes in history. Even still, all of these things that happen before the second half of the seventieth week are merely the beginning of birth pangs.

All of this begs the question: Where are the contractions leading? Or more specifically, who or what is being birthed? For that matter, who is the mother, and when will the birth take place? We'll get to all that in the next chapter. First, let's see what else Jesus said would happen when the second half of the seventieth week finally begins with the greatest travail:

> "Then they will deliver you to tribulation, and will kill you, and you will be hated by all nations because of My name. At that time many will fall away and will betray one another and hate one another. Many false prophets will arise and will mislead many. Because lawlessness is increased, most people's love will grow cold. But the one who endures to the end, he will be saved. This gospel of the kingdom shall be preached in the whole world as a testimony to all the nations, and then the end will come.
> —*MATTHEW 24:9-14*

Tribulation, persecution, martyrdom, apostasy, betrayal, false prophets misleading many, increasing lawlessness, love growing cold. All of this has been going on for the last two thousand years in waves of pain caused by Braxton Hicks contractions, but it will begin in earnest when the final 3.5-year period begins. And just to be sure that the disciples understood the exact timeframe that He was referring to, Jesus expounded even further:

> "**Therefore** when you see the ABOMINATION OF DESOLATION which was spoken of through Daniel the prophet, standing in the holy place (let the reader understand), then those who are in Judea must flee to the mountains. Whoever is on the housetop must not go down to get the things out that are in his house. Whoever is in the field must not turn back to get his cloak. But woe to those who are pregnant and to those who are nursing babies in those days! But pray that your flight will not be in the winter, or on a Sabbath. For then there will be a great tribulation, such as has not occurred since the beginning of the world until now, nor ever will. Unless those days had been cut short, no life would have been saved; but for the sake of the elect those days will be cut short.
> —*MATTHEW 24:15-22*

The abomination of desolation is the event that will reveal the ultimate manifestation of the antichrist and kick off the greatest period of tribulation in history, including all of the persecution, martyrdom, apostasy, betrayal, and false prophet deception mentioned earlier. We'll talk more about this event in the next book. In the context of Matthew 24, it all sounds quite terrible, to say the least. But before you write off the final 3.5 years as hell on earth, let's apply the wisdom of perspective to these verses.

First, remember the context. Jesus was on the Mount of Olives overlooking the city of Jerusalem He had just cursed moments earlier. He was answering questions about the prophesied destruction of Jerusalem in the context of a seventy-week prophecy that was given directly to the nation of Israel and her holy city. In a physical sense, the abomination of desolation itself will take place in the Jewish temple within the physical city of Jerusalem. The initial and main focus of the ensuing tribulation will be the people of Israel. That is why Jesus said, "Then those who are in Judea must flee to the mountains," and "Pray that your flight will not be in the winter, or on a Sabbath." Both of those statements only make sense for those who are physically living in Israel at the time.

Don't get me wrong. I'm not saying that the Body of Christ won't experience great tribulation. We certainly will. But the main focus of Christ's warnings is for Israel, just as the main focus of Daniel's seventy-weeks prophecy is Israel. Israel will be the epicenter, though waves of persecution will emanate out from there to much of the world. So the Church will experience the great tribulation, but as we shall see shortly, the Church is offered a different path *through* the tribulation than Israel.

Second, notice what else Jesus said would be happening during that time: The gospel of the kingdom would be "preached in the whole world as a *testimony* to the nations, and *then* the end" would come. This is a simple statement with immense implications. It won't just be the gospel of salvation being preached. It will be the gospel of the kingdom. The good news about the coming King and His power and authority to bring healing, order, and redemption to the earth will be preached. The gospel of the kingdom is about entering His rest and becoming one with Him. It is the message of God's ultimate plan for creation. And this preaching won't be some desperate message from those just barely clinging to their hope for an afterlife in heaven. No, this message will be a *testimony* to the nations. We can only testify to that which we have seen and touched and experienced. Moreover, effective testimony requires evidence. In other words, the true testimony of the kingdom will require demonstrations of the King's character, power, and authority by those who have already tasted the fruit of the age to come and who are living in the reality of the Kingdom of God. When the great tribulation begins, those who have already learned to partner with the King through the trials and tribulations of life will be positioned to leverage that earned authority to great effect when it is needed most.

Don't miss the sequence here. The end will only come after the testimony of the coming kingdom is preached to the whole world. Don't get it twisted. The end is not the abomination of desolation, nor the great tribulation. The end means the end of the seventieth week. As we'll see in future chapters, the end is the final outpouring of God's wrath upon the kingdom of the beast, followed immediately by the physical return of Christ. That means that the bondservants of Christ will be actively and effectively preaching the gospel of the kingdom throughout the final 3.5 years. During the very time when the beast is trying (and failing) to establish his own kingdom, portions of the Body of Christ will be overcoming his kingdom on multiple levels and in many ways. More on this later.

> When the great tribulation begins, those who have already learned to partner with the King through the trials and tribulations of life will be positioned to leverage that earned authority to great effect when it is needed most.

Lastly, notice what Jesus said about the end of the great tribulation: "Unless those days had been cut short, no life would have been saved; but for the sake of the elect those days will be cut short." Jesus used the past tense here— "unless those days *had been* cut short" —because the length of the great tribulation is already determined, and God has already decided that it will not last as long as the enemy would like. Yes, the beast will be given a measure of authority to act for the final 3.5 years. This timeframe is set in stone, decreed from heaven, and known by the powers of light and darkness. But the great tribulation itself—the concerted, focused, final outpouring of Satan's wrath upon anything and everything that resembles Jesus—that wrath will be cut short and end well before the end of the seventieth week. In other words, the great tribulation will be less than 3.5 years.

DISCIPLINE FOR THE HOLY PEOPLE

We'll see exactly what that means in a later chapter. Right now, I want to return our focus to that final 3.5-year period. We've seen some of the bad stuff that will happen during that timeframe, but we have yet to define its purpose. In a moment I'll show you a much better lens through which to view those 3.5 years. But first I want to reframe what we've just discussed about the antichrist.

Despite how it may look, the second half of the seventieth week is not a playground for evil. It is not all about great tribulation, and it is certainly not all about the antichrist. For all of his boastful arrogance and grandiose machinations, everything the beast will attempt to do will only end up working into the hand of the true King.

To that end, I believe there are two main reasons that God allows the antichrist to have a level of authority during the final 3.5 years. One involves Israel, which we'll look at now, and the other involves the Church, which we'll look at in the next chapter.

The antichrist is meant to scourge the nation of Israel in much the same way that God used Nebuchadnezzar to discipline Israel at the beginning of the seventy-week prophecy. The final 3.5 years will be the ultimate discipline in preparation for the ultimate outpouring of God's mercy for His original covenant people:

> He will speak out against the Most High and **wear down the saints of the Highest One**, and he will intend to make alterations in times and in law; and they will be given into his hand for a time, times, and half a time.
> —*DANIEL 7:25*

> ... it would be for a time, times, and half a time; and as soon as they finish **shattering the power of the holy people**, all these events will be completed.
>
> I heard, but I did not understand. So I asked, "My lord, what will be the outcome of these things?"

> He said, "Go your way, Daniel, for these words are concealed and sealed up until the end time. **Many will be purged, purified and refined**, but the wicked will act wickedly; and none of the wicked will understand, but those who have insight will understand.
> —*DANIEL 12:7-10*

Both of these passages are specifically referring to Israel. In the context of the book of Daniel, the "saints of the Highest One" and the "holy people" are references to the natural branches, not the wild branches. Please don't just substitute Christians for holy people here and think that the rest of the verse applies as-is. Yes, there is a spiritual application of these verses that applies to Christians that we will see soon enough, but that perspective requires more context. The concept of the power of Israel being completely shattered fits very naturally with the purpose of Israel's allotted seventy weeks.

Think of it like this: when Israel rejected Christ they were broken off from the root. Paul specifically said that "*some* of the branches were broken off." The original disciples and much of the early Church were Jews who embraced the Messiah. These remained connected to the root as natural branches in the Body of Christ. But the majority of Israel rejected Jesus and the nation remains estranged from Him to this day. Those who cling to their Jewish faith continue to trust in a limited understanding of the old covenant because of what Paul called "partial blindness." Essentially, they are holding to a form of godliness but denying its power.

But God is faithful. He has not rejected Israel. To do so would violate His nature and impugn His character. They are broken off from the life of Christ, but to the degree that they continue to trust in God's original promise of a Messiah—even if they don't yet recognize Jesus as that Messiah—a measure of life remains that has partially sustained Israel for the last two thousand years. After all, they are *partially* blind not totally blind. It's as if these branches are barely alive, clinging to the hope of a life that is both right in front of them and wholly unrecognizable to them. But at least that means they are not completely dead or there would be no grafting them back into the root.

That is where the antichrist comes in. The power of the holy people must be completely shattered before they will be desperate enough to embrace the true Messiah that their ancestors killed in their blindness and arrogance. Their hope in the law of Moses without the fulfillment of Jesus must be broken. The vision and prophecy must be sealed up.

Remember in the last chapter when I described one of the most common interpretations of the seventieth-week covenant? Many believe that it is a future event that begins when the prince who is to come signs a seven-year peace treaty with Israel. Although I don't entirely agree with that construct, there is a sense in which it could still apply as a secondary layer to the main interpretation. While the seventieth week began with Christ's ministry, a time may come in the final years leading up to the second half of the seventieth week when Israel does enter into a peace treaty with the antichrist before they know his true identity, especially if he can offer an opportunity to rebuild their temple. This would be before the abomination of desolation and before he is revealed to be a beast and a tyrant.

> For all of his boastful arrogance and grandiose machinations, everything the beast will attempt to do will only end up working into the hand of the true King.

In that scenario, the final straw of their rebellion would be the embracing of a false messiah only to have him turn around and desecrate their temple, which is the very symbol of their strength and connectivity to God through the law of Moses, and the final legitimacy crutch upon which they still lean. Whether a peace treaty is involved or not, we know that the physical event of the abomination of desolation will happen in the temple in Jerusalem. At that point, Israel will find itself backed into a corner and facing the greatest time of trouble and the greatest choice in their history. Some will flee into the wilderness where they will be purified, refined, and prepared to fall on the rock when He returns. Others will knowingly embrace wickedness until their final destruction at the end of the seventieth week.

If you consider the various ways that Israel resisted the contractions that brought forth Christ during His incarnation, then it makes sense that she will respond similarly when the Braxton Hicks contractions that comprise the more than two thousand-year gap between the first and second halves of the seventieth week give way to the real labor pains. Perhaps that is when Israel will respond with one final desperate attempt to resist the coming birth and hold on to her imaginary independence. But the power of her resistance will be broken, and then the mercy of God will flow to her in the form of a birth.

It is important to note that when we reference Paul's declaration that "all Israel will be saved," we are talking about Israel as a nation, or as a general body of people. That does not mean that every single human of Israeli descent, or every single person physically descended from the bloodline of Abraham, or every individual living in the land of Israel will turn to Christ at the time. Free will is the main variable. Just as free will determined which of the natural branches were cut off, free will determines which will be grafted back in. And just as the majority of Israel followed their leadership in rejecting Christ two thousand years ago because of their spirit of slavery, the majority will finally embrace a spirit of sonship at the end to be grafted back into the Olive Tree.

And so we return to the big questions: Where are the contractions leading? Who or what is being birthed? Who is the mother? And when will the birth take place relative to the seventieth week? Let's dig in …

CHAPTER 16

THE SEVENTIETH WEEK - PART 3: THE PAROUSIA OF CHRIST

or - "I do not think it means what you think it means ..."

T here are multiple facets to the birth alluded to in Matthew 24, and many angles from which it can be viewed. When the hourglass of the seventieth week is finally started again and the second half of the seventieth week begins, the Braxton Hicks contractions that have impacted the world in waves of pain for the last two thousand years will finally give way to the intense labor of true birth pangs.

If you are thinking the labor is obviously leading to the coming of Jesus, you are not wrong. After all, most of what Jesus described in Matthew 24 was in response to the question, "What will be the sign of your coming, and of the end of the age?" So yes, the labor pains are leading to the coming of Jesus at the end of the age, but there is so much to His coming than just His physical return to earth. And there is so much more to the birthing process than just pain. Especially for the Church, who is His Body.

Let's go back to Matthew 24 to find more clues about the final 3.5 years of contractions:

> Then if anyone says to you, 'Behold, here is the Christ,' or 'There He is,' do not believe him. For false Christs and false prophets will arise and will show great signs and wonders, so as to mislead, if possible, even the elect. Behold, I have told you in advance. So if they say to you, 'Behold, He is in the wilderness,' do not go out; or, 'Behold, He is in the inner rooms,' do not believe them. **For just as the lightning comes from the east and flashes even to the west, so will the coming of the Son of Man be.**
> —*MATTHEW 24:23-27*

The idea of false christs and false prophets showing great signs and wonders fits well with what the book of Revelation says about the final 3.5 years. We'll come back to that in a later chapter. Right now I want to draw your attention to one pivotal phrase that sets the tone for everything else Jesus says in the remaining verses of Matthew 24: "For just as the lightning comes from the east and flashes even to the west, so will the coming of the Son of Man be."

This passage is often interpreted to mean that Christ's return will happen

There is so much to His coming than just His physical return to earth. And there is so much more to the birthing process than just pain. Especially for the Church, who is His Body.

unexpectedly and suddenly, like a flash of lightning across the sky. There may be a kernel of truth to that perspective, but it does not capture the entirety of the point Jesus was making about His coming.

Christians have debated this verse since the time of the early church fathers. The phrase itself is oddly constructed and makes little sense in context. Does lightning come from the east and flash to the west? Perhaps you could say that some lightning flashes from one end of the sky to the other, but if Christ's point was simply that His return would be instantaneous, or impossible to predict, or visible to everyone like a bolt of lightning across the sky, surely a clearer example could have been used. Why east to west? The phrase doesn't fit with Jesus' style of simple, contemporary, unpretentious examples that explain deep spiritual truths. There has to be something more to what He was saying.

"Just as lightning comes from the east and flashes even to the west, so shall the coming of the Son of Man be." This wording is taken from the New American Standard Version. Most of the other popular translations use similar language that highlights the characteristics of lightning. I am no Greek scholar, but at the risk of stepping out of bounds or sounding immensely arrogant, I don't think Jesus was comparing His return to the nature of lightning here, at least not in the sense or with the emphasis that modern science understands lightning. I know that is a bold statement, so let me explain my reasoning.

My argument is mainly one of context, which I'll show you in a minute. But first, we need to broaden our vocabulary by drilling down on three specific words in the verse: lightning, flashes, and coming.

WORDS IN CONTEXT

The Greek word for lightning here could also have been translated as a bright shining or a glare. Even when it is rendered as lightning in other verses the focus seems to be more about the illumination caused by the lightning, or the power of the lightning to light up the surrounding darkness, than it is about the actual bolt of electricity itself.

Consider that the same Greek word (*astrapé*, Strongs 796) was used to describe the illuminating rays of a candle that we earlier described as a metaphor for our human spirit:

> If therefore your whole body is full of light, with no dark part in it, it will be wholly illumined, as when the lamp **illumines** you **with its rays.**"
> —*LUKE 11:36*

Astrapé is also used to describe the overwhelming shining that emanated from the face of an angel of the Lord at Christ's empty tomb on resurrection Sunday:

> And behold, a severe earthquake had occurred, for an angel of the Lord descended from heaven and came and rolled away the stone and sat upon it. And his appearance

[or countenance, in other translations] was like **lightning**,
and his clothing as white as snow. The guards shook for
fear of him and became like dead men.
—*MATTHEW 28:2-4 (BRACKETED TEXT MINE)*

"For just as lightning comes from the east and flashes even to the
west." So lightning here isn't necessarily a bolt of electricity, but rather
something that shines intensely bright. As bright as lightning when it
illuminates the night sky.

That's not the only difficult word in this verse. The Greek word
translated here as *flashes* occurs thirty other times in the New Testament,
and every other time it is rendered either as *appearing* or *shining*. Here
are just a few examples:

Then Herod secretly called the magi and determined from
them the exact time the star **appeared**.
—*MATTHEW 2:7*

But when Herod died, behold, an angel of the Lord **appeared** in a dream to Joseph in Egypt, and said,
—*MATTHEW 2:19*

And then the sign of the Son of Man will **appear** in the
sky, and then all the tribes of the earth will mourn, and
they will see the SON OF MAN COMING ON THE CLOUDS
OF THE SKY with power and great glory.
—*MATTHEW 24:30*

In His right hand He held seven stars, and out of His
mouth came a sharp two-edged sword; and His face was
like the sun **shining** in its strength.
—*REVELATION 1:16*

and the light of a lamp will not **shine** in you any longer;
and the voice of the bridegroom and bride will not be
heard in you any longer; for your merchants were the great
men of the earth, because all the nations were deceived by
your sorcery.
—*REVELATION 18:23*

So the word translated in Matthew 24:28 as flashes (*phainetai*, Strongs 5316) doesn't necessarily fit with the characteristics of a flash of lightning either. It actually seems like the opposite of the instantaneous nature of lightning. The word conveys more about the process of light appearing or being made manifest and visible to others. It comes from the same Greek root as the word John used for Christ's appearing, which will not just be a momentary blip of an event but rather a process of unveiling that culminates in a permanent and abiding revelation:

> Beloved, now we are children of God, and it has not **appeared** as yet what we will be. We know that when He **appears**, we will be like Him, because we will see Him just as He is.
> —*1 JOHN 3:2*

It is also important to understand that the Greek word used by Jesus to describe His *coming* is a noun rather than a verb (*parousia*, Strongs 3952), and it literally means presence, a being near, or an advent. New Testament authors used other Greek words in other places to describe the specific action and unique event of Christ's physical return, but whenever *parousia* is used, the focus is on the reality and impact of His presence during the period of His Unveiling. It is the perfect companion to the concept of His appearing. The Greek word leaves room for a progressive revealing of Himself rather than just a one-time instantaneous event. And if you recall our discussion about the presence of I AM in the burning bush, and the work of the Spirit of the Fear of the Lord to prepare us for uniting with Him in rest, then this word *parousia* fits well with those concepts.

Taking all of that together, perhaps Jesus actually said something like, "For just as the intense brightness comes from the east and its appearance shines even to the west, so shall the presence of the Son of Man be." Again, I'm no Greek scholar, but it sounds like Jesus was comparing His coming to the rising sun rather than saying that His return would be instantaneous and unpredictable. And I am not alone in this perspective, as I've read other Bible commentators comparing Christ's return to the rising sun, even if they took a different path to arrive at their conclusions.

THE PATH OF THE SUN

Please understand that I'm not just parsing words or nitpicking unnecessary details. This is an important difference that directly influences our view of everything else we see in Matthew 24. The rising sun comparison is significant on many levels. It speaks of an inexorable process over a determined period in which light overwhelms darkness. It is neither sudden, nor a magic wand, nor an instant cure. It is a progression built on the natural and spiritual principles of God's Word cast onto the canvas of creation at the beginning:

> But the path of the righteous is like the light of dawn, That shines brighter and brighter until the full day.
> —*PROVERBS 4:18*

> So we have the prophetic word made more sure, to which you do well to pay attention as to a lamp shining in a dark place, until the day dawns and the morning star arises in your hearts.
> —*2 PETER 1:19*

The path of the sun from east to west is a poignant illustration of the principles and process of Christ's Unveiling, and it ties directly into the most prominent prophetic picture in Scripture: the concept of the Day of the Lord. Consider the following:

> Now we request you, brethren, with regard to the coming [*parousia*] of our Lord Jesus Christ and our gathering together to Him, that you not be quickly shaken from your composure or be disturbed either by a spirit or a message or a letter as if from us, to the effect that **the day of the Lord** has come. Let no one in any way deceive you, for it will not come unless the apostasy comes first, and the man of lawlessness is revealed, the son of destruction, who opposes and exalts himself above every so-called god or object of worship, so that he takes his seat in the temple of God, displaying himself as being God.
> —*2 THESSALONIANS 2:1-4 (BRACKETED TEXT MINE)*

Do you see the similarities between this passage and Matthew 24? The disciples asked Jesus about the signs of His coming (*parousia*), and He answered by describing birth pang events—including the abomination of desolation—before explaining that His *parousia* would be like the light of the rising sun. Paul understood all of this, so when the Thessalonians experienced some Braxton Hicks contractions of persecution and became concerned that they had somehow missed the coming (again, *parousia*) of Jesus, Paul pointed out that the travail of the great tribulation had certainly not yet started, so there was no way they could have missed the *parousia* of Jesus.

> It sounds like Jesus was comparing His coming to the rising sun rather than saying that His return would be instantaneous and unpredictable.

Without diving too deeply down another rabbit hole, I'll also mention that this 2 Thessalonians passage destroys the false narrative still taught in some Christian circles that the entire Church age is the millennial reign of Christ. In some ways, this was the very deception that Paul was addressing with the Thessalonians. Any attempt to theologically escape either the pain or the glory of the final 3.5 years is a tremendously shortsighted perspective of slavery rather than sonship. But I digress.

THE DAY OF THE LORD

All of that is helpful corroboration of our end-times sequence, but perhaps less obvious is the sequence inherent in the idea of "the day of the Lord." Notice that Paul directly associated Christ's *parousia* with the day of the Lord. Why is that important, and what does it tell us about His coming?

Consider the simple relationship between the rising of the sun and the concept of a day. In our Western model, the twenty-four-hour day technically starts at midnight. In another sense, we sometimes think of our functional day as starting at dawn. But in God's sequencing, a day starts at sundown and continues till the following sundown. This construct was deeply ingrained in the Hebrew culture from the repeated declaration in the book of Genesis that "there was evening and there was morning" on each day of creation, and it was reinforced by many precepts in the law of Moses. Likewise, shouldn't we expect "the day of the Lord" to begin with a period of darkness before progressing to the dawn, and eventually the full light of day? In other words, the day of the Lord won't just appear out of nowhere shining like high noon.

Maybe this will make more sense if we review a few more references to the day of the Lord. The Old Testament prophets spoke of it as a coming day of judgment and recompense. So ubiquitous was this idea in Scripture that it was often simply referred to as "the day." The day was primarily seen as the outpouring of God's wrath to purge the earth of wickedness, though some of the prophets also connected it with the coming of Messiah to establish His kingdom at the end of the age:

> Behold, the day of the LORD is coming, cruel, with fury and burning anger, to make the land a desolation; and He will exterminate its sinners from it.
> —*ISAIAH 13:9*

> Alas for the day! For the day of the LORD is near, and it will come as destruction from the Almighty.
> —*JOEL 1:15*

> A day of darkness and gloom, A day of clouds and thick darkness. As the dawn is spread over the mountains, So there is a great and mighty people; There has never been anything like it, Nor will there be again after it to the years of many generations.
> —*JOEL 2:2*

> For the day of the LORD draws near on all the nations. As you have done, it will be done to you. Your dealings will return on your own head.
> —*OBADIAH 1:15*

> Be silent before the Lord GOD! For the day of the LORD is near, For the LORD has prepared a sacrifice, He has consecrated His guests.
> —*ZEPHANIAH 1:7*

A day of wrath is that day, A day of trouble and distress, A day of destruction and desolation, A day of darkness and gloom, A day of clouds and thick darkness,
—*ZEPHANIAH 1:15*

"For behold, the day is coming, burning like a furnace; and all the arrogant and every evildoer will be chaff; and the day that is coming will set them ablaze," says the LORD of hosts, "so that it will leave them neither root nor branch. But for you who fear My name, the sun of righteousness will rise with healing in its wings; and you will go forth and skip about like calves from the stall. You will tread down the wicked, for they will be ashes under the soles of your feet on the day which I am preparing," says the LORD of hosts.
—*MALACHI 4:1-3*

The references go on and on throughout the Old Testament. Again, the common themes were judgment, destruction, darkness, and wrath, with a few hints of hope sprinkled in every once in a while.

Now let's layer in the perspective of the New Testament apostles who had insight into the mystery of Christ. We've already seen Paul directly associate the coming (*parousia*) of our Lord Jesus Christ with the day of the Lord. What else did they say?

But do not let this one fact escape your notice, beloved, that with the Lord one day is like a thousand years, and a thousand years like one day. The Lord is not slow about His promise, as some count slowness, but is patient toward you, not wishing for any to perish but for all to come to repentance.

But the day of the Lord will come like a thief, in which the heavens will pass away with a roar and the elements will be destroyed with intense heat, and the earth and its works will be burned up.

Since all these things are to be destroyed in this way, what sort of people ought you to be in holy conduct and godliness, looking for and hastening the coming of the day of God, because of which the heavens will be destroyed by burning, and the elements will melt with intense heat! But

according to His promise we are looking for new heavens
and a new earth, in which righteousness dwells.
—2 PETER 3:8-13

Peter highlighted the destruction of the day of the Lord while also framing that destruction as the first step toward the creation of a new heavens and new earth. The unveiling of Christ, which includes His *parousia*, will bring both. Notice that Peter said the day of the Lord would come like a thief, but then exhorted us to look for and hasten the coming of that day. Now compare that peculiar juxtaposition of ideas to Paul's description of Christ's coming:

> Now as to the times and the epochs, brethren, you have no need of anything to be written to you. For you yourselves know full well that the day of the Lord will come just like a thief in the night. While they are saying, "Peace and safety!" then destruction will come upon them suddenly like labor pains upon a woman with child, and they will not escape. But you, brethren, are not in darkness, that the day would overtake you like a thief; for you are all sons of light and sons of day. We are not of night nor of darkness; so then let us not sleep as others do, but let us be alert and sober.
>
> For those who sleep do their sleeping at night, and those who get drunk get drunk at night. But since we are of the day, let us be sober, having put on the breastplate of faith and love, and as a helmet, the hope of salvation. For God has not destined us for wrath, but for obtaining salvation through our Lord Jesus Christ, who died for us, so that whether we are awake or asleep, we will live together with Him. Therefore encourage one another and build up one another, just as you also are doing.
> *—1 THESSALONIANS 5:1-11*

Did you catch all of that?! The day of the Lord; sons of day; labor pains; drunk versus sober; thief in the night; wrath versus salvation. Paul weaves together so many different analogies in this passage that it can make your head spin. Let's focus on the central theme: "the day of the Lord will come just like a thief in the night." Paul wasn't revealing anything new here. This whole passage is borrowed from Christ's teaching on the Mount of Olives. We haven't gotten to this part of Matthew 24 yet, but let's skip ahead to see where Paul derived his language:

> "Therefore be on the alert, for you do not know which day your Lord is coming. But be sure of this, that if the head of the house had known at what **time of the night the thief was coming**, he would have been on the alert and would not have allowed his house to be broken into. For this reason you also must be ready; for the Son of Man is coming at an hour when you do not think He will.
> —*MATTHEW 24:42-44*

"A thief in the night." What does that mean? Does that simply mean that the return of Christ is imminent, unexpected, and instantaneous? Not exactly. Think about how a thief breaks into a house. It happens under the cover of darkness, slowly, methodically, carefully, and quietly so as not to awaken the owners. It is not imminent because it requires a particular time of night; it is not unexpected if we are warned ahead of time; and it only seems instantaneous if we sleep through the warnings and awake in the morning to find our house already plundered. So the answer entirely depends on our perspective and response to the warning.

That is why Paul described two distinct sets of people who will experience the day of the Lord in two very different ways. On the one hand are those who are in darkness, who sleep at night, who are not alert or sober as it relates to Christ's coming. The night in this context speaks of the deep depravity that will cover the earth like midnight at the beginning of the second half of the seventieth week when the man of lawlessness sets up the abomination of desolation. Many will be swept away by that deception as they become drunk on darkness, rejecting the principles of God's nature and imbibing deeply from the defiled chalice of secular and religious humanism.

Eventually, the deepest darkness will give way to the dawning of the day of the Lord. Unfortunately, the children of darkness will sleep through the beginning stages of the rising sun of Christ's Unveiling, and they will not perceive the transformative illumination that progressively accompanies His *parousia*. By the time they awake to what is going on, it will be too late. Because they were not alert and sober, they will experience the day of the Lord as a thief that came at night, and they will awaken to the unexpected and instantaneous day of wrath and destruction from the Almighty. Paul also described this as the day overtaking them like the most intense pains of a woman in the midst of delivering a child, but we'll dig deeper into that analogy in the next chapter.

On the other hand, the Body of Christ is not in darkness, and the day of the Lord is not meant to overtake us like a thief. We are called to be on the alert, to stay awake during the deep darkness, and to remain sober. We are called to watch for the dawn, to long for the sunrise, to stare intently at the magnificence of its kaleidoscopic beauty as it slowly, steadily, progressively begins to unfold with colors of God's essence that we have never imagined.

> It is not imminent because it requires a particular time of night; it is not unexpected if we are warned ahead of time; and it only seems instantaneous if we sleep through the warnings and awake in the morning to find our house already plundered.

That's what the *parousia* of Christ is all about. When we talk about the return of Christ, we often focus on the crescendo of the first resurrection in which our bodies will be instantaneously transformed into immortal, new creation bodies after the likeness of Jesus' resurrection body. That is not a bad thing to focus on, and we will certainly discuss that aspect of our glorious hope in the next book. That resurrection will be like the full brightness of the noonday sun, and it is the salvation that Paul says we are destined to obtain through our Lord Jesus Christ. But before the event of the resurrection, there will first come a dawn, and a sunrise, that will bring a period of progressive, unprecedented, unimaginable, experiential revelation of Christ's nature. Let's not miss the necessary principles and process that are meant to prepare us for the resurrection.

IN THE SAME WAY

Jesus had much more to say in Matthew 24 about the the day of the Lord, the resurrection, and His coming. We'll unpack those verses later in the series when we're ready to view them in the context of the book of Revelation, but first I want to drive home the progressive process of Christ's unveiling from a different angle.

Remember that this entire discussion of Christ's *parousia* is in the context of the final 3.5 years of Daniel's prophecy of the seventieth week. In the next chapter we are going to dig into the pattern of Christ's earthly ministry to build a better framework for the final 3.5 years and understand how and where His *parousia* fits into the timeline. To set the stage for that discussion, consider this description of Christ's ascension:

> And after He had said these things, He was lifted up while they were looking on, and a cloud received Him out of their sight.
>
> And as they were gazing intently into the sky while he was departing, behold, two men in white clothing stood beside them;
>
> And they also said, "Men of Galilee, why do you stand looking into the sky? This Jesus, who has been taken up from you into heaven, will come in just the same way as you have watched Him go into heaven."
> —*ACTS 1:9-11*

Jesus is going to return to the earth in the same way that the disciples watched Him leave. What does that mean? Does it simply mean that His physical return to earth will look like His first-century ascension? Yes, but only if we look at the *entire pattern* of His ascension.

According to Revelation 19:11, Jesus will return to the earth triumphantly, riding a white horse, having eyes of fire, wearing many crowns, followed after by the armies of heaven, judging the earth with righteousness, and making war with His enemies. This is a significant departure from the Acts 1:9 picture of Jesus peacefully being lifted into the clouds. So let's zoom out. Christ's second coming *will* mirror His original ascension but on a broader scale. The pattern for His return can be seen in the preceding verses of Acts 1:

> To [His disciples] He also presented Himself alive, after His suffering, by many convincing proofs, appearing to them over a period of forty days, and speaking of the things concerning the kingdom of God.
> —*ACTS 1:3*

> And after He had said these things, He was lifted up while they were looking on, and a cloud received Him out of their sight.
> —ACTS 1:9

So after His initial years of ministry, and after His suffering and resurrection, Jesus appeared to His disciples many times, in many ways, over a period of forty days. During that time He manifested the nature of His resurrection body, taught about the kingdom of God, and prepared them for the baptism of the Holy Spirit. It was only after this period of intimate manifestation that Jesus ascended into the clouds.

Can you see the pattern? His return will be similar. If we view the 3.5 years of Christ's earthly ministry as the general pattern of His end-times Unveiling, then the forty-day period between His resurrection and ascension is a model for His end-times *parousia*.

Based on the context of Daniel's seventy-weeks prophecy, the final 3.5 years of this age will be a time of intense manifestation of the kingdom of God through the Body of Christ on earth. Then, toward the end of that season, there will be an even more intense manifestation of the new creation during the earliest hours of Christ's *parousia* as the sunrise of His coming begins to paint the horizon with the living fire of God's presence. I'll explain exactly what I mean by that statement over the next few chapters.

But before the event of the resurrection, there will first come a dawn, and a sunrise, that will bring a period of progressive, unprecedented, unimaginable, experiential revelation of Christ's nature. Let's not miss the necessary principles and process that are meant to prepare us for the resurrection.

CHAPTER 17

THE PARABLE OF THE UNVEILING - PART 1:
THE WOMAN AND THE MALE CHILD

or - "More birth pangs?!"

In previous chapters we saw how God will use the second half of the seventieth week to shatter the power of the nation of Israel, to remove every last legitimacy crutch the Jewish people have leaned on to keep from falling on Christ, and to disabuse His original covenant people of their slave mindset so that they can finally embrace their full birthright as the natural branches of His Body.

Now let's focus on the Church. What path will the Body of Christ take at the end? Will the beast have authority and success against the Church? Is the power of the betrothed Bride of Jesus meant to be shattered along with that of the natural branches? The short answer is ... it depends. What do I mean by that? The full answer gets to the very heart of the Unveiling of Jesus, so to fully understand the Church's role during the second half of the seventieth week we need to pull in threads from the heart of the book of Revelation. And to do that we first need to talk more about that birth metaphor.

Remember, in Matthew 24 Jesus used the metaphor of birth to describe the signs of His coming and the end of the age. Wars, ethnic strife, famines, earthquakes, persecutions, tribulations, and even death were all mentioned as pains brought on by contractions. In the most basic sense, you could say that the contractions are leading to the second coming of Christ to rule over the earth as King of Kings. That is the obvious meaning, and we'll see some of that in the book of Revelation, but there are other treasures hidden in the birth metaphor that will expand our capacity to experience and participate in Christ's Unveiling.

Let's set the stage with another passage from Paul's writings:

> For you have not received a spirit of slavery leading to fear again, but you have received **a spirit of adoption as sons** by which we cry out, "Abba! Father!" The Spirit Himself testifies with our spirit that we are children of God, and if children, heirs also, heirs of God and **fellow heirs with Christ**, if indeed we suffer with Him so that we may also be glorified with Him.
>
> For I consider that the sufferings of this present time are not worthy to be compared with the glory that is to be revealed to us. For the anxious longing of the **creation waits eagerly for the revealing of the sons of God**. For the creation was subjected to futility, not willingly, but because of Him who subjected it, in hope that the creation itself also will be set free from its slavery to corruption into the freedom of the glory of the children of God. For we know that **the whole creation groans and suffers the pains of childbirth** together until now. And not only this, but also we ourselves, having the first fruits of the Spirit, even we ourselves groan within ourselves, **waiting eagerly for our adoption as sons, the redemption of our body**. For in hope we have been saved, but hope that is seen is not hope; for who hopes for what he already sees? But if we hope for what we do not see, with perseverance we wait eagerly for it.
> —ROMANS 8:15-25

There are bountiful, multifaceted treasures here, but let's stay focused on the theme of birth. The whole of creation is suffering the pains of childbirth. That includes the heavens and the earth, the sky and the water, the physical and spiritual realms, the animals, and of course humankind. All of these are experiencing the pains of childbirth together. Matthew 24 showed us the form of these pains. But to what end?

Precision matters here. Paul said that "creation was subjected to futility." What does that mean? It's not so much that creation itself is pregnant, but rather that God has made the first creation an unwilling yet absolutely necessary instrument to enforce the pressures and pains of childbirth upon us, the children of God, who make up the Church, His Body. That is why later on in Romans 8:28 we read:

> And we know that God causes all things to work together for good to those who love God, to those who are called according to His purpose. For those whom He foreknew, He also predestined to become conformed to the image of His Son, so that He would be the firstborn among many brethren.
> —*ROMANS 8:28-29*

Jesus is the Firstborn, a title that is profound on multiple levels. Colossians 1:15 calls Him "the firstborn of all creation," not because He was actually born but because all things in heaven and earth were created through Him and for Him. That means that the entire universe was derived from the essence of Jesus. Therefore He is before all things, and in Him, all things hold together. He is preeminent in every conceivable way. That is mind-blowing on its own, but it doesn't stop there:

> He is also head of the body, the church; and He is the beginning, the firstborn from the dead, so that He Himself will come to have first place in everything.
> —*COLOSSIANS 1:18*

Jesus is also the Firstborn from the dead. Through His death and resurrection, Christ became the prototype of a brand-new creation. That is what Paul was referring to in Romans chapter 8. So not only is Jesus the Firstborn of the original creation, but He is also the Firstborn of a new creation that is superior in every way to the original.

As the Firstborn, Jesus is the pattern we are meant to follow. And God causes all things to work together in our lives to bring this about. That doesn't mean He simply takes the bad things and turns them into good. Neither does God cause of all the bad that happens to us. Remember free will? God has established the fundamental principles of reality, and within that frame, many different wills initiate cause and effect in our lives.

He doesn't initiate everything that happens to us, but He does filter it. For those who love Him and are called according to His purposes, He goes beyond the automatic operation of principles. Cause and effect are still applied—we still reap what we sow, and we are still impacted by the choices of others—but God takes all of that and causes it to work together toward a purpose. He doesn't cause every circumstance, but He does cause them all to work together for our good by presenting us with opportunities to grow while providing the grace we need to find the path through to maturity.

This dynamic is part of what it means for creation to be "subjected to futility." God's love for us is so great, His confidence in the goodness of His divine character so absolute, and His desire for us to fully partake in the goodness of that character so compelling, that He was willing to subject all of creation to the temporary futility of being a tool to mold us into His image.

Think about it this way: the whole purpose of the first creation is to act as a womb. It is a womb designed to operate on the natural and spiritual laws of nature that reflect God's character. As the Unveiling unfolds and new aspects of Christ's nature are revealed, creation will respond appropriately with contractions meant to bring about transformation in that area. And wherever free will has violated God's principles or twisted His nature or ignored His laws, creation will produce commiserate amounts of pain and tribulation associated with the contractions to give our free will reason to come into alignment with God's character.

That is why Paul said that creation is eagerly awaiting the revealing of the sons of God. This idea of becoming sons of God is deep and wide and often misunderstood, but for now, let's just focus on the picture that Paul drew in Romans chapter 8. Paul specifically correlated the concept of the sons of God with being "fellow heirs" with Christ, meaning we will be glorified with Him "if indeed" we suffer with Him. So sonship requires suffering before inheritance. I realize that I haven't exactly defined what this sonship is yet, but I'm just pointing out that to become sons in the mold of the firstborn requires us to voluntarily embrace suffering. Remember that as we move forward because it is a central principle in this chapter, and it is one of the main principles that Christ modeled for us throughout His ministry.

So what is the endgame of these birth pangs throughout creation? From one perspective, the contractions are leading to the coming King and His coming kingdom. From another perspective, we could also say that the contractions are working to bring forth the new creation. They are also working to reveal the sons of God, bring the Body of Christ into alignment with the Head, and prepare His Bride for marriage by forming His nature in His people. However you look at it, the travail is ultimately for our benefit. Jesus will return in the fullness of time when His Bride has made herself ready, so the pressures and tribulations, and even the pains, should be met with hope and expectation. It is all about making us ready, which in turn will hasten His coming.

> He doesn't cause every circumstance, but He does cause them all to work together for our good by presenting us with opportunities to grow while providing the grace we need to find the path through to maturity.

A GREAT SIGN

With all of that in mind, we are now going to reach into the book of Revelation to help complete our outline of the seventieth week. Think of these remaining chapters as an initial foray into the forest of the Unveiling to spy out the topography of the land. We will overlay this information with the grid and coordinate system of the seventieth week to finish our map. We are only dipping our toe into the Unveiling right now; we'll jump in with both feet in the next book.

Our focus here will be Revelation chapter 12, which is the beginning of a passage that stands outside the main flow of events like an interlude in the middle of the intensity. We'll start by reading through the entire chapter, and then circle back around to walk through verse by verse as we did with Daniel 9 and Matthew 24. This is a large block of Scripture to read at once, but it is important to understand the entire context before we unpack it further:

A great sign appeared in heaven: a woman clothed with the sun, and the moon under her feet, and on her head a crown of twelve stars; and she was with child; and she cried out, being in labor and in pain to give birth.

Then another sign appeared in heaven: and behold, a great red dragon having seven heads and ten horns, and on his heads were seven diadems. And his tail swept away a third of the stars of heaven and threw them to the earth. And the dragon stood before the woman who was about to give birth, so that when she gave birth he might devour her child.

And she gave birth to a son, a male child, who is to rule all the nations with a rod of iron; and her child was caught up to God and to His throne.

Then the woman fled into the wilderness where she had a place prepared by God, so that there she would be nourished for one thousand two hundred and sixty days.

And there was war in heaven, Michael and his angels waging war with the dragon. The dragon and his angels waged war, and they were not strong enough, and there was no longer a place found for them in heaven. And the great dragon was thrown down, the serpent of old who is called the devil and Satan, who deceives the whole world; he was thrown down to the earth, and his angels were thrown down with him. Then I heard a loud voice in heaven, saying,

"Now the salvation, and the power, and the kingdom of our God and the authority of His Christ have come, for the accuser of our brethren has been thrown down, he who accuses them before our God day and night.

"And they overcame him because of the blood of the Lamb and because of the word of their testimony, and they did not love their life even when faced with death.

"For this reason, rejoice, O heavens and you who dwell in them. Woe to the earth and the sea, because the devil has come down to you, having great wrath, knowing that he has only a short time."

And when the dragon saw that he was thrown down to the earth, he persecuted the woman who gave birth to the male child. But the two wings of the great eagle were given to the woman, so that she could fly into the wilderness to

her place, where she was nourished for a time and times and half a time, from the presence of the serpent. And the serpent poured water like a river out of his mouth after the woman, so that he might cause her to be swept away with the flood. But the earth helped the woman, and the earth opened its mouth and drank up the river which the dragon poured out of his mouth. So the dragon was enraged with the woman, and went off to make war with the rest of her children, who keep the commandments of God and hold to the testimony of Jesus.
—*REVELATION 12:1-17*

That's a lot to digest, but we'll take it slowly and only use what we need for our map at this time. For all of its heavenly imagery and deep spiritual meaning, the path we will take through Revelation in the next book will often be straightforward and literal. But Revelation chapter 12 stands separate as a sign that must be interpreted metaphorically. I like to think of Revelation 12 as the Parable of the Unveiling. In a sense, it is an allegorical outline of the seventieth week, and in this outline, we find that the entire drama revolves around a birth.

In the very first verse, we see a great sign that has two different interpretations. Well, there are more than two interpretations, but we are only going to focus on two: the woman as Israel, and the woman as the Church. Both perspectives are legitimate and equally important to the Unveiling of Jesus.

Beyond this great sign, we also see two other characters directly related to the woman: the "son, a male child" who she gives birth to, and the "rest of her children" mentioned at the end of the chapter. We'll talk about the relationship between these three in a moment, but understanding the great sign of the woman is the key that unlocks the rest of the parable. Viewing the woman as Israel highlights the first half of the seventieth week. Viewing the woman as the Church highlights the second half of the seventieth week.

We need to unpack both of these interpretations to fill out our seventieth-week outline, but our goal right now is not to interpret every aspect of every symbol but to find the underlying theme and uncover a portable principle or two to take on our journey. We'll start with the natural branches and then circle back around to see the parable in light of the Church.

There is one more point I need to mention. As we progress through the parable we'll find two main patterns emerging: the fractal of two and the fractal of three. Remember, the fractal of two deals with giving and receiving. First God gives so that we can receive, and then in response we give and God receives. This general sequence of growth is seen in the two halves of the seventieth week and reflected in the two main interpretations of Revelation 12, both of which work together to present a fuller picture of the book of Revelation.

Within that sequence of growth, we'll also find a deeper understanding of God's plan for His people by viewing the woman, the male child, and the rest of her children through the fractal of three. Remember, the fractal of three deals with the internal relationship of systems, like the spirit, soul, and body of a human, or God expressed as Father, Son, and Holy Spirit, or the temple made up of holy of holies, inner court, and outer court. When we apply the fractal of three to either Israel or the Church, we'll find that they both have three different but interrelated parts and each part of Israel and the Church will be impacted differently by the seventieth week. Don't worry about making sense out of all of these symbols right now. Just keep the fractals in the back of your mind as we go back to the beginning of the parable.

> I like to think of Revelation 12 as the Parable of the Unveiling. In a sense, it is an allegorical outline of the seventieth week, and in this outline, we find that the entire drama revolves around a birth.

THE WOMAN AS ISRAEL

> A great sign appeared in heaven: a woman clothed with the sun, and the moon under her feet, and on her head a crown of twelve stars; and she was with child; and she cried out, being in labor and in pain to give birth.
> —*REVELATION 12:1-2*

In the natural sense, the woman clothed with the sun, with the moon under her feet, with a crown of twelve stars, was the nation of Israel during the first sixty-nine weeks of Daniel's prophecy. To be more precise, the woman represents what we might call faithful Israel, or that part of the nation of Israel that clung to the promise of a coming Messiah. She was pregnant with this promise of Messiah, and all of the pressures and pains of her decreed sixty-nine weeks were meant to prepare her for the birth.

> Then another sign appeared in heaven: and behold, a great red dragon having seven heads and ten horns, and on his heads were seven diadems. And his tail swept away a third of the stars of heaven and threw them to the earth. And the dragon stood before the woman who was about to give birth, so that when she gave birth he might devour her child.
> —*REVELATION 12:3-4*

Another sign, this one maybe not so great. The dragon is Satan, as we are told in a later verse. Don't worry about the seven heads and ten horns for now; they'll be defined at another time. The stars are likely fallen angels or some other form of spiritual beings subservient to the enemy, but that's also not our focus right now.

Satan did everything he could to influence various internal enemies and external empires during Israel's sixty-nine weeks to intimidate and bully the nation in an attempt to abort the birth of the Messiah or to eventually devour Him as a baby before He could rule the earth.

> And she gave birth to a son, a male child, who is to rule all the nations with a rod of iron; and her child was caught up to God and to His throne.
> —*REVELATION 12:5*

Satan failed, and in the fullness of time, Israel brought forth the Messiah. This is an obvious reference to the birth of Jesus Christ, but I suggest that we look deeper than the obvious because there is more to see here than just the physical birth of baby Jesus in a manger. Remember, we're talking about the firstborn, so let's look for His pattern to better understand our own path as we are conformed to His image.

THE BEGINNING OF SONSHIP

Consider the wording: "she gave birth to *a son, a male child*." The focus here is not physical gender but spiritual relationship, rights, and responsibilities. Women and men, boys and girls, young and old alike are all called to become sons of God. Sonship is a position, an inheritance, and a responsibility in relationship with the Father. Yes, it was something Jesus was born with, but it was also something He had to grow into over the course of His life and ministry. In a sense, the early years of Jesus' life were preparation for sonship.

According to the Mosaic law, Levites were not permitted to begin their tabernacle ministry until the age of thirty, and although Jesus was not a Levite, His work as a High Priest according to the order of Melchizedek (see Hebrews 5:10) began the same way. Sometime around His thirtieth birthday the Father proudly affirmed His maturity and declared Him ready for ministry:

> After being baptized, Jesus came up immediately from the water; and behold, the heavens were opened, and he saw the Spirit of God descending as a dove and lighting on Him, and behold, a voice out of the heavens said, "This is My beloved Son, in whom I am well-pleased."
> —MATTHEW 3:16-17

The Father's affirmation came before Jesus had preached a single sermon or performed a single miracle. Everything that Jesus did from that point forward was built on His established sense of identity and legitimacy. But even then, at the beginning of His ministry, there was a sense in which He was not yet perfected. Yes, of course, Jesus was spotless and sinless, but He had not yet inherited His birthright nor entered into everything He was called to be as the only begotten Son. Consider the following:

> Although He was a Son, He learned obedience from the things which He suffered. And having been made perfect, He became to all those who obey Him the source of eternal salvation,
> —HEBREWS 5:8-9

Again, the wording is fascinating: "*Although* He was a Son[.]" Obedience is not the goal of sonship, but it is a necessary ingredient. Obedience is for children. And it must be combined with difficulty and testing to produce maturity. Obedience is about becoming conformed to the Father's character through the difficulties of life. The ultimate goal of the process is not to produce obedient children or well-behaved robots. It is to produce mature, liberated, creative "sons" who have discovered their design in the crucible of life and can be trusted to reproduce the Father's nature in everything they do as they utilize all of the resources they have inherited. Jesus provided the perfect example of this process in action:

> Have this attitude in yourselves which was also in Christ Jesus, who, although He existed in the form of God, did not regard equality with God a thing to be grasped, but emptied Himself, taking the form of a bond-servant, and being made in the likeness of men. Being found in appearance as a man, He humbled Himself by becoming obedient to the point of death, even death on a cross. For this reason also, God highly exalted Him, and bestowed on Him the name which is above every name, so that at the name of Jesus EVERY KNEE WILL BOW, of those who are in heaven and on earth and under the earth, and that every tongue will confess that Jesus Christ is Lord, to the glory of God the Father.
> —*PHILIPPIANS 2:5-11*

So Jesus did reach a milestone of maturity around the age of thirty when the Father affirmed His Sonship, but then He had to work out that Sonship through a process of obedience that carried Him all the way to the cross. The perfection of His Sonship included temptation, persecution, tribulation, and eventually both death and resurrection. Through His death He redeemed the original creation, and through His resurrection He inaugurated a new and better creation. And it is only in His resurrection—His rebirth as the new creation Man—that we find the full meaning of the birth in Revelation 12.

Consider the following verses that correlate the travail and birth metaphor with Christ's ministry, suffering, and resurrection rather than His initial birth as a baby:

> Jesus knew that they wished to question Him, and He said to them, "Are you deliberating together about this, that I said, 'A little while, and you will not see Me, and again a

little while, and you will see Me'?" Truly, truly, I say to you, that you will weep and lament, but the world will rejoice; you will grieve, but your grief will be turned into joy.

"Whenever a woman is in labor she has pain, because her hour has come; but when she gives birth to the child, she no longer remembers the anguish because of the joy that a child has been born into the world. Therefore you too have grief now; but I will see you again, and your heart will rejoice, and no one will take your joy away from you.
—*JOHN 16:19-22*

"But **God raised Him from the dead**; and for many days He appeared to those who came up with Him from Galilee to Jerusalem, the very ones who are now His witnesses to the people.

"And we preach to you the good news of the promise made to the fathers, that God has fulfilled this promise to our children in that **He raised up Jesus**, as it is also written in the second Psalm, 'YOU ARE MY SON; **TODAY I HAVE BEGOTTEN YOU.**'
—*ACTS 13:30-33*

So when Revelation 12 says that "the woman gave birth to a son, a male child," it's not so much talking about His birth in a Bethlehem manger. Embedded in that statement is the entire process of Christ's perfection, beginning with the Father declaring Him the beloved Son, followed by the public testing of His sonship during His earthly ministry, and culminating with His rebirth and exaltation to the right hand of the Father. All of these together are essential elements of the process of sonship, and they represent the pattern of the firstborn during the first half of the seventieth week. God intends for us to understand and emulate this pattern during the second half of the seventieth week:

For it was fitting for Him, for whom are all things, and through whom are all things, **in bringing many sons to glory**, to perfect the author of their salvation through sufferings. For both He who sanctifies and those who are sanctified are all from one Father; for which reason He is not ashamed to call them brethren,
—*HEBREWS 2:10-11*

Before we move on, take a moment to ponder the type of sonship that Jesus modeled during His ministry. Before the incarnation, He existed in the form of God. He was unlimited in every way. Omniscient, omnipresent, omnipotent. From that place, He emptied and humbled Himself to take human form. And not just any human. He took the form of a bondservant. He wasn't born in a palace with great financial wealth. He went from having everything to having nothing, yet He never complained, and He never embraced a poverty mindset. Instead, He was able to accomplish all things because He recognized the potential in the raw materials that the Father brought to Him. As a Son and a bondservant, He knew that all things belonged to the Father, and so He lacked for nothing as He did the Father's will. Imagine what it would look like for us to live with that same type of abandon!

Viewing the woman as Israel highlights the first half of the seventieth week. Viewing the woman as the Church highlights the second half of the seventieth week.

CHAPTER 18

THE PARABLE OF THE UNVEILING - PART 2: THE BIRTH

or - "Come and see!"

The 3.5-year ministry of Christ is the linchpin that ties together the natural and spiritual interpretations of Revelation chapter 12. It is the general pattern of sonship established by the First-born and the most important key to understanding the purpose, focus, and result of the entire seventieth week of Daniel.

More on that in a moment, but first we need to return to the story of Israel in Revelation chapter 12 and find out what happened after the Son was born:

> Then the woman fled into the wilderness where she had a place prepared by God, so that there she would be nourished for one thousand two hundred and sixty days.
> —REVELATION 12:6

Remember that we are currently viewing this drama through the lens of Israel as the woman and Christ as the Son. In the timeline of the seventy-week prophecy, this verse begins in the middle of the seventieth week, after Christ's death, burial, and resurrection and, of course, after Israel was cut off from Christ. It was at that time that the general period of destruction and desecration began for Israel. You could say that Israel has been in a wilderness ever since they rejected Christ but, just as we saw in Matthew 24, the greatest period of destruction and persecution won't begin until the second half of the seventieth week begins and the abomination of desolation is unleashed. That was why Jesus exhorted the inhabitants of Jerusalem and Judea to flee to the mountains in the middle of the seventieth week when they saw the abomination of desolation standing in the Holy Place. That is when Israel—or at least those Jews who have no interest in bowing to the antichrist—will literally flee to the wilderness to a place prepared by God for the final 1,260 days.

We know that Israel's wilderness period correlates with the second half of the seventieth week, and we've already seen that during that time the antichrist will be allowed a level of authority to "shatter the power of the holy people." But how does any of that fit with the pattern of sonship that Christ established through His ministry? If Jesus faithfully preached and effectively demonstrated the power of the coming kingdom during His 3.5-year ministry, what does that say about the second half of the seventieth week?

THE WOMAN AS THE CHURCH

To answer that question we need to circle back around to the beginning of Revelation chapter 12 and layer in our second metaphor. Let's try this again:

> A great sign appeared in heaven: a woman clothed with the sun, and the moon under her feet, and on her head a crown of twelve stars; and she was with child; and she cried out, being in labor and in pain to give birth.
> —*REVELATION 12:1-2*

We've seen the pattern of the Firstborn. Now let's see how this great sign applies to the revealing of the sons of God—the many brethren who are predestined to be conformed to His image. From that perspective, the pregnant woman is the Body of Christ, and the pains of her labor are the very pains referred to in Matthew 24, Romans 8, and elsewhere.

The Church, His Body, has been experiencing Braxton Hicks contractions for the last two thousand years, but her real labor will ramp up right before the start of the second half of the seventieth week. That is the picture we see here in Revelation chapter 12: the Church crying out in labor and in pain to give birth as the beginning of the second half of the seventieth week approaches.

> Then another sign appeared in heaven: and behold, a great red dragon having seven heads and ten horns, and on his heads were seven diadems. And his tail swept away a third of the stars of heaven and threw them to the earth. And the dragon stood before the woman who was about to give birth, so that when she gave birth he might devour her child.
> —*REVELATION 12:3-4*

The dragon is still the devil, and here he is seen trying to intimidate the Church, to influence and delay the birth, and ultimately to devour the child at the time of delivery. Again, Satan has been doing this for the last two thousand years, and that posturing will continue to grow more blatant and aggressive the closer we get to the end.

> And she gave birth to a son, a male child, who is to rule all the nations with a rod of iron; and her child was caught up to God and to His throne. Then the woman fled into the wilderness where she had a place prepared by God, so that there she would be nourished for one thousand two hundred and sixty days.
> —*REVELATION 12:5-6*

This is where things start to get exciting. Remember the pattern of the Firstborn. The first half of the seventieth week began when Jesus came up out of the Jordan River and the Father declared, "This is My beloved Son ..." For the next 3.5 years, He went around teaching and demonstrating the kingdom of God while proving Himself to be a faithful Son with all of the people, resources, and tasks the Father had given Him to steward. It was only after He completed His work on the cross that He experienced the resurrection and then eventually ascended into heaven to inherit His full birthright as Son.

Likewise, the birth of the male child will usher in the second half of the seventieth week, but it will only represent the *beginning* of the revealing of the sons of God. The revealing of the sons of God will take the entire second half of the seventieth week, and it will only culminate in the resurrection at the very end.

All this begs a few important questions. First, if the woman represents the Church, who does the male child represent? Second, what exactly does it mean that the child was caught up to God and to His throne? Is this simply a reference to the resurrection at the very end? And why would the Church have to flee into a wilderness for the final 3.5 years?

THE MALE CHILD AT THE END

Let's take these one by one. Who is the male child? Simply put, right before the start of the second half of the seventieth week, those Christians who have already joined themselves to the Lord as bondservants—who have leaned into the greatest seasons of trials and tribulations and persecutions of life as though they were His provision; who have taken full advantage of those beginning birth pangs described in Matthew chapter 24—those Christians will emerge from the Church as mature sons ready to step into their season of ministry. We've seen them described by the apostle Paul as the sons of God. In the book of Revelation, we'll also see them described as the overcomers and the bondservants of the Lamb. I also like to think of them as the first-fruits Bride, but we'll have to wait until book two to unpack those concepts. For now, we're mainly focusing on the characteristics of their sonship.

Like the Firstborn, these mature "sons" will launch into the final 3.5 years of this age teaching and demonstrating the kingdom of God on earth with the character, wisdom, authority, and power of Christ. If I understand correctly, they will be an organic and decentralized movement of mature Christ followers all over the world, each one helping to prepare the way for the kingdom of God with tools derived from their own unique journey, using whatever resources and spheres of influence the Father provides. I use the word *movement* lightly because it will include men, women, and children from every country, ethnicity, and culture, with no organizational structure or spiritual head other than the King of Kings. We'll unpack their role and relationship with the rest of the Church soon.

CAUGHT UP

Next question: In what way will these sons be caught up to God and to His throne? Again, think of the pattern of the Firstborn. Let's take some time to dig into this one. What happened when Jesus came up from the baptismal water as the mature Son?

> After being baptized, Jesus came up immediately from the water; and behold, the heavens were opened, and he saw the Spirit of God descending as a dove and lighting on Him, and behold, a voice out of the heavens said, "This is My beloved Son, in whom I am well-pleased."
> —*MATTHEW 3:16-17*

The heavens were opened, and the Spirit of God descended on Him. Notice that it never says the heavens ever closed again. Jesus lived under an open heaven for His entire 3.5 years of ministry. Not only that, but the Spirit of God descended and stayed with Him. That means the fullness of the seven spirits of God—those flames burning before the throne of God—abided in fullness with Christ Jesus. With the eyes of His spirit fully enlightened, Jesus received the full spectrum of God's light directly from the throne room and shone it into the world around Him, while the seven eyes of His spirit were able to perceive the surrounding world with perfect clarity. He maintained full access to the resources of heaven, and He brought that open heaven with Him everywhere He went.

In a spiritual sense, Jesus was caught up to God and to His throne at the moment of His baptism. That is when He became connected to the power and authority of the kingdom of God as the beloved Son. From that time on He walked under an open heaven, connected directly to the Father's heart, drawing deeply from the power of the Holy Spirit. When He completed His work on the cross 3.5 years later and rose again, He became the Firstborn of the new creation. When He physically ascended to the Father's right hand, He completed the final stage of the pattern of Sonship. And that is the basic sequence that the Revelation 12 sons will follow as well. The initial birth and catching up to God's throne is not the rapture. They will still be on earth, but they will walk under an open heaven, empowered by the seven spirits of God, connected to the Father's heart, fully exercising the authority of Christ:

> But God, being rich in mercy, because of His great love with which He loved us, even when we were dead in our transgressions, made us alive together with Christ (by grace you have been saved), and raised us up with Him, and seated us with Him in the heavenly places in Christ Jesus,
> —*EPHESIANS 2:4-6*

According to the righteous law of the universe, all Christians are legally seated with Christ in heavenly places the moment we are born again, but having a legal right to something is not the same as actually possessing it, let alone knowing how to exercise it. Jesus was born in Bethlehem as the only begotten Son of God, but it wasn't until His baptism that He fully stepped into the responsibility of that role and began manifesting that reality on earth. The same will be true for the portion of the Body of Christ that is ready to become the male child in Revelation chapter 12.

Can you imagine the implications?! What will happen when this movement of Christians emerges from the Church to step into mature sonship, fully engaging in their birthright to sit with Christ in heavenly places? The impact will literally shake the heavens and earth:

> And there was war in heaven, Michael and his angels waging war with the dragon. The dragon and his angels waged war, and they were not strong enough, and there was no longer a place found for them in heaven. And the great dragon was thrown down, the serpent of old who is called the devil and Satan, who deceives the whole world; he was thrown down to the earth, and his angels were thrown down with him. Then I heard a loud voice in heaven, saying,
>
> "Now the salvation, and the power, and the kingdom of our God and the authority of His Christ have come, for the

accuser of our brethren has been thrown down, he who accuses them before our God day and night.

"And they overcame him because of the blood of the Lamb and because of the word of their testimony, and they did not love their life even when faced with death.
—*REVELATION 12:7-11*

Remember, this passage is in the context of the great sign of the woman giving birth to the male child. The immediate result of the birth will be a war in which Satan and his angels are kicked out of heaven and cast down to the earth. That sounds immense, but what does it mean? What are the practical ramifications of such an event? We need to camp here for a moment because this will take some time to unpack.

THE HEAVENS

First, let's back up and ask a fundamental question. Where does the majority of Revelation 12 take place? Remember, the great sign appeared *in heaven*. The whole drama with the woman and the male child transpires in heaven, as does the subsequent war. But how can there be war in heaven? Have you ever wondered about that? Psalm 115:16 says that "the highest heavens belong to the LORD, but the earth he has given to mankind." If God inhabits heaven, how can Satan and his angels camp out there, let alone resist the will of God in that realm? And what even are the *highest* heavens?

The simplest answer is that there is more than one heaven. The Bible suggests that there are at least three heavens. Much of the theology of multiple heavens is derived from 2 Corinthians 12, in which Paul describes being caught up into the *third* heaven. The third heaven was a paradise where he heard indescribable words and received revelations of the Lord Jesus

> All Christians are legally seated with Christ in heavenly places the moment we are born again, but having a legal right to something is not the same as actually possessing it, let alone knowing how to exercise it.

Christ. The majority of Paul's insight into the mystery of God was probably derived from this visit to the third heaven.

If there is a third heaven, then it stands to reason that there is also a second heaven and a first heaven. And although the Bible doesn't use the term second heaven, the book of Revelation does refer to a place called *midheaven* which, as we'll see later in this series, fits perfectly with what we're about to discuss about the second heaven.

There are various theories about the nature of the three heavens. Are they hierarchical levels? Are they separated spatially? Do they exist chronologically in time? Are they realms, or are they dimensions that occupy the same space? I don't know how to parse all of that out from the biblical record, so we'll stick with what can be reasoned clearly from Scripture.

The first heaven is commonly considered to be the physical atmosphere surrounding the Earth, though a case could be made to include the moon, planets, and stars beyond the Earth as well.

The second heaven is a bit more mysterious. Ephesians 1:20-21 (NKJV) says that Jesus sits at the right hand of the Father "far above every principality and power and might and dominion." Based on Paul's experience we can assume that both paradise and the throne of God reside in the third heaven. Darkness has no power, authority, or station in the third heaven, so it stands to reason that the devil and his angels principally rule from the second heaven.

If you are interested in digging deeper, I recommend applying the fractal of three. In that frame, the third heaven correlates with the characteristics of the Father, the human spirit, and the holy of holies. The second heaven correlates with the characteristics of the Son, the human soul, and the inner court. And of course, the first heaven correlates with the characteristics of the Holy Spirit, the human body, and the outer court. In the interest of time, I'm not going to unpack that here, but I encourage you to ruminate on the parallels.

I believe the second heaven is the realm in which the majority of Revelation chapter 12 transpires. The second heaven is the arena of the soul. It is the domain of emotions and thoughts. It is the realm of ideas and concepts that shape our mindset and dominate our worldview. I'm not saying that the second heaven is our soul, just that our souls are most directly impacted by influences that exist in the second heaven.

In that frame, consider some of these classic spiritual warfare verses. As you read, keep in mind that wherever we see the word "world" in these verses, the Greek word is typically some form of the word *kosmos,* which has more to do with the second heaven than with the physical earth:

> We know that we are of God, and that **the whole world lies in the power of the evil one**.
> —*1 JOHN 5:19*

> For our struggle is not against flesh and blood, but against the rulers, against the powers, against the **world** forces of this darkness, against **the spiritual forces of wickedness in the heavenly places**.
> —*EPHESIANS 6:12*

> in whose case **the god of this world has blinded the minds of the unbelieving so that they might not see the light of the gospel of the glory of Christ**, who is the image of God.
> —*2 CORINTHIANS 4:4*

> And you were dead in your trespasses and sins, in which you formerly walked according to the course of this world, **according to the prince of the power of the air**, of the spirit that is now working in the sons of disobedience.
> —*EPHESIANS 2:1-2*

> We are destroying **speculations and every lofty thing raised up against the knowledge of God**, and we are taking every thought captive to the obedience of Christ,
> —*2 CORINTHIANS 10:5*

The picture the apostles are painting here is one of a dark spiritual atmosphere that envelopes the earth like a shroud of confusion and lies. This veil is perpetrated in the second heaven by the spiritual forces of wickedness who seek to blind human minds from the light of the gospel of Christ. These rulers and powers and world forces of darkness are usually considered to be fallen angels led by Satan—the prince of the power of the air—who have raised up speculations and lofty ideas against the knowledge of God. The war in Revelation 12 is a battle for this arena, a struggle for dominion over the second heaven and the ability to influence minds and emotions through either freedom or tyranny.

Consider Isaiah's famous description of Lucifer's fall, and notice how similar it is to Revelation 12:7-11:

> "How you have fallen from heaven,
> O star of the morning, son of the dawn!
> You have been cut down to the earth,
> You who have weakened the nations!
> "But you said in your heart,
> 'I will ascend to heaven;
> I will raise my throne above the stars of God,
> And I will sit on the mount of assembly
> In the recesses of the north.
> 'I will ascend above the heights of the clouds;
> I will make myself like the Most High.'
> "Nevertheless you will be thrust down to Sheol,
> To the recesses of the pit.
> —ISAIAH 14:12-15

The traditional interpretation of this passage is that Satan, seen here as Lucifer, or the star of the morning, rebelled against God and was cast out of heaven sometime during the dawn of creation. At least that's what I was taught in Sunday school. That may very well be true, and within that frame, the war described in Revelation chapter 12 can legitimately be viewed as a past event in which Satan was cast out of God's presence in the third heaven after his initial rebellion. Yet even if Lucifer's original fall is echoed in these verses, the main expression of the war is still to come.

The full context of Isaiah 14 and Revelation 12 are both very clearly set in the future. Isaiah's prophecy is specifically described as a taunt spoken by God's covenant people over Satan as they enter the millennial reign of Christ, and the surrounding verses

> The second heaven is the arena of the soul. It is the domain of emotions and thoughts. It is the realm of ideas and concepts that shape our mindset and dominate our worldview.

strongly suggest that Satan's fall from heaven is directly related to events that transpire at the end of the age.

So perhaps in one sense Satan and his angels are already expelled from their original roles in the third heaven, if they ever lived there, but there remains a further expulsion from their domain in the second heaven in the future. And as I'll explain in a moment, the expulsion applies to both halves of the seventieth week. In other words, Satan was temporarily cast down during Christ's 3.5-year ministry, and he will

> Satan was temporarily cast down during Christ's 3.5-year ministry, and he will be cast down permanently during the second half of the seventieth week when the sons of God begin their ministry.

be cast down permanently during the second half of the seventieth week when the sons of God begin their ministry. The Revelation 12 war in heaven is simply a behind-the-scenes look at the spiritual mechanics of how Satan is cast down and the impact of that displacement on the second heaven and the earth.

THE EXERCISE OF SONSHIP

It is important to understand that the war is not a separate event that takes place outside the drama of the male child's birth. It is the direct result of the male child stepping into sonship and beginning to walk in an open heaven, connected to the throne room, enlightened and empowered by the seven spirits of God, and exercising the full authority of the Firstborn.

It is always the exercise of mature sonship that displaces Satan. We see this most clearly in the pattern of the Firstborn. Let's review the events after Christ's baptism because they represent the practical, substantial results that we should expect during the second half of the seventieth week when a group of saints begins walking in the full reality of being seated with Christ in heavenly places.

To set the scene, remember that after coming up out of the Jordan River, Jesus was immediately led by the Holy Spirit into the wilderness for forty days to be tempted by the devil. Every detail of Christ's temptation in the wilderness is pertinent to His pattern of sonship, but that is a discussion for another time. Right now, we are just looking at the general shape of events.

The Gospel of Luke says that He entered the wilderness full of the Holy Spirit, but after overcoming the tempter He left the wilderness full of the *power* of the Spirit. In other words, there was a conversion factor in the wilderness. The experience took what He had received from the Father and converted it into something He could give to the world around Him. Or if you fancy more playful language, Jesus' wilderness temptation was a graduate-level class on the dance of receiving and giving.

Now skip forward to one of the first examples of the power of Christ's Sonship impacting the surrounding cosmos:

> I t is always the exercise of mature sonship that displaces Satan.

> Philip found Nathanael and said to him, "We have found Him of whom Moses in the Law and also the Prophets wrote—Jesus of Nazareth, the son of Joseph." Nathanael said to him, "Can any good thing come out of Nazareth?" Philip said to him, "Come and see."
>
> Jesus saw Nathanael coming to Him, and said of him, "Behold, an Israelite indeed, in whom there is no deceit!" Nathanael said to Him, "How do You know me?" Jesus answered and said to him, "Before Philip called you, when you were under the fig tree, I saw you." Nathanael answered Him, "Rabbi, You are the Son of God; You are the King of Israel." Jesus answered and said to him, "Because I said to you that I saw you under the fig tree, do you believe? You will see greater things than these." And He said to him, "Truly, truly, I say to you, you will see the heavens opened and the angels of God ascending and descending on the Son of Man."
> —*JOHN 1:45-51*

This is one of my favorite passages in all of Scripture. The subtext is so rich, and the seventieth-week parallels run so deeply, that it is worth taking the time to unpack. It starts with a skeptical Nathanael doubting that a man from backwoods Nazareth could amount to anything special. But after responding to an invitation to "come and see," Nathanael enters Jesus' presence and almost immediately recognizes Him as the Son of God. This before witnessing any miracles or persuasive teachings, and well before Peter's famous proclamation, "Thou art the Christ, the Son of the living God" (Matt. 16:16 KJV).

Oh sure, Jesus spoke a prophetic word to Nathanael about sitting under a fig tree, but that on its own was hardly enough to convince a pragmatic Israelite like Nathanael. How could Nathanael have such life-altering revelation and confidence without evidence? I suggest it was a byproduct of the open heavens surrounding Jesus that displaced the resident darkness from the second heaven.

Think about Nathanael's initial reaction *before* meeting Jesus: "Can any good thing come out of Nazareth?" In today's culture, we might call that racism, or at the very least bigotry. Yet Jesus called him an Israelite in whom there is no deceit. Other translations say no guile, no treachery, or that he had complete integrity. The idea is that Nathanael had a pure heart and that the eyes of his spirit were singularly focused on the truth. But how could that be true given the clutter of his prejudice? As we'll see in a moment, perhaps the prejudice wasn't his junk.

Obviously, many of our wrong ideas, bad attitudes, and ungodly thought processes *are* the result of our own decisions. Garbage in, garbage out. When we fill our minds with worldly influences, or when we focus on things that are not true and noble and just and pure as Paul described in Philippians 4:8, then our minds darken over time. The eyes of our spirit become less clear, and in that place, what comes out of our mouths can easily be defiling to ourselves and others. But I don't think Nathanael's prejudiced statement about Nazareth came from internal darkness. So if it wasn't his junk, where did it come from? In this case, I believe it was second-heaven junk.

When Nathanael was far away from Jesus, sitting under the fig tree, his perspective was subject to the prevailing spiritual forces in that area. The cultural lies and prejudice perpetrated by the enemy and embraced by the local people created a darkness of destructive assumptions that were difficult to break through, even for a truth seeker and otherwise well-intentioned Israelite. Yet to his credit, despite the weight of prejudice that pressed in around his soul from the second heaven, Nathanael responded wisely to an immense invitation when his brother said, "Come and see." Spoiler alert: the words "come and see" are incredibly significant in the context of the book of Revelation, but we'll have to wait until later in our journey to see why.

Now think about Jesus' statement when Nathanael first arrived: "Behold an Israelite in whom there is no deceit." How's that for a greeting? Jesus spoke directly to Nathanael's inner man, describing his core desire, and legitimizing his identity all in a single salutation. And then Jesus followed it up with a very peculiar statement: "Before Phillip called you, **while you were under the fig tree**, I saw you." Nathanael was moved by Christ's first statement and forever changed by the second. But why? What was the significance of Christ's second statement about the fig tree? Sure, it demonstrated that He had supernatural knowledge, but was that enough to move Nathanael from skeptic to worshipper in one breath?

THE FIG TREE

There was a spiritual subtext to Jesus mentioning the fig tree, and it again connects the pattern of the Firstborn to Revelation chapter 12. I don't know if Nathanael's mind grasped the entire significance of Christ's words, but based on his response, his spirit certainly did.

To understand the spiritual dynamic that Jesus was addressing, consider these words written by the prophet Isaiah about the coming day of the Lord:

> And **all the host of heaven will wear away**,
> And the sky will be rolled up like a scroll;
> All their hosts will also wither away
> As a leaf withers from the vine,
> **Or as one withers from the fig tree**.
> —ISAIAH 34:4

Sometimes a fig tree is just a fig tree, and other times it is also a spiritual object lesson. In this verse, the fig tree represents the heavens—both the natural heaven and the second heaven. The figs (or perhaps the leaves) represent the physical stars in the first heaven, as well as the powers and principalities that rule from the dimension of the second heaven. I suspect that many fascinating insights into the nature of the spiritual forces in the second heaven can be derived by unpacking the nature of a fig tree, but that is a study for another time.

So in Isaiah 34 and other places, we find that one vital feature of the day of the Lord is that His *parousia* will cause the spiritual forces of wickedness in heavenly places to be cast down from their domain like leaves and figs falling from a tree. At that time the veil that they have perpetrated will come down as well. The shroud of accusations, deceit, confusion, depression, frustration, and other pressures that we wrestle against will fall from the spiritual atmosphere. There may also be a physical manifestation of falling stars, meteors, asteroids, comets, or other astronomical phenomena, but those will merely be a sign of what is happening in the spirit. The apostle John echoed this reality:

> and the stars of the sky fell to the earth, as a fig tree casts its unripe figs when shaken by a great wind.
> —*REVELATION 6:13*

I believe Jesus had this dynamic in mind when he said, "Before Phillip called you, when you were under the fig tree, I saw you." He had seen Nathanael sitting under the fig tree, perhaps in a vision or impression or some other prophetic experience, but the hidden significance of the picture was not lost on Him. He saw Nathanael's purity, his desire for truth, but He also saw the spiritual principalities in that area like a canopy above him blocking Nathanael's ability to perceive the light as clearly as he desired. All of that fell away the moment Nathanael stepped into Jesus' orbit.

There was no darkness above and around Jesus. He was the anchor of a spiritual portal that extended from Earth, straight through the second heaven, and into the throne room in the third heaven. The only darkness—the only lies or deceit or demonic influence—that existed in His presence were the internal ones that people willfully brought with them. And Nathanael didn't have any of those. So when Jesus called out Nathanael's purity of spirit and then indicated by His fig tree statement that He understood the source of Nathanael's prejudice—that it had simply been external, second-heaven stuff and not his own junk—Nathanael was able to respond without shame as his eyes were instantly opened: "You are the Son of God! You are the King of Israel!"

Are you getting the picture? The very act of Jesus stepping into His position as mature Son forced the spiritual powers of wickedness to be temporarily dislodged from the second heaven and to lose their greatest position of influence over the human soul. As a result of this transaction, Jesus' interactions with people were even more impactful than they would have been otherwise. It was like pushing the mute button on a blaring stereo when you were trying to have an intimate conversation. All of the external distractions were eliminated so that nobody could have any excuse for not hearing the gospel of the kingdom as it flowed from the lips of the King. People could still bring their own internal junk and personal demons to the encounter, but nothing could prevent them from experiencing the fullness of Christ's love except their own free will.

T here was a conversion factor in the wilderness. The experience took what He had received from the Father and converted it into something He could give to the world around Him.

CHAPTER 19

THE PARABLE OF THE UNVEILING - PART 3: TIME TO CLEAR THE AIR

or - "Wow, the colors are so vibrant!"

Now let's return to Revelation chapter 12 and apply the pattern of the Firstborn to the birth of the sons of God. If it was true of Jesus during the first half of the seventieth week, it will be true in some fashion of His many brethren who will step into the maturity of sonship during the second half of the seventieth week. As I mentioned earlier, when that movement of mature Christians emerges from the Church to step into their full birthright, the impact will first shake the heavens and then the earth. Here is another look at the passage describing the immediate aftershocks:

> And there was war in heaven, Michael and his angels waging war with the dragon. The dragon and his angels waged war, and they were not strong enough, and there was no longer a place found for them in heaven. And the great dragon was thrown down, the serpent of old who is called the devil and Satan, who deceives the whole world; he was

thrown down to the earth, and his angels were thrown down with him.

Then I heard a loud voice in heaven, saying, "Now the salvation, and the power, and the kingdom of our God and the authority of His Christ have come, for the accuser of our brethren has been thrown down, he who accuses them before our God day and night.

"And they overcame him because of the blood of the Lamb and because of the word of their testimony, and they did not love their life even when faced with death.
—*REVELATION 12:7-11*

I don't pretend to understand the exact mechanics involved between humans walking in sonship and the angels of God waging war in heaven, but the two are intimately connected throughout Scripture. Remember what Jesus said to Nathanael? You will see "the heavens opened, and the angels of God ascending and descending on the Son of Man" (John 1:51). Everything Jesus did on earth He did as a man —a humble bondservant blazing the trail for His Body who would come after Him.

We see the same principle at work on a slightly larger scale when Jesus sent the seventy disciples ahead of Him to the surrounding cities in preparation for His visit:

The seventy returned with joy, saying, "Lord, even the demons are subject to us in Your name." And He said to them, "I was watching Satan fall from heaven like lightning. Behold, I have given you authority to tread on serpents and scorpions, and over all the power of the enemy, and nothing will injure you.
—*LUKE 10:17-19*

The seventy were sent out without money or physical provision and were expected to act like sons of God, creatively using the resources around them and accessing the provision of heaven as they preached and demonstrated the good news of the kingdom of God. These were new disciples walking in a relatively immature level of sonship, yet the results were a localized dislodging of the principalities and powers in each area they traveled.

I don't know if Jesus was saying that He literally saw Satan himself falling from heaven while the seventy were doing their thing. Perhaps He was simply highlighting a general principle that walking in the creativity of sonship creates a spiritual portal to third-heaven resources and that the process naturally results in the displacement of second-heaven powers that stand in the way. Either way, I imagine the entire scene with the seventy reminded Jesus of what He had seen in the heavenlies on the day of His baptism. We know He saw the heavens opened at that time, but perhaps He also observed Satan actually falling to the earth, forcibly displaced from his position of influence in the second heaven like a dragon with clipped wings. This fits with the Revelation 12 narrative, and it makes sense considering Jesus was immediately led into the wilderness by the Spirit to wrestle with the newly earth-bound tempter, where He essentially treaded on the serpent by overcoming Satan's three temptations.

My point is that perhaps Jesus had His own wilderness experience in mind when He excitedly proclaimed to the seventy after they had returned from their mission:

> Nevertheless do not rejoice in this, that the spirits are subject to you, but rejoice that your names are recorded in heaven."
>
> At that very time He rejoiced greatly in the Holy Spirit, and said, "I praise You, O Father, Lord of heaven and earth, that You have hidden these things from the wise and intelligent and have revealed them to infants. Yes, Father, for this way was well-pleasing in Your sight.
> —*LUKE 10:20-21*

"Rejoice that your names are recorded in heaven!" Why was Jesus so passionate about this? He had just watched them walk in a level of sonship that reminded Him of Himself and represented a picture of things to come at the end of the age. He had just watched them demonstrate the kingdom of God on earth and plant seeds in human hearts that would spring up to eternity. He had just watched them exercise dominion over demonic forces. Why refocus the whole thing on their names being recorded in heaven?

Perhaps Jesus was highlighting one of the fundamental characteristics of sonship: Sons derive their identity and legitimacy from knowing they are pleasing to the Father, not from their accomplishments. Their accomplishments flow out of the Father's love, not the other way around. This is elementary but cannot be overstated. Sons receive to give; they don't give to receive. Sons are freed from the need to achieve recognition, status, or acceptance because they have already received these and much more from the Father.

And from that fearless place of liberated creativity, they are clear-minded enough to see the Father's provision for building the kingdom, even when it comes in the form of raw materials and unrefined resources that require faith, discipline, and even sacrifice to unpack.

> S ons derive their identity and legitimacy from knowing they are pleasing to the Father, not from their accomplishments.

Now imagine that dynamic on steroids, multiplied by many thousands, or even tens of thousands, at the end of the age when a whole host of humans around the earth step into fully mature sonship after the pattern of the Firstborn. The impact will be felt worldwide. The dragon and his angels will not be strong enough, and there will be *no place* left for them in the second heaven.

THE FOG IS LIFTED

Think about the significance of the prince of the power of the air permanently losing every inch of his heavenly domain. When Satan and his angels are cast down to earth, the impact will be felt in both the spiritual and physical realms:

> Then I heard a loud voice in heaven, saying, "Now the salvation, and the power, and the kingdom of our God and the authority of His Christ have come, for the accuser of our brethren has been thrown down, he who accuses them before our God day and night.
> —REVELATION 12:10

Again, the arena is the second heaven. With that insidious voice of the accuser of the brethren now removed, and with his incessant shroud of shame and frustration and lies excised, the entire world will benefit from the open heavens brought on by the sons of God. This event will allow for the ultimate fulfillment of Christ's prediction in Matthew 24:14—"This gospel of the kingdom shall be preached in the whole world as a testimony to all the nations, and then the end will come."

We've seen the gospel preached throughout the world for the last two thousand years, but we haven't seen anything like what is coming when the early stages of Christ's *parousia* begin with the initial revealing of the sons of God. Not only will the reality of the coming kingdom be effectively preached and demonstrated on an epic scale, but the message will be heard and received by worldwide multitudes whose minds and emotions will suddenly be cleared from all second-heaven veils. The spiritual airwaves will be wide open, and as a result, many human souls will be more receptive to the Truth.

I don't mean to suggest that everyone will receive Christ, nor that the final 3.5 years will lack spiritual warfare, conflict, difficulty, persecution, and tribulation. All of those will exist in the most extreme measures, but the primary battlefield will shift from heaven to earth:

> And they overcame him because of the blood of the Lamb and because of the word of their testimony, and they did not love their life even when faced with death. For this reason, rejoice, O heavens and you who dwell in them. Woe to the earth and the sea, because the devil has come down to you, having great wrath, knowing that he has only a short time."
> —*REVELATION 12:11-12*

"Rejoice, O heavens and you who dwell in them." Is this just referring to God's angels and the saints who have already passed into eternity? I don't think so. Remember the arena. The initial battle is for dominion in the second heaven, and the sons of God will be victorious on that stage. Both the woman and the male child will then enjoy the fruit of that dominion, in as much as their souls will no longer be subject to the accuser of the brethren. That truly will be a reason to rejoice, just as Jesus rejoiced when the seventy demonstrated a similar triumph on a smaller scale in Luke 10.

Speaking of the seventy disciples, think about the order in which Jesus described the impact of their sonship. First, Jesus pointed to the heavenly impact: "I was watching Satan fall from heaven like lightning." Then, He pointed to the resulting earthly impact: "Behold, I have given you authority to tread on serpents and scorpions, and over all the power of the enemy, and nothing will injure you." It was as though they had shaken loose the demonic forces from the heavenly realm like unripe figs, but then they had to deal with the resulting increase in direct demonic activity on earth as well.

EVE RESTORED

We've already seen this same pattern in the life of Jesus. The enemy was cast down from the second heaven when Jesus stepped into Sonship, but then Jesus immediately entered the wilderness for a chance to tread upon the serpent on earth. He did this to take back the earthly authority that Adam had abdicated for mankind in the Garden of Eden.

Adam and Eve were created for sonship. They were blessed with authority over the entire earth, and although that authority did not initially extend into the heavenly realms, they still enjoyed open heavens by virtue of their pure and unfettered access to God, who walked in the garden with them.

I don't know if it was the initial creation of Adam, or the subsequent revealing of Eve, or God's proclamation of their joint commission to rule over the earth, but I suspect that one of these events triggered Satan's first rebellion and fall from heaven. Perhaps he finally understood mankind's design when he saw Eve separated from Adam's side, and he became jealous at the implication that we were destined to be united with God in Christ's Body. Whatever the reason, in the very next scene we see the devil on earth manifesting as a crafty serpent.

When Adam and Eve listened to the serpent's twisted temptations, they were subjugating themselves to Satan, effectively giving him access to their earthly authority. Then, when they chose to hide rather than run to God for mercy, their souls succumbed to the trap of shame, effectively empowering Satan to stand between them and God as the accuser of the brethren in the second heaven. In other words, it may have been mankind's hiding that gave Satan the authority as prince of the power of the air in the first place. Perhaps it was Adam's spiritual abdication that empowered the serpent to grow wings like a dragon.

So when Jesus came out of the baptismal waters as the beloved and well-pleasing Son representing Adam perfectly reconciled to the Father, it was a direct repudiation of the accuser of the brethren, and it caused Satan to fall from the second heaven to earth. That is why Jesus immediately entered the wilderness after His baptism—He had to face Satan manifested on earth as Adam did, and He needed to overcome the same direct temptations to reclaim mankind's original earthly birthright for Himself. He was undoing Adam's mistake in reverse order of the original sin.

If that was the pattern of the Firstborn, we should expect the same for the sons of God during the second half of the seventieth week. The sequence of events is designed to reverse the effects of the fall of mankind in Eden. After all, if Jesus overcame the enemy during the first half of the seventieth week as a picture of Adam restored, the Body of Christ must also overcome during the second half of the seventieth week as a picture of Eve restored.

Notice that John mentioned three specific reasons that the male child and the woman will overcome the dragon: "because of the blood of the Lamb and because of the word of their testimony, and they did not love their life even when faced with death." These three principles follow the fractal of three and represent God's strategy for fully overcoming the enemy's attack against our spirit, soul, and body. It is the same underlying strategy that Jesus used to overcome the three temptations in the wilderness. Woven together, these form the catalyst that will lead to the initial birth of the sons of God, and they will empower every victory that follows during the final 3.5 years. We'll unpack this strategy later, but for now, let's press forward in Revelation 12 to complete our outline of the seventieth week.

> Woe to the earth and the sea, because the devil has come down to you, having great wrath, knowing that he has only a short time."
>
> And when the dragon saw that he was thrown down to the earth, he persecuted the woman who gave birth to the male child.
> —*REVELATION 12:12-13*

"Woe to the earth and the sea." This foreboding passage coincides with the beginning of the great tribulation described in Matthew 24.

When the birth of the male child displaces all of the second-heaven powers, Satan and his angels will be forced to manifest on the earth. At that time, the dragon will leverage the earthly authority of fallen mankind by directly empowering two humans—the man of lawlessness and the false prophet—forming an unholy trinity of sorts. Revelation chapter 13 describes these two as the beast that comes up out of the sea and the beast that comes up out of the earth. Once again, we'll have to wait until later in our journey to unpack these symbols and their corresponding principles. On the surface, it may sound terrifying, but the message of these verses is actually highly encouraging for two reasons.

First, remember the whole purpose of the latter half of the seventieth week:

> but He, having offered one sacrifice for sins for all time, SAT DOWN AT THE RIGHT HAND OF GOD, waiting from that time onward UNTIL HIS ENEMIES BE MADE A FOOTSTOOL FOR HIS FEET.
> —HEBREWS 10:12-13

Now combine that verse with this one:

> Thus says the LORD, "Heaven is My throne and the earth is My footstool. Where then is a house you could build for Me? And where is a place that I may rest?
> —ISAIAH 66:1

"Earth is My footstool." It is necessary for Satan to be cast down to earth because it is on earth where he will be made a footstool for the feet of Jesus *before* Jesus returns. Sometimes we think that Jesus is coming back to overcome the kingdom of darkness, but that is not entirely true. Yes, He will deliver the final blow with the sword of His mouth when He physically returns to earth, but He has already overcome all the power of the enemy. He has successfully reversed the fall of Adam, and now He sits in heaven with confident anticipation as we—His Body on earth—learn how to appropriate His power and authority. When a small portion of the Church represented by the emerging male child causes the entire kingdom of darkness to fall to earth, it will initiate the ultimate final exam for the whole Body of Christ. Final exams are hard, but they also mean graduation is right around the corner.

There is another reason why the enemy falling to earth is actually a good thing. Think about it like this: earth is not a position of strength for Satan. The dragon's greatest tactical advantage is air power. Unlike mankind, he was not designed to have authority over the physical realm. His only earthly authority is derived from mankind's fall, and he leverages sin-enslaved humans to great effect, like a hidden puppet master wielding our birthright for his own mischief. That is why he prefers a second-heaven domain—from that higher realm Satan can cast his arrogant ideas and wicked concepts in such a way that entire cultures are blinded from the knowledge of God. The position affords him protection from direct assault, greater offensive reach, and more bang for the buck. But on earth his influence is greatly reduced as his attack vector shifts from the soul toward the body. On earth the dragon must adapt to the role of earth-bound serpent, where his attack requires more direct contact.

> If Jesus overcame the enemy during the first half of the seventieth week as a picture of Adam restored, the Body of Christ must also overcome during the second half of the seventieth week as a picture of Eve restored.

So when Satan is cast to earth he will lose a tremendous amount of leverage over the human soul, and then he will be forced to rely on brute force and the seeds he had previously sowed into the hearts of mankind to influence the masses. He will no longer be in position to sow new seeds on a wide scale from an elevated position in the second heavens.

POSITION OF WEAKNESS

Perhaps you're wondering where the antichrist and the one-world government fit into all of this. Yes, Satan does want a one-world government through which he can dominate the earth, but he wants it on his own terms. He desperately wants to rule from the heavenlies like God. Previous evil empires with world-conquering aspirations like ancient Babylon, Persia, Greece, Rome, and even Nazi Germany were his attempts to establish his kingdom from a position of strength so that he could exterminate the seed of God before they reached a level of maturi-

ty in Christ that would shatter his hold on the second heaven and reduce his influence. He has spent millennia concocting and testing various schemes through any available means to bend, twist, accelerate, or
otherwise circumvent God's timeline and accomplish his objectives before the fullness of God's time—that is, before the birth of the male
child:

> He will speak out against the Most High and wear down
> the saints of the Highest One, and he will intend to make
> alterations in times and in law; and they will be given into
> his hand for a time, times, and half a time.
> —DANIEL 7:25

This verse is specifically about the antichrist at the end of the age
after the dragon has been cast down to earth, but it also exposes Satan's
underlying fear throughout the ages. The dragon wants to establish his
kingdom on his terms, in his timeframe, from his current position of
strength in the second heaven. When he and all his angels lose that
strategic position, it will be a humiliating disaster for his plans. He
knows the Scriptures. He knows that once he is cast down to earth, he
only has 3.5 years before Christ returns and he is locked away in the
bottomless pit. Giving his authority and power directly to the antichrist
and false prophet is a contingency plan—his last-ditch attempt to steal,
kill, and destroy as much as possible before his humiliation is completed. Even in that final stage of desperation, he will *intend* to extend his
allotted time and stretch the boundaries of his earthly authority beyond
God's design, but it won't work, and as we will see, his failure will be
spectacular.

I don't mean to sugarcoat any of this. It is certainly true that Satan's
second-heaven campaign will be at least partially successful before he is
cast down to earth. There is no getting around that. At the beginning of
the second half of the seventieth week, his seed will have already been
spread far and wide, and many will have already internalized his deception. The result will be something that we'll refer to as the *nature of the
beast,* which is a worldview completely devoid of God's love, God's
principles, and everything that makes us a reflection of the divine nature. It is the natural devolution of mankind that happens when the
eyes of our spirit are completely darkened and cut off from the sevenfold light that shines in the face of Christ.

When a human spirit is utterly separated from the Source, it grows so weak and inconsequential that eventually the person is little more than a wild animal, reacting to every bodily urge and base desire that comes along. And the most tragic part of this deception is that it leaves the human spirit so blinded by self-focus that it boasts in its own emaciated powerlessness. In that state, people will be easy marks for Satan and his angels when they come to earth.

It is necessary for Satan to be cast down to earth because it is on earth where he will be made a footstool for the feet of Jesus *before* Jesus returns.

Having made that disclaimer, we need to understand that not every unbeliever will embrace the nature of the beast. Those who have maintained some semblance of love for truth will suddenly find clarity where confusion and frustration previously reigned in their minds. Even in the midst of great tribulation, these will be primed to receive the gospel of the kingdom from the sons of God under an open heaven. At that time, the enemy will be more powerless than at any other point in history to silence, dampen, or even slow the message of the coming King.

Satan has no desire to enter his final 3.5 years of freedom from this position of weakness, but that is exactly what the birth of the sons of God will force upon him. So many eschatological theories focus on the inexorable rise of a one-world government growing behind the scenes until the antichrist steps out from the shadows to begin his 1,260-day tyrannical reign. That is not *entirely* wrong, but it is a grievously incomplete and skewed perspective. The dragon has a skilled PR department in the second heaven, and his messaging team has preemptively spun his coming great loss as a victory. That kind of propaganda is merely his attempt to threaten, oppress, and wear down the saints to abort the birth of the male child. Don't listen to it!

We will spend some time in the next book unpacking how the nature of the beast eventually empowers the antichrist's one-world government, though I promise it will only be a small subplot to the Unveiling of Jesus Christ as we journey through the book of Revelation. For now, I'll just acknowledge that the enemy will effectively wield blustery words and displays of power to intimidate and control world systems after Satan loses his heavenly domain. But take heart because, like all bullies, his carefully crafted facade will crumble before courageous men and women who walk in sonship.

The dragon has a skilled PR department in the second heaven, and his messaging team has preemptively spun his coming great loss as a victory. That kind of propaganda is merely his attempt to threaten, oppress, and wear down the saints to abort the birth of the male child. Don't listen to it!

CHAPTER 20

THE PARABLE OF THE UNVEILING -
PART 4: THREE PROTAGONISTS

or - "Which one am I?"

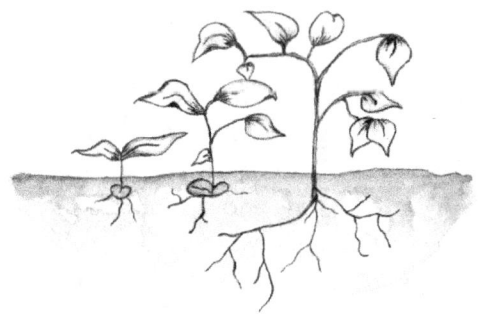

W e've spent the last few chapters looking at Revelation
chapter 12 as a parable describing the general shape of
the Unveiling of Jesus Christ. To this point, we have used
the bifocal of Israel and the Church, following both perspectives to
view the birth of the male child as Christ stepping into His earthly
ministry and the sons of God being revealed at the end of the age.
Both paths converged in the middle of the seventieth week of Daniel's
prophecy.

The shapes of these events are like topographical markers on the
metaphorical map we've been building throughout this book. These are
loose analogies, but they help to define the structure and purpose of the
tools we need for our impending expedition through the book of Revelation. This entire book has been equipping us for that journey into the
heart of the Unveiling of Jesus, and this topography is the final piece
that we need before embarking on that journey in book 2. We are al-

most there, but first we need to extend the topography through the rest of Revelation chapter 12.

Here is a quick reminder of where we left off:

> And they overcame him because of the blood of the Lamb and because of the word of their testimony, and they did not love their life even when faced with death.
>
> "For this reason, rejoice, O heavens and you who dwell in them. Woe to the earth and the sea, because the devil has come down to you, having great wrath, knowing that he has only a short time."
> —*REVELATION 12:11-12*

So at this point, the male child has been born, the dragon has been cast to earth, and the woman has fled into the wilderness. And then begins the season of the dragon's wrath on earth, which is the short period that Jesus referred to as the "great tribulation" (not to be confused with the wrath of God that will transpire later in the book of Revelation during the Day of the Lord). So what does the dragon's wrath mean for the woman and her other children? Would Jesus really allow His Bride to experience something so terrible? And where is the male child in all of this?!

A BETTER KIND OF OBEDIENCE

We will get to all of that shortly, but first I ask you to follow me into one more digression. I've already said this multiple times, but it especially bears repeating as we look at the second half of the seventieth week: perspective is everything! The enemy knows this and has spent millennia perfecting his ability to control the narrative. Satan would have us believe that the end times begin when his anointed one rises to power, but that is not how it works. The end begins when the sons of God come forth and shatter his dominion in the heavenlies, forcibly casting him down to earth. The accuser of the brethren must first lose his greatest position of influence over the human soul, and only then will he be released to begin his desperate and ill-fated campaign of wrath upon the earth.

Consider the "great tribulation" in light of that reality. The very term conjures fear and trembling for some Christians and ignorant apathy for others. But what if the great tribulation was designed for our benefit? What if the dragon's wrath was allowed because God planned to appropriate it for His agenda despite the enemy's plans? Remember the Firstborn:

> Although He was a Son, He learned obedience from the
> things that He suffered
> —*HEBREWS 5:8*

What kind of obedience did Jesus need to learn from suffering? He wasn't rebellious, nor did He require affliction to adjust His behavior. Instead of thinking about obedience from the perspective of a slave, or with the expectation of punishment, we need to view it through the lens of sonship and priesthood, since that is the greater context of this verse in Hebrews. Take a moment to read the whole passage with me:

> For every high priest taken from among men is appointed on behalf of men in things pertaining to God, in order to offer both gifts and sacrifices for sins; **he can deal gently with the ignorant and misguided, since he himself also is beset with weakness**; and because of it he is obligated to offer sacrifices for sins, as for the people, so also for himself. And no one takes the honor to himself, but receives it when he is called by God, even as Aaron was.
>
> So also Christ did not glorify Himself so as to become a high priest, but He who said to Him, "YOU ARE MY SON, TODAY I HAVE BEGOTTEN YOU"; just as He says also in another passage, "YOU ARE A PRIEST FOREVER ACCORDING TO THE ORDER OF MELCHIZEDEK."
>
> In the days of His flesh, He offered up both prayers and supplications with loud crying and tears to the One able to save Him from death, and He was heard because of His piety. **Although He was a Son, He learned obedience from the things which He suffered.** And having been made perfect, He became to all those who obey Him the source of eternal salvation, **being designated by God as a high priest according to the order of Melchizedek.**
> —*HEBREWS 5:1-10*

"According to the order of Melchizedek." Melchizedek was something of an enigma in the Old Testament. Little is known of his origin beyond the fact that he was the king of Salem and priest of God Most High. For you Tolkien fans, Melchizedek is the Tom Bombadil of ancient Jewish history—he makes a single, scene-stealing appearance early in the life of Abraham and is never seen or heard from again. David mentions him in a messianic prophecy in Psalm 110, and the book of Hebrews expounds on this Psalm, suggesting his appearance is an early prophetic shadow—or type—of Jesus Christ.

A deep discussion of the Melchizedek priesthood is beyond the scope of this book, but I simply want to point out that there are two types of obedience hidden in the subtext of this passage and throughout much of the book of Hebrews. There is the obedience associated with the Levitical priesthood, and there is an altogether different kind of obedience associated with the Melchizedek priesthood.

The Levitical priesthood, while righteous and appropriate for its time, was a God-ordained reciprocation of Israel's slave mindset. The very covenant that the Levitical priesthood served was a temporary tutor given to rebellious children. Like remedial education or boarding school, it was built on strict rules and explicit instructions designed to keep the student on the straight and narrow until their maturity caught up with their age. As such, the officiators of that covenant had to be experts in the law and exemplary adherents to every precept, and they were measured by how well they followed every command. They learned the ins and outs of that law through discipline, suffering, and intentional training, and they were often motivated by the fear of judgment for failure. To sum that all up, the obedience of the Levitical priesthood looked a lot like slavery to the fruit of the tree of the knowledge of good and evil.

On the other hand, the Melchizedek priesthood has no detailed instruction manual in Scripture, no book of ordinances outlining right and wrong, and no required ceremony for membership. The Melchizedek priesthood is about mature sonship, and its only laws are intentionally vague to invite creativity from those who desire to reflect the divine character:

> A new commandment I give to you, that you love one another, even as I have loved you, that you also love one another.
> —*JOHN 13:34*

> For you were called to freedom, brethren; only do not turn your freedom into an opportunity for the flesh, but through love serve one another. For the whole Law is fulfilled in one word, in the statement, "YOU SHALL LOVE YOUR NEIGHBOR AS YOURSELF."
> —*GALATIANS 5:13-14*

Obedience in the Melchizedek priesthood looks like freedom. It is not *just* about God's character or principles or standard of righteousness—it is about those aspects of divinity being expressed through humans who have come into alignment with their God-given design. It is not about right and wrong or good and evil; it is about life flowing through us to the rest of creation. It is about feeling our way through the wild and spontaneous dance of receiving and giving the light of the seven spirits of God in whatever unique pattern of steps He has customized for our individual journey.

> The Melchizedek priesthood is about mature sonship, and its only laws are intentionally vague to invite creativity from those who desire to reflect the divine character.

That is why Christ had to suffer. It wasn't so much about learning how to be God, or how to be one with the Father. It was mostly about learning how to sympathize with our weaknesses through experience, which was the only way He could earn the authority to become the perfect High Priest of a new covenant that would have the life-giving power to bring humanity into the freedom of maturity. In other words, He had to learn how to dance as a human so that He could also be the perfect dance instructor for the rest of humanity. In that way, His sufferings weren't intended to teach Him what to do; they were meant to prove the pathway from immaturity to maturity, from slavery to sonship, and from the old creation to the new.

Jesus embraced every circumstance the Father brought to Him. Some were accompanied by pain, and some pain was greater than others, but He embraced them all as the productive pressures of contractions. He trusted the process because He trusted the Father. And He wasn't a passive observer, but an active participant with the contractions, using them to His benefit and for the benefit of those around Him.

The tribulations at the end of the age—the very contractions of the Unveiling of Jesus—should be viewed in the same way. Suffering is an opportunity to identify with Jesus and be conformed to His image. Please understand that I'm not advocating for a defeatist or masochist mentality! God does not delight in our pain, and we do not need to seek out tribulation. Suffering is not a fruit of the Holy Spirit, and being downtrodden is not a badge of honor or a mark of legitimacy. And yet the fact remains that through many tribulations we will enter the kingdom of God. These pressures are an opportunity for us to become overcomers because they force us to find new and creative ways to lean into Him while the eyes of our hearts are enlightened to see His provision.

So let us adjust our perspective. Let us not fear the coming difficulties, and let us not imagine a rapture that spares us from the very pressure that God has orchestrated to perfect us. We *will* be delivered, but it will be the delivery of new birth *through* the contractions, not delivery *from* the contractions.

> Let us not fear the coming difficulties, and let us not imagine a rapture that spares us from the very pressure that God has orchestrated to perfect us.

THREE SECTIONS

Okay, now we can return our focus to Revelation chapter 12:

> And when the dragon saw that he was thrown down to the earth, he persecuted the woman who gave birth to the male child.
>
> But the two wings of the great eagle were given to the woman, so that she could fly into the wilderness to her place, where she was nourished for a time and times and half a time, from the presence of the serpent.
>
> And the serpent poured water like a river out of his mouth after the woman, so that he might cause her to be swept away with the flood.
>
> But the earth helped the woman, and the earth opened its mouth and drank up the river which the dragon poured out of his mouth.

> So the dragon was enraged with the woman, and went
> off to make war with the rest of her children, who keep the
> commandments of God and hold to the testimony of Jesus.
> —*REVELATION 12:13-17*

We already read in the preceding verses that the woman fled to the wilderness and the dragon was cast to earth, but here the vision drills down to provide more detail for those events. We'll focus on those specifics shortly, but first notice that we now have three protagonists as the objects of the dragon's wrath: the male child, the woman, and the rest of the woman's children. Using the fractal of three that we discussed earlier, these three can be seen as the three parts of the Body of Christ. Just as the Godhead has three members, and a human being is made up of three interrelated parts, and the tabernacle had three sections, there is a sense in which the Church also has three sections. And just as the various expressions of the fractal of three focus on different aspects of the form, function, and interrelationship of the three parts, there are many legitimate lenses through which we can view the three sections of the Body of Christ.

Right now, we will focus on the three sections as a general picture of the progression of our spiritual maturity, or the level of our Christlikeness. To put it more succinctly, the male child, the woman, and the woman's other children represent the three categories of Christians that will be alive on earth at the end of the age. That is not all they represent, but that is the lens we are using in this book.

From that perspective, whether you know it or not, and whether you regularly attend a formal church service or not, if you are born again, your current spiritual maturity can be compared to one of the three sections of the tabernacle. I'll explain what I mean by that in a moment. The hope is that as we mature in our relationship with the Godhead, we move from outer court to inner court to holy of holies. But that is largely dependent on our responses to the trials and pressures of life, as well as our willingness to embrace the discipline that refines our ability to see Christ more clearly because in Him dwells all the fullness of the Godhead bodily. Everyone does not mature at the same rate, and unfortunately, some people never grow at all after being born again.

Don't get me wrong, all three sections of the Church will eventually arrive at the same general destination, fully prepared, unified, and transformed as a Bride made ready for her Bridegroom by the very end. But each of these categories of believers will enter the second half of the seventieth week at dramatically different levels of maturity, and each will endure the travail and suffering of that season in distinctive ways, and therefore each will have a unique experience with the progression of Christ's unveiling. We'll look at the general shape of their separate paths in a moment, but first, we need to take a step back to get a clearer description of these categories.

THE INNER COURT

We will start with the woman, since that is where Revelation 12 starts. The woman coincides with the inner court section of the tabernacle of Moses, also known as the Holy Place. The Holy Place was a fully enclosed tent that sat inside the walls of the outer court. And nestled inside the heart of the Holy Place tent was a second fully enclosed tent called the holy of holies. So in a sense, the inner court contained the holy of holies within its womb, just as the woman contained the male child within her womb.

Everything inside the Holy Place was consecrated as holiness unto the Lord, and only the consecrated Levitical priests were allowed to enter, and they only to perform their service to God. In the same way, the woman represents the portion of God's people who are fully consecrated to His service, who have devoted not just their external actions

> Just as the Godhead has three members, and a human being is made up of three interrelated parts, and the tabernacle had three sections, there is a sense in which the Church also has three sections

but also their internal lives to Him. Whereas the outer court was generally about dealing with sin, the inner court was generally about cultivating divine character through the temple service. This category of inner court Christianity isn't just for ordained clergy, pastors, priests, evangelists, or other full-time ministers—it is for any Christian of any age, race, background, industry, or career who desires to embrace the commitment of a Bride betrothed to Christ, and who desires to serve His Body. After all, the inner court is all about betrothal, which we'll see in book 2. Having said that, the form and function of the Levitical priesthood in the Holy Place is indicative of the maturity level of this portion of the Body of Christ.

This mature woman is not a reference to any specific denomination. She represents many streams of the faith who will be faithfully serving God just before the period of Christ's Unveiling begins. It is possible that the advanced stages of her labor pains will break down the superficial divisions that exist in the Church today, though I suspect that the deepest denominational strife and infighting will not heal until the accuser of the brethren is cast out of the second heaven by the birth of the male child.

Remember that just before the birth, Revelation 12 described the woman as "clothed with the sun, and the moon under her feet, and on her head a crown of twelve stars." This is a picture of a faithful, glorious, and mature Church. Faithful because she is resolved to carry the seed of God to full term; glorious because her righteous acts are garments shining like the sun to reveal many aspects of God's nature to the universe; mature because she has conquered the moon.

If that last image is not immediately clear, think of it like this: according to Genesis chapter 1, God made the moon to govern times and seasons. The fact that the moon is under her feet in a position of subjugation means that she has leveraged the seasons of her contractions enough to literally hasten the coming of the day of the Lord. In other words, she has used the seasons well and redeemed the time given to her.

The crown of twelve stars speaks of the God-ordained authority structure that has governed the institution of the Christian Church since the time of the first-century apostles. The original apostles were wise master builders who established a foundational system and spiritual structure for the young church based upon the principles they learned from the Old Testament and observed in the life of Christ. It is a system that has allowed the Church as an institution to survive and persist through two thousand years of persecution, both from external assault and internal abuse. This system, with its many variations across denominations and tribes, has at times been used to cause both strife and unity, turmoil and order, abuse and protection for many generations, but despite the mixture, the general principles upon which the system was built will continue to serve the woman well through the end of this age and into the next.

In many ways, the woman represents the pure and faithful aspects of the local church system as delineated by the first-century apostles, with all its leadership and organizational structures that provide common ground for Christians to come together, work together, grow together, and impact culture with greater numbers. She also represents the people who have faithfully embraced and utilized that system to expand the kingdom of God on earth.

I'm not saying that every Christian who is a member of a local church at the end of the age will be considered part of the woman, nor am I suggesting that church membership is required to be in this inner court company of Christians, but in general the woman is the culmination of the church age that began almost two thousand years ago on the day of Pentecost.

THE HOLY OF HOLIES

Now think of the male child as the holy of holies section of the tabernacle. The believers in that category will be those who have fully embraced the Braxton Hicks contractions—the common trials and tribulations of life—as motivation to grow in the grace and knowledge of the Lord *before* the second half of the seventieth week begins. These will have already presented their bodies as a living sacrifice to God by embracing a bondservant lifestyle (the goal of the outer court season of maturity), and they will have already embraced an inner court bridal relationship with Christ. When they reach full maturity, they will metaphorically step into the holy of holies, and that "birth" into full sonship will initiate the second half of the seventieth week. It's important to note that they will step into the holy of holies as priests according to the order of Melchizedek rather than the Levitical priesthood.

The holy of holies was a place of rest and unity with God. According to the law of Moses, only the high priest was allowed to enter, and even he could only enter once a year on the Day of Atonement. Because the presence of God rested on the mercy seat above the ark of the covenant within the holy of holies, and because no human could stand in His presence, there is a rabbinical tradition that the high priest actually underwent a temporary divine transformation to become one with God when he stepped beyond the veil so that he could perform his high priest duties without suffering instant death.

Whether or not that is literally what happened with the Old Testament Levitical high priest on the Day of Atonement, it is a perfect picture of the transformation that this category of Christians will undergo when they spring forth as the male child at the end of the age. They will be united with Christ, the first part of the Body to attain the full maturity of the Head. They will represent a first-fruits harvest of the kingdom of God, demonstrating the power of the age to come, and they will show the way forward to the rest of the Church.

Remember Christ's words to the seventy disciples after they returned from their mission of sonship? "Behold, I have given you authority to tread on serpents and scorpions, and over all the power of the enemy, and nothing will injure you." That is the level of dominion that this movement of mature sonship will walk in on earth during the final 3.5 years as they preach and demonstrate the kingdom of God. During that time, they will be beyond the dragon's ability to harm, which is why verse thirteen in Revelation chapter 12 says that the dragon will persecute the woman who gave birth to the male child—not the male child himself.

A MORE MATURE STRUCTURE?

Consider what these details suggest about the male child and his relationship with the woman. Just as the male child is no longer inside the woman after his birth, the end-times sons of God will also exit the general structure of the institutional church. They will still be members of the universal Body of Christ interacting with organic Christian community, but the traditional church structure modeled after the Levitical priesthood will no longer be a suitable habitat to support the purposes for which they are called. If that concept sounds controversial or even dangerous, consider the words of the apostle Paul:

> He who descended is Himself also He who ascended far above all the heavens, so that He might fill all things. And He gave some as apostles, and some as prophets, and some as evangelists, and some as pastors and teachers, for the equipping of the saints for the work of service, to the building up of the body of Christ; **until we all attain** to the unity of the faith, and of the knowledge of the Son of

God, to a mature man, to the measure of the stature which
belongs to **the fullness of Christ**.
—*EPHESIANS 4:10-13*

Apostles, prophets, evangelists, pastors, teachers—all are gifts given
to equip the individual members of the Church so that the entire Body
is edified. Their gifts are meant to reproduce their nature throughout
the rest of the Body, but the end goal was never meant to be a permanent clergy class modeled after the Levitical priesthood, nor a laity class
of spectators sitting back watching the priests do the dirty work. Remember, that is how the nation of Israel responded to God's offer on
Mount Sinai, and that is why God patiently gave them the temporary
tutor of the Mosaic law administered by the Levitical priesthood.

We are meant to outgrow the need for these temporary equipping
ministries on an individual and corporate level as we experience the Unveiled Christ and step into the full measure of His maturity. The end-
times sons of God will be early adopters of this reality, blazing a trail of
hope for the rest of the Body of Christ. And they won't look like a kingdom of *Levitical* priests working within the confines of the institutional
church system. They will look like a kingdom of *Melchizedek* priests,
serving the purposes of the kingdom of God outside of the traditional
church structure, leveraging all of their gifts, resources, and vocations to
impact culture in real and transformational ways.

Remember the model of the Firstborn. How much life, equipping,
blessing, protection, or authority did Jesus ever receive from the Jewish religious system? On the one hand, His parents steadfastly fulfilled
the law of Moses, bringing Him to Jerusalem after His birth for the
firstborn dedication, and every year afterward for the appropriate
feasts. As a baby He was blessed in the temple by Simeon and Anna,
and as a child of twelve He sat in the temple listening and asking
questions of the teachers. So perhaps He did receive some level of nurture from the system in His early years. But either way, that time offi-
cially came to an end when He was baptized into Sonship. From that
point forward His spiritual and emotional sustenance came primarily
from His relationships with the Father and the Holy Spirit, and sec-
ondarily from His small community of trusted friends like Mary,
Martha, and Lazarus, and perhaps even Peter, James, John, and any
others with whom He enjoyed spending time. He continued to visit
the temple in Jerusalem and various local synagogues from time to

time, but only to reach the lost sheep of Israel, and always with a message that antagonized the religious leaders while simultaneously honoring the divine principles upon which their system was originally built.

However you look at it, the established Jewish religious authority structure and system of "worship" did nothing to enable, enhance, or legitimize Christ's ministry. I'm not even talking about the twisted, greedy, hypocritical, self-righteous, slave mindset of religious humanism that the Pharisees embraced. I'm talking about the foundational system itself—the "seat of Moses" upon which the scribes and Pharisees sat. It was a God-ordained and righteous system, and to the degree that it still adhered to its Godly moorings, it was a blessed and effective conduit of God's grace to the world. And yet it was wholly inadequate to support the fullness of God's plan for creation. It was just a temporary tutor. Its most important role was to bring forth Christ and then to bequeath the principles inherent in its original inception to the nascent Christian Church as she found her footing on the world stage.

Don't worry, I'm not suggesting that the end-times church will outgrow the foundation installed by the first-century apostles and prophets. That foundation is solid and will persist even through the millennial reign of Christ. In other words, the woman won't lose her crown of twelve stars after the male child's birth. She may even come to understand and appreciate that crown even more.

What I am saying is that foundations are meant to be under the surface, and they shouldn't have more than a general impact on the form of the final building. Once they are laid, the focus needs to shift away from the foundation. And that is what will finally happen after the birth of the male child.

To whatever extent the Church has treated the foundation of the apostles and prophets like the Israelites treated the law of Moses—leaning on the system the way an insecure slave leans on rules for survival—to that degree she has stunted her growth and prevented herself from being counted as part of the male child.

I say all this out of respect and love for a system that God has blessed for millennia. But in many cases the various institutional church systems in place on the earth today are disproportionally self-focused, simply by virtue of the energy and resources that are constantly required to maintain their structure. Such systems do not resemble the pattern of the Firstborn and simply cannot support the full glory of what the Body of Christ will become before the end.

I recognize that I am painting with a massive brush when a finer tip might be more appropriate. Remember, we're only dealing with topography here. What I'm describing is simply the general shape of things at the end, not exact details applying equally to every church and every Christian. I'm also being intentionally vague about what exactly constitutes the foundation of the apostles and prophets, which aspects of the institutional church will change, and which will stay the same. There are many reasons for that, not the least of which is that there is too much that I don't see clearly yet. We will revisit this topic in the next book to discuss some specific aspects of the church's transformation that I think I do understand in the context of the book of Revelation, but even so, it is not given to me to tear down another person's work. My purpose is to cast vision for what can and will be.

To that end, it is important to understand the male child's general role in the woman's transformation. We'll dig into some of the mechanics in a moment because their example of radically free and creative sonship will combine with the pressures of the great tribulation to drive the woman to finally and fully unpack the deeper principles embedded in the apostles' foundation. And that is when she will be forced to shed the institutional church system in favor of something more organic and nimble and kingdom-focused. Something modeled after the male child, who is of course modeled after Jesus Christ.

I can't tell you exactly what she will look like; history has never seen a fully mature Body of Christ. As glorious as the first-century Church was, for all of her powerful exploits, expeditious growth, and transformational influence, the Church was still only an infant during that season. Over the subsequent centuries, she has gone through various stages of growth, teenage rebellion, identity crisis, self-discovery, and more recently, a slow and painful rediscovery of her roots. But her greatest season of growth is reserved for the second half of the seventieth week, because only then will she be mature enough to experience and understand the Unveiled reality of her betrothed Bridegroom like never before.

Revelation chapter 21 describes the holy city of New Jerusalem coming down out of heaven from God, prepared as a Bride adorned for Her Husband. Among other things, this is a profound picture of the

Church after she is finally fully fitted together. We are not going to dig into that description right now, but suffice it to say that she will bear little resemblance to any of the Old Testament temples or New Testament churches of the last two thousand years, though both influences will be celebrated in her architecture. As we'll see in a moment, it is the birth of the sons of God that initiates the final season of change to the Church's form, and this must happen for her to become what she is destined to be.

THE OUTER COURT

If the woman represents the faithful, advancing, overcoming portions of the institutional church around the world, and the male child represents a first-fruits harvest of believers walking in the fullness of Christ's sonship outside of the structure of the institutional church, then who are the rest of the woman's children?

This category of Christians contains those who, for various reasons, remain in an outer court relationship with God. They are born again, having accepted Christ's sacrifice for their salvation, but they go no further. Like the Israelites who were delivered from Egypt but continued to embrace a slave mindset in an illusion of separation, these are the Christians who have yet to fully embrace the spiritual disciplines of the outer court bondservant which would have led them into the shelter of the inner court tent.

In the context of Revelation chapter 12, these "other children" are clearly separated from the woman, especially considering that the dragon had to leave his persecution of the woman to go attack the other children. Likewise, many of the believers in this category will not only be outside of the institutional church system, but they will be separated from the life-giving relationships found in any healthy, organic, Christian community, and therefore they will be outside of the protection offered by the covered Holy Place.

There are any number of factors that could keep a believer in the outer court. In some cases, these will be Christians who have left the inner court in response to abusive and exploitive leadership, or out of bitterness over Christian hypocrisy. Some shrink back over time because their particular religious experience is ineffective and powerless against the trials of life, and others simply leave to pursue the "pleasures" of Babylon.

Not everyone in the outer court will be backslidden or lukewarm. During the second half of the seventieth week, the outer court will also be populated with a massive number of new converts who will flood into the kingdom of God as a result of the testimonies of the male child and the woman. The open heavens perpetrated by the sons of God will provide the clarity that many souls will be hungering for during the great tribulation, and so they will courageously embrace the gospel of Jesus Christ, hoping to escape the impending wrath of God. We'll talk more about this dynamic in a later chapter.

In both cases, whether brand new or complacent Christians, the outer court represents the immature offspring of the woman who have yet to embrace the disciplines and productive contractions that produce the character of Christ over time and lead to a more fulfilling experience of His life.

I hasten to say that the lines between these three categories of spiritual maturity are rarely obvious, and they can be especially difficult to discern from the outside. Church attendance is probably the least reliable metric. Not every Christian who regularly attends a church meeting is at an inner court maturity level, and not every Christian who has left the institutional church is an outer court Christian. Some outer court believers are faithful members of a local church, and many newborn believers quickly progress in maturity, while those who are currently hidden in the womb as prenatal sons of God are all over the map as far as their relationship to the institutional church. Although it is generally important to understand these three sections of the Body of Christ, it is not my place to label any individual, church, denomination, or movement. In the fullness of time everyone's deeds will be made manifest, and only then can we know each other by our fruit. But if you are tempted to judge another person's fruit before the time, just remember the words of Paul:

> For who among men knows the thoughts of a man except the spirit of the man which is in him? Even so the thoughts of God no one knows except the Spirit of God.
> —*1 CORINTHIANS 2:11*

> But he who is spiritual appraises all things, yet he himself is
> appraised by no one.
> —*1 CORINTHIANS 2:15*

Above all, remember that every person who is born again is a member of the Body of Christ, and all three portions of the Body are precious to the Lord Jesus. They may take different paths through the Unveiling and even inherit different rewards at the end, but they will all be His.

As glorious as the first-century Church was, for all of her powerful exploits, expeditious growth, and transformational influence, the Church was still only an infant during that season.

CHAPTER 21

THE PARABLE OF THE UNVEILING - PART 5: OF WRATH AND WINGS AND WILDERNESSES

or - "Can you give me an example?"

N ow that we have a foundational understanding of the three categories of believers described in Revelation chapter 12, it is time to examine their unique paths through the second half of the seventieth week. We'll start with a small step back to set the stage, and then we'll weave in a few more parallel examples from Scripture to enrich our understanding of the narrative. This three-part discussion will complete the topography of our map and draw us into the beginning stages of our journey.

AFTER THE PUSH

When we first saw the woman, she was crying out from the pains of advanced labor. It was a glimpse of the end-times inner court church in the most difficult stages of transition, about to give birth to something new and exciting and totally mysterious to her. Into the chaos and anxiety of that scene appeared a monstrous dragon, postering to cause a miscarriage or to devour the child at birth. Talk about a traumatic situation for an expectant mother!

Now consider the woman/church *after* the birth. The fruit of her labor didn't produce a tiny baby to coddle and nurture, nor a young spiritual movement to protect and disciple. Instead, she found a fully mature son who immediately left her established system to attend to the Father's work. And then the woman witnessed this "sons of God" movement exercising intimacy with Christ, spiritual maturity, and effective authority over the works of the enemy, all of which she was ill-equipped to follow.

After all the drama surrounding the birth, this sounds like a recipe for severe postpartum depression, especially when you consider that the entire spectacle up until this point had taken place in the second heaven—which is the realm of soul and all of the soul's thoughts and emotions—and in that realm there was still a menacing dragon wielding accusation as a weapon. I expect in that moment the insidious dragon will be desperate to misbrand the woman as a second-class failure and a castaway.

Such may be the precarious position of much of the Church around the world after the birth of the sons of God. Fortunately for her, the spiritual authority of the male child will immediately release the archangel Michael and the armies of heaven to evict the dragon and his followers from their threatening position. And so the blaring, destabilizing, shame-inducing voice of the dragon will be silenced in the heavenly realms at the very moment when the Church will be at her most vulnerable. But that is not the end of the story. Let's read through the rest of the chapter again to see what happens after the dragon is cast to earth:

> And when the dragon saw that he was thrown down to the earth, he persecuted the woman who gave birth to the male child.
>
> But the two wings of the great eagle were given to the woman, so that she could fly into the wilderness to her place, where she was nourished for a time and times and half a time, from the presence of the serpent.
>
> And the serpent poured water like a river out of his mouth after the woman, so that he might cause her to be swept away with the flood.

But the earth helped the woman, and the earth opened its mouth and drank up the river which the dragon poured out of his mouth.

So the dragon was enraged with the woman, and went off to make war with the rest of her children, who keep the commandments of God and hold to the testimony of Jesus.
—*REVELATION 12:13-17*

The general sequence of events is simple, but here is a quick outline to make sure we are all on the same page:

1. The dragon is cast to earth.
2. He initiates (or intends to initiate) persecution against the woman.
3. The woman is given wings to begin her escape to the wilderness.
4. The dragon/serpent pours water out of his mouth after the woman.
5. The earth helps the woman by swallowing the flood.
6. The enraged dragon goes off to make war with her other children.

Again, the sequence is straightforward, though the symbolism is nuanced and requires wisdom and some finesse to unpack. To that end, we'll spend these final chapters drilling down on each of these events while using a familiar Old Testament story to navigate the contours.

At this point, you've heard my disclaimer about the seed nature of the Word of God, so I don't need to tell you that there are other legitimate interpretations of these signs. I'm using the frame that most passionately captures my heart, but other perspectives may highlight complementary facets of the divine plan. Even so, I do believe that the perspective I am about to share is the most appropriate use of the frame we've built for understanding, hastening, and experiencing Christ's Unveiling at the end of the age. If you prefer another frame, I simply ask you to weigh everything we're about to discuss and then overlay it with your existing viewpoint. You may find that it contradicts some beliefs and aligns with others. Either way, I pray that it will establish and strengthen your faith in powerful and unexpected ways!

DRAGON WINGS?

We've already talked about how and why the dragon is cast to the earth, but notice that after his excommunication the dragon is also referred to as the serpent. It is almost as if the dragon's wings were ripped off when the male child stepped into his rightful authority, and from that point on, the serpent's power and authority were relegated to that which he could personally and directly influence in the physical realm.

To be fair, the text never actually says that the dragon had wings when he was in the heavens. I am assuming wings because that is the classic picture of a dragon, and it fits with the imagery of him being in the heavens and then being cast down to earth, and it aligns with the biblical concept of Satan as the current prince of the power of the air. But either way, my point is applicable: After the birth of the male child, the dragon will lose his second-heaven superiority.

It is also fascinating that just after the newly earthbound dragon/serpent begins directing his attack against the institutional Church, the woman will be given her own set of wings to escape into the wilderness away from the persecution. More on that in a moment.

First, it is important to understand that the wrath of the dragon, directed first at the woman and then at the woman's other children, correlates with the great tribulation described by Jesus on the Mount of Olives:

> "Therefore when you see the ABOMINATION OF DESOLATION which was spoken of through Daniel the prophet, standing in the holy place—let the reader understand—then those who are in Judea must flee to the mountains. Whoever is on the housetop must not go down to get things out of his house. And whoever is in the field must not turn back to get his cloak. But woe to those women who are pregnant, and to those who are nursing babies in those days! Moreover, pray that when you flee, it will not be in the winter, or on a Sabbath. For then there will be a great tribulation, such as has not occurred since the beginning of the world until now, nor ever will again. And if those days had not been cut short, no life would have been saved; but for the sake of the elect those days will be cut short.
> —*MATTHEW 24:15-22*

Again, heavy stuff for sure, though I hasten to remind you that the great tribulation is merely a useful blip on the radar of Christ's Unveiling. We will talk about the details of the great tribulation in the next book when our full expedition into the book of Revelation finally extends beyond our current reconnaissance mission. Don't worry, we won't shy away from topics like the abomination of desolation, the mark of the beast, and the blood of the martyrs in the next book, but I'm saving all of that for when we have a fuller perspective of the Unveiling to combat the enemy's boasts.

> It is almost as if the dragon's wings were ripped off when the male child stepped into his rightful authority, and from that point on, the serpent's power and authority were relegated to that which he could personally and directly influence in the physical realm.

The only reason I'm bringing you back to Matthew chapter 24 now is to drive home the connections we made in previous chapters between the seventieth week and Christ's prophecies, and because we are going to refer back to these verses shortly when we talk about the woman's wilderness and the persecution of the rest of her children.

EAGLE'S WINGS

Back to Revelation chapter 12. Shortly after the great tribulation begins, the woman is given two great wings of the eagle to flee into the wilderness, where she will be nurtured away from the presence of the serpent. Let's camp here for a moment. What are the two wings of the great eagle? Do they represent a particular nation? Two nations? A specific spiritual power? An organization? A philosophy? I've read many interesting theories, and I have some of my own, but right now, I'm less interested in specifically identifying the wings than I am in understanding how they fit into the greater narrative of the woman moving from where she is to where she needs to be.

Remember, the whole point of tribulation is maturation. At the start of the second half of the seventieth week, the woman will still need time and pressure and nurture to reach the full maturity of Christ, but apparently, she won't need to experience the full measure of the dragon's wrath to get there. That is where the eagle's wings come in.

Wings often speak of freedom. Unless they are caged, birds have unparalleled maneuverability and freedom to go and do as they please.

But in the case of the woman, freedom of maneuverability seems secondary, considering that the wings are given to her for the primary purpose of transportation from point A to point B. So although freedom plays a role, there is more to the imagery.

An eagle's physiology, combined with their mastery of various atmospheric forces, enables them to fly to great heights, cover great distances, reach impossible locations, and even carry heavy cargo without crippling expenditures of energy. They adapt to the winds, air currents, and barometric pressures, and they use them to their advantage to accomplish feats of strength and endurance in an arena that other creatures cannot. And this natural mastery of first-heaven forces is symbolic of second-heaven authority.

In that light, consider this famous prophecy by Isaiah:

> Why do you say, O Jacob, and assert, O Israel,
> "My way is hidden from the LORD,
> And the justice due me escapes the notice of my God"?
> Do you not know? Have you not heard?
> The Everlasting God, the LORD, the Creator of the ends
> of the earth does not become weary or tired.
> His understanding is inscrutable.
> He gives strength to the weary,
> And to him who lacks might He increases power.
> Though youths grow weary and tired,
> And vigorous young men stumble badly,
> Yet those who wait for the LORD
> Will gain new strength;
> **They will mount up with wings like eagles**,
> They will run and not get tired,
> They will walk and not become weary.
> —*ISAIAH 40:27-31*

The larger context of this prophecy is all about the immensity of God's strength and His ability to fulfill His promises of transformation through the unveiling of Jesus, even when our faith is withering under the threat of unjust persecution. In that context, the wings of eagles represent a tireless strength and an abundant provision to accomplish that which seems impossible from the perspective of earthbound creatures who are oppressed by the prince of the power of air.

THE EXODUS PARALLEL

With all of that in the back of your mind, come with me back to Exodus chapter 19. The entire Exodus story foreshadows Christ's Unveiling on multiple levels and from multiple perspectives. You may recall that we visited part of the Sinai story in previous chapters to add context to Daniel's seventy-week prophecy, and we will return to different parts of Exodus in the next book, but right now I want to grab just a few threads that apply directly to our Revelation 12 narrative:

> When they set out from Rephidim, **they came to the wilderness of Sinai and camped in the wilderness**; and there Israel camped in front of the mountain. And Moses went up to God, and the LORD called to him from the mountain, saying, "This is what you shall say to the house of Jacob and tell the sons of Israel: 'You yourselves have seen what I did to the Egyptians, and how **I carried you on eagles' wings, and brought you to Myself**. Now then, if you will indeed obey My voice and keep My covenant, then you shall be My own possession among all the peoples, for all the earth is Mine; and you shall be to Me a kingdom of priests and a holy nation.' These are the words that you shall speak to the sons of Israel."
> —*EXODUS 19:2-6*

Do you see the Revelation chapter 12 parallels? The woman crying out in the pains of labor is like the nation of Israel crying out to God for deliverance from hundreds of years of Egyptian bondage before the exodus. The dragon seeking to devour her child is like the Pharaohs—or more accurately, the second-heaven spiritual forces that influenced the Pharaohs to hold generations of Hebrews in bondage and even to commit infanticide at the time of Moses's birth. The birth of the male child is like Moses's commissioning at the burning bush, and the war to cast the dragon out of heaven is like the ten plagues humbling the gods of Egypt and breaking Pharaoh's strength.

God used Moses to demonstrate the superiority of His kingdom over all the second-heaven powers of Egypt. And once those powers were shaken loose, something else happened that was almost as amazing as the ten plagues:

> Now the sons of Israel had done according to the word of
> Moses, for they had requested from the Egyptians articles
> of silver and articles of gold, and clothing; and the Lord
> had given the people favor in the sight of the Egyptians, so
> that they let them have their request. Thus they plundered
> the Egyptians.
> —*EXODUS 12:35-36*

The nation of Israel—this collection of impoverished Hebrew slaves, a culturally reviled and racially despised group of second-class citizens—were inconceivably gifted tremendous provision by the very system that had enslaved them for hundreds of years, and by the very people whose economy had just been devastated by the Hebrews' God.

We don't know how much was given to the Israelites that day, but considering there were over 600,000 Hebrew men (and who knows how many women and children) asking their Egyptian neighbors for gifts, it must have been a staggering transfer of wealth and resources, and it was likely a major factor in Pharaoh's decision to pursue them to the Red Sea. You might even say that this plundering was God's way of baiting Pharaoh into the trap.

From Israel's perspective, imagine the effect that this sudden and miraculous influx of abundance must have had on their spiritual, emotional, and physical health! Just one day earlier they were generationally impotent slaves to an unstable, stone-hearted tyrant, with little hope of freedom and barely enough resources to survive a wilderness journey, even if they could escape. The next day they were hightailing it out of Egypt with the wealth of their oppressors at their disposal. What did this turn of events do for their faith, their view of God, and their capacity to understand the immensity of His kingdom? Their national psyche was still deeply wounded from generations of slavery, and they would shortly resort to that ingrained slave mindset, but without this demonstration of miraculous provision, would they have had the emotional stamina to make it beyond the borders of Egypt in the first place? The plundering of Egypt was the wind beneath their wings.

Now, back to the two wings of the great eagle. In the wilderness of Sinai, God referenced what He had done to the Egyptians as part of the process by which He carried Israel on eagle's wings and brought them to Himself. The most obvious stage of Israel's deliverance transpired at the far end of the Red Sea when Pharaoh's army was obliterated by the collapsing walls of water, but in a sense, the process of that deliverance began the moment Moses and Aaron first stepped into Pharaoh's court and proclaimed to the earthly and heavenly rulers:

> And afterward Moses and Aaron came and said to Pharaoh, "Thus says the Lord, the God of Israel, 'Let My people go that they may celebrate a feast to Me in the wilderness.'"
> —EXODUS 5:1

From that moment on, each of the plagues, the resulting devastation of the Egyptian economy, the humiliating powerlessness of Egyptian cosmology, and the eventual plundering of Egyptian wealth and provisions were all part of the great deliverance process that cleared out the second heaven so that God could send the eagle's wings to carry Israel all the way through the Red Sea to the foot of a mountain in the wilderness of Sinai. There He would introduce her to her true birthright and present her with a path to sonship that would eventually lead her into the promised land.

Now take all of that and apply it to the woman. The inner court portion of the end-times Church will experience a similar process of deliverance beginning shortly after the male child is birthed into the sonship of Christ. At the very moment when the woman is most vulnerable, exhausted from the birth, and facing the threat of persecution from the dragon, her fortunes will suddenly change for the better. Just as Pharaoh finally acquiesced after the Passover plague on the Egyptian firstborn, the dragon will lose his amplified position of accusation when he is cast to the earth by the sons of God exercising the authority of the Firstborn. And once the air is finally clear, God will send the two wings of the great eagle to give the woman the spiritual, emotional, and physical strength she needs to complete her flight into the wilderness.

I know that I said we would not discuss the specifics of the great tribulation until the next book, but I encourage you to meditate on what kind of supernatural provision the inner court portion of the Church might receive right before the season of the dragon's wrath on earth. Remember the Exodus parallel: Israel was granted favor to plunder the wealth of Egypt on the very day that she escaped its system. This plundering was a direct result of the way God humiliated the false gods of Egypt through Moses. The Egyptian people had just seen every false god they had trusted—every ungodly principle they had built their lives on—shaken to the core. Their entire national psyche was destabilized, and in that "open heavens" climate God was able to give the Israelites pity and even favor in the eyes of their oppressors. The Church will have a similar experience right before the great tribulation begins.

> When the Church gives birth to the sons of God movement and all the powers of the second heaven are shaken, the entire world will take notice, and then favor and provision will flow to her.

When the Church gives birth to the sons of God movement and all the powers of the second heaven are shaken, the entire world will take notice, and then favor and provision will flow to her. And when the dragon sees the magnitude of the influence he has lost, his desperate jealousy will be so reckless that it will ultimately lead to his undoing (think Pharaoh's armies at the Red Sea), but that's a topic for the next book.

THE DRAGON'S DESPERATION

Now let's move on to consider the general shape of the dragon's attack against the woman:

> And when the dragon saw that he was thrown down to the earth, he persecuted the woman who gave birth to the male child.
>
> But the two wings of the great eagle were given to the woman, so that she could fly into the wilderness to her place, where she was nourished for a time and times and half a time, from the presence of the serpent.
>
> And the serpent poured water like a river out of his mouth after the woman, so that he might cause her to be swept away with the flood.
>
> But the earth helped the woman, and the earth opened its mouth and drank up the river which the dragon poured out of his mouth.
> —*REVELATION 12:13-16*

At the risk of belaboring the obvious, please remember the chronology. First, the dragon attempts to persecute the woman. Then the woman receives wings so that she can flee into the wilderness. Then the serpent pours out water after the woman. Then the earth helps the woman. It is important to understand that the serpent's flood is separate and subsequent to the dragon's initially intended persecution. The Greek word translated as "persecuted" in verse 13 is often translated as "pursued," and it has the connotation of chasing after someone with malicious intent to persecute. Like Pharaoh pursuing the Israelites to the Red Sea, the dragon's wrath toward the woman will contain all the threatening sound and fury of persecution with none of the physical payoff.

Remember, by this point, the dragon will have already lost his heavenly domain. The woman will have already escaped his "accuser of the brethren" influence, and she will be in the process of receiving wings to escape his presence altogether. That is why verse 13 still refers to the dragon instead of the serpent. The initial stage of the dragon's persecution will still be on the soul level, and it will end when the woman is given eagle's wings to overcome.

On the other hand, the serpent's attack begins after the woman is given wings to escape to the wilderness. This begs the question: how could a flood of water emanating from the mouth of an earthbound serpent threaten a woman with wings? Is it simply that she hasn't yet taken flight? In other words, is this description of the serpent's attack merely adding further detail to the dragon's persecution that was first mentioned in verse thirteen? This is unlikely considering that the woman is saved from the serpent's flood by the earth's assistance rather than by her flight (we'll talk more about the earth's assistance later). Again, this description of the serpent's flood must be separate and subsequent to the dragon's initial persecution.

So how is the woman threatened by the serpent's flood if she has already taken flight? If she is mid-flight, she couldn't be swept away. If she is resting somewhere on the ground before reaching her final wilderness destination (which is a silly proposition given the implied endurance of wings from the "great eagle"), she could have simply taken flight again to escape. No, the simplest and most obvious answer is that the woman is already safely hidden away in her wilderness, and the serpent's flood is his final, frantic, and ultimately vain campaign to overwhelm the entire earth with his putrefying influence in a desperate attempt to somehow reach the woman's secret refuge. But as we'll see shortly, the dragon's crusade against the woman will fail when the earth itself swallows his defilement in direct response to the unfolding of Christ's Unveiling.

L ike Pharaoh pursuing the Israelites to the Red Sea, the dragon's wrath toward the woman will contain all the threatening sound and fury of persecution with none of the physical payoff.

CHAPTER 22

THE PARABLE OF THE UNVEILING - PART 6: TRIUMPHANT TRIFECTA OF TRIBULATION

or - "Let's not shrink back!"

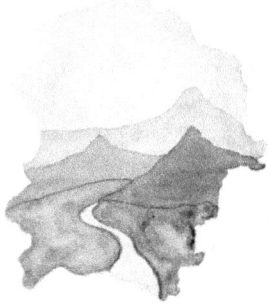

W
e still have some unanswered questions to fill out our Revelation 12 topography. What is the woman's wilderness? What is the serpent's flood? How does the earth help the woman? Where is the male child during all this? What happens to the woman's other children? In these last chapters, we'll unpack each of these questions as a final training for the journey that begins in earnest in book 2.

Let's start with the wilderness. What is it? Where is it? Does the wilderness represent a physical place to which the Church will literally flee at the beginning of the second half of the seventieth week? Considering that we are talking about the Body of Christ worldwide, a singular physical wilderness seems highly unlikely. Could different parts of the Body in different parts of the earth flee to different wildernesses? Perhaps. At the very least I expect different parts of the Body will have different wildernesses tailored to their own specific needs, but I'll explain what I mean by that in a moment.

One of the most fundamental aspects of any wilderness is seclusion. We see this with the Israelites after the Exodus, and with Christ after His baptism. In the wilderness, external influences are minimized to maximize our encounter with God—an encounter that initiates healing, testing, discipline, and transformation to prepare us for the conquest of the promised land. That much is clear in the pattern of Scripture. But will the woman's wilderness be a set of secluded physical safe havens to which she must travel, or will she only "flee" in a figurative sense, as one finding an emotional and spiritual lifeline in the midst of their trials? I don't know, but I suspect some combination of both will apply.

Revelation 12 describes the wilderness as a place prepared by God and a place of nourishment from the presence of the serpent. It also prophesies that the woman will be there for 1,260 days, or a time, times, and a half a time, which corresponds with the entire second half of the seventieth week. Whether that equates to a literal 3.5 years or some longer season is impossible to know for sure.

Just as with the eagle's wings, there are a plethora of theories about the nature, location, length, and even the timing of the woman's wilderness. Some view the wilderness as a general description of the historical Dark Ages. Others see the entire church age between the first-century ascension and the second coming of Christ as a wilderness period. Many other theories focus either on Israel's diaspora or various periods of Christian persecution over the centuries. When you remember the seed nature of prophecy, and that there are different legitimate ways to interpret the identity of the woman herself, then there are certainly multiple valid ways to understand her wilderness throughout Church history because each of these are prenatal examples of the final fulfillment at the end of the age.

It is all about the frame you choose. In this book, our primary frame is God's eternal plan to derive a suitable companion by summing up all things in Christ. So we will stay focused on the Church's future wilderness during the second half of the seventieth week as a reflection of Christ's 3.5-year ministry, however long that period ends up being. Our goal at this point is not so much to identify the specific location and duration of that final wilderness but to understand its purpose, and to see how God will use it to accomplish His plan in and through the Church. In other words, we are seeking to unpack the principles of the wilderness. This is important because, in a moment, we'll see how the three sections of the Body of Christ will experience the wilderness at the end of the age in very different ways, and how the way we interact with the smaller training-wildernesses of life that God presents to each of us today will propel us toward that final wilderness as either the male child, the woman, or the woman's other children.

To that end, the Exodus parallel has more wisdom to share. In one sense, Israel's forty-year wilderness experience is a cautionary tale of God's discipline against a perpetually unbelieving, grumbling, rebellious, and idolatrous generation who refused to enter into their promised land. But futility was not the original purpose of Israel's wilderness. God intended the Sinai wilderness to be a temporary season of intense isolation, pressure, and revelation for the purpose of transformation.

The wilderness was meant to reveal God and to reveal Israel. It wasn't just for God to reveal Himself; He could have done that anywhere. He intentionally delivered Israel into an isolated crucible where there were few outside influences or second-heaven forces to distract and obstruct. The only darkness in the wilderness was the internal darkness they brought with them. There were a few external enemies in the wilderness, but those attacks were allowed by God as strategic opportunities for Israel to grow in the areas where God was revealing Himself. In other words, every aspect of Israel's wilderness was customized to force their internal darkness to the surface so they could deal with it and grow up as God revealed the light of His character.

Israel's entire wilderness experience revolved around an encounter with I AM at the foot of Sinai. They were a generation who only knew of Him from ancient stories and indirect observations, so God reintroduced Himself in a tangible and irresistible way at Sinai. He brought them there to make an offer—a covenant proposal to fulfill the original promises given to Abraham. It was a triune offer to lead them into bondservanthood, betrothal, and sonship to prepare them to possess the promised land.

The wilderness could have been a short season of spiritual, emotional, and even physical nourishment. From the constant reality of God's presence in a pillar of fire and a cloud of smoke, to the miraculous water from a rock, to daily bread from heaven, to the exciting task of building a dwelling place for God, the people of Israel were meant to be nourished with reminders of His character and glory in ways that could help them gradually escape their dependence on the Egyptian system that had perversely enslaved and sustained them for generations. But Israel failed to recognize His nourishment, refused to enter His rest, and were forced to wander for forty years.

To be clear, I'm not suggesting that God failed in His endeavor just because Israel rebelled in the wilderness and incurred His wrath. He understood Israel's situation and knew exactly what He was getting. Multi-generational slaves had little grid to comprehend the immensity of their place in His cosmic plan and couldn't be expected to fully rise to the occasion. But maybe that was the point. Everything that happened to the natural branches happened as an example for our benefit.

Moses was an incomparable spiritual giant—a hero of the faith who walked closer to God than perhaps anyone else in the Old Testament—and yet his ministry still represented the absolute best that mankind could reach while still tethered to the fruit from the tree of knowledge of good and evil. It was only through Christ's work on the cross that Adam's fallen nature was put to death, along with the poverty-inducing, shame-inflicting effects of the forbidden fruit. In Christ we are invited not only to eat from and be tethered to the spiritual tree of life but also to become one with Him who is the source of all life and knowledge.

Leaving behind the old nature and being joined to Christ's new nature is both an instantaneous legal transaction in the spirit realm through choice and a lifelong process of transformation that requires the daily choice to take up our cross and follow Him. That is where the wilderness comes in. The wilderness takes what is settled legal truth in the court of heaven and converts it to effective reality in our lives.

I mentioned this earlier, but recall Christ in the wilderness. Luke's Gospel tells us that after the Father affirmed His sonship during baptism, Jesus entered the wilderness "full of the Holy Spirit," but after His wilderness experience, He returned to Galilee "in the **power** of the Spirit." In other words, He entered the wilderness full of the knowledge of His Sonship, but He left the wilderness with fully proven character, equipped to demonstrate His Sonship. The trials and temptations and subsequent nourishment Jesus received in the wilderness took that which was already declared and true and settled in the Father's heart and established it in substantive reality. Another way to think of this is that the wilderness is the special space where God draws human will into alignment with His will. Or as the writer of the book of Hebrews inferred, the wilderness is where we learn how to enter His rest.

The ultimate purpose of the woman's wilderness at the end of the age—and to a smaller degree the purpose of every mini wilderness we experience during the trials of life—is to demolish our dependency on the fruit from the tree of the knowledge of good and evil and the associated shame of the old nature so that we can be transformed into God's suitable companion through the unfiltered power of Christ's Unveiling.

THE CONVERSION FACTOR

So why does God use a wilderness to accomplish such miraculous metamorphosis? I mean, beyond the solitary environment and the singular focus it provides? Couldn't He unveil Himself to the Church anywhere? Why go through the trouble of preparing a place in the wilderness and orchestrating world events to miraculously draw her away to that place? Why not meet her where she is, in full view of an unbelieving world? The answer is found in the essence of the wilderness itself.

By definition, a wilderness is undefiled, uninhabited land, free from human civilization and ownership, and insulated from the comforts, conveniences, and pleasures of the world. There are no grocery stores in the wilderness, no Starbucks or shopping malls or movie theaters or sporting events to feed our soul and body. And in that protected place of raw material, we are invited to trust in God's lovingkindness, to recognize His abundance, and to be sustained by every word that proceeds from His mouth.

Some type of fasting is inherent in every wilderness. And I'm not just talking about fasting from food or water. Those are legitimate types of fasting, but there are many other things we can fast, such as media, entertainment, music, speech, comfort, sleep, etc.

Fasting is about embracing powerlessness and lack in order to align with the reality of Christ's strength and provision. Said another way, fasting helps to ween us from our dependence on the twisted "Egyptian" world systems that are built on the fruit from the tree of knowledge of good and evil. It is an essential ingredient for realigning the eyes of our spirit to see Christ in the way that He wants to reveal Himself, and only by beholding Him do we receive the full benefit of the wilderness conversion factor.

Jesus entered His wilderness with zero internal darkness, willingly embracing a forty-day fast as a Son led by the Holy Spirit, and as a result, He left the wilderness equipped with the fullness of the seven spirits of God to preach and demonstrate the kingdom with power. On the other hand, Israel entered their wilderness still captivated with internal darkness, and God had to force them to go without food, water, and other comforts numerous times to bring all of that to the surface. In the end, their transformation was vastly diminished because their response fell far short of sonship.

Consider the broader parallel of the Exodus. Israel was baptized into Moses when they passed through the Red Sea (see 1 Corinthians 10:2), and then they immediately entered a period of fasting and testing when they followed Moses into the wilderness. First, they had no water in the wilderness of Shur (see Exodus 15), then they had no food in the wilderness of Sin (see Exodus 16). Then another shortage of water. Then a surprise test in the form of an attack from the opportunistic Amalekites (see Exodus 17). At each turn, God provided in miraculous ways that should have nourished much more than just their bodies, and at each turn, the Israelites shrank from the challenge of sonship, grumbling like powerless slaves and totally missing the point for forty years, until they died and a new generation was willing to embrace God's covenant offer.

Compare that to Christ who willingly embraced the most extreme wilderness experience imaginable without grumbling or compromise. He overcame every test and needed only forty days to fully absorb and convert the Father's immense baptismal declaration into nourishment that would sustain and empower Him for the remaining 3.5 years of His ministry.

These examples apply on many levels to the wilderness seasons that the Holy Spirit leads us into at various times in our lives. I'm not talking about the difficulties we sometimes create for ourselves with our own foolish decisions. I'm talking about the concentrated periods of spiritual, emotional, or physical testing and scarcity that we inevitably enter when we follow the leading of the Holy Spirit. The types of difficulties and oppositions we encounter when we seek to emulate the Father with creative initiative flowing out of the gifts He has placed in us for the goal of seeing His life and character expanded in the world around us.

Those seasons of tribulation always result in positive transformation when we embrace them as sons rather than slaves.

To the degree that we cling to delusions of separation in a given area of our lives, God will often leverage a specially crafted wilderness so that we can experience the necessary pain of fasting and testing in that area. If we embrace that temporary pain as lovingkindness from an abundant Father, our delusions gradually fall away, and we begin to see Him more clearly in the mirror of God's Word. Israel largely failed in this area, but let's not be arrogant toward the natural branches. Haven't we all responded similarly in many of our own wilderness trials, prolonging or repeating some lessons altogether?

HOW TO PREPARE?

With all of that in mind, let's return to our Revelation 12 narrative. We already know that much of the Body of Christ on earth during the second half of the seventieth week will be led into the ultimate wilderness season for the purpose of ultimate transformation. But what kind of testing will they face?

At the very least the Church will have to fast from many of the provisions and comforts of the fallen world systems while in her final wilderness. I'll leave you to ponder exactly what that means and how that could look in your own life. Whether or not our generation is alive when that time comes is beside the point. Our goal should be to look for and hasten the coming of the Day of the Lord. How we each prepare for that day should flow from personal introspection with the Holy Spirit, and I suspect the answer will look different in different geographical areas, and require different responses from different parts of the Body of Christ. We are not all the same, and we are not meant to be.

Whatever paths we take as we follow the Holy Spirit, just remember that adopting a survivalist mindset out of fear is not the path of sonship. If we want to be prepared for the coming Day of the Lord, we would do well to start by embracing our current wildernesses with expectation, learning how to trust and identify the Father's infinitely abundant provision in the face of apparent scarcity and powerlessness. He is going to provide for His Body either way, just as He provided for Israel as she left Egypt, but it is up to us whether or not we are transformed by the process.

ONE SIZE DOES NOT FIT ALL

Before we move on, it is important to remember that unlike the nation of Israel after the Exodus, the Church's wilderness during the second half of the seventieth week won't be a single physical location. As I mentioned earlier, the entire Body of Christ on earth isn't going to camp out together in some physical desert location. If the woman's wilderness flight does represent some level of physical exodus, then at the very least we must be talking about many different regions of safety throughout the earth. It is also possible that the woman's wilderness will be more metaphorical, representing a trial of isolation and lack that doesn't necessarily require physical relocation. Most likely it will be some combination of both depending on where you are in the world.

Either way, I find it enlightening to think of the woman's wilderness in light of the Romans chapter 12 description of the seven different parts of the Body of Christ named after the seven redemptive gifts: prophet, servant, teacher, exhorter, giver, ruler, and mercy. Paul described these in the context of the body being made up of different members, each graced with different gifts and purposes. Well, these seven different "members," or aspects of the Body, will also have different wildernesses tailored to their specific needs based on the precise way the Bridegroom wants to reveal Himself during His Unveiling.

> If we want to be prepared for the coming Day of the Lord, we would do well to start by embracing our current wildernesses with expectation, learning how to trust and identify the Father's infinitely abundant provision in the face of apparent scarcity and powerlessness.

In the next book, we'll see how the letters to the seven churches represent invitations to each of these seven portions of the Body to follow the Holy Spirit into their own custom wilderness. Keep that in the back of your mind as we move forward and let it enlarge your appreciation of God's vast creativity to transform His people.

While the fractal of seven in this context highlights the different designs and gifts of the Body as expressions of the divine character, the fractal of three emphasizes the three stages of a Christian's relationship with the Trinity, with His people, and with the rest of creation. So even though each of the seven colors of the Church will have unique wilderness trials, within the continuum of those seven wildernesses the members will still find themselves in one of three categories based on their response: the holy of holies, the inner court, or the outer court. I should mention that all of this also applies at an individual level to the seven portions of our spirit, but we'll see more about that in the next book.

From the corporate perspective, consider what the wilderness means for the three different sections of the Body of Christ entering the second half of the seventieth week. On the one hand, Revelation chapter 12 specifically states that the wilderness is a place prepared for the woman and that the woman is given the two wings of the great eagle to fly there. That suggests that the final wilderness is mainly intended as a crucible for the inner court portion of the Church, but that doesn't mean that the male child and the woman's other children won't also interact with the wilderness.

The best way to understand how the three categories of Christians will experience the final wilderness is by returning to our familiar model of Israel after the Exodus. Think of Moses and Joshua as examples of the holy of holies portion of the Church (the male child). Aaron, the Levitical priesthood, and to some degree the entire tribe of Levi, are examples of the inner court portion (the woman). And the other eleven tribes of Israel generally represent the outer court (the woman's other children). All three groups entered the wilderness, but their responses to the trials, and their subsequent experiences, were significantly different.

THE SONS IN THE WILDERNESS

Remember that Moses had already spent forty years in the wilderness before He ever met I AM at the burning bush. And he didn't just experience some random wilderness of lesser consequence—he sojourned for forty years in the very same Sinai wilderness that Israel would enter after the Red Sea deliverance. Moses had already embraced its trials and experienced its conversion factor. He was well acquainted with its contours and knew of its power to deliver a person from their reliance on Egypt and their addiction to the fruit from the tree of knowledge of good and evil, and it was in that very wilderness where he received his commission at the burning bush.

Moses had already learned something of the principles of sonship in his wilderness, so by the time he led the children of Israel into their wilderness, he was there as a shepherd and as an example of maturity, and he was able to encounter the "unveiling" of God's character in ways that the rest of the nation was ill-prepared to receive.

This is a perfect picture of what the male child will experience at the end of the age. Consider that Israel's wilderness journey forced Moses to continually grow in intimacy with God (a bridal position) to more effectively and creatively shepherd the people (a position of sonship). Likewise, the sons of God will have already embraced their own wilderness, and they will be perfectly positioned to lead the rest of the Body of Christ into her wilderness, though they will also have to continue growing through the final wilderness.

Just as Moses was permitted to see God on Mount Sinai, in this final wilderness the sons of God will experience the progressive Unveiling of Christ with fully enlightened spiritual eyes. In that state, they will be visible examples of Christ's nature to the rest of creation. So the sons of God won't be there so much for the trials and pain—though there will be some of that—but rather to help facilitate the Body of Christ's experience of the Unveiling.

THE WOMAN IN THE WILDERNESS

Unlike the male child, the woman will enter the second half of the seventieth week with much less wilderness experience. I'm not saying the inner court saints will have never been tested through the trials of life, nor matured through those lessons, but they will have never fully embraced its solitude and fasting and inherent pain in an effort to find God to the same degree as the sons of God.

Again, consider the differences between Aaron and Moses before the Exodus. Moses spent an entire generation hidden away from both Israel and Egypt in the crucible of the wilderness. What about Aaron? Aaron apparently spent his life in Goshen laboring among the people of God, but still marinated in slavery under the oppressive Egyptian system. The lessons hidden for us in that juxtaposition are immense, but I'll leave you to ponder them with the Holy Spirit on your own.

I find it fascinating that God did eventually draw Aaron into the wilderness to meet Moses at Mount Horeb shortly after Moses's commissioning at the burning bush *before* sending them both back to Goshen (see Exodus 4:27). It must have been important for Aaron to have some degree of wilderness experience outside of Egypt before he could participate with Moses in the emancipation of Israel. We can only imagine what this encounter did for Aaron as he stepped outside the purview of the spiritual darkness over Egypt—maybe for the first time in his life—to find his brother alive and divinely commissioned to deliver Israel. This short time with Moses in the proto-wilderness must have been enough to enlarge Aaron's spirit for the coming battles, and perhaps it even

> Just as Moses was permitted to see God on Mount Sinai, in this final wilderness the sons of God will experience the progressive Unveiling of Christ with fully enlightened spiritual eyes. In that state, they will be visible examples of Christ's nature to the rest of creation.

contributed to his greater-than-average faithfulness (compared to the rest of Israel) when they entered the wilderness after the Exodus.

So will it be for the woman as she enters the wilderness of the second half of the seventieth week. Unlike the rebellious generation of Israelites who perished in their wilderness because they refused to enter God's rest, the inner court of the Body of Christ will embrace the trials and benefit from the conversion factor that leads to walking in sonship. After all, Revelation 12 tells us that the final wilderness is a place prepared for the woman's nourishment and protection. It is a womb for her to experience the Unveiling. Through the lens of Exodus, it is fundamentally about disabusing the people of God from their slavery so that they can experience the fullness of His covenant offer. And as we'll see in the next book, the end goal of the wilderness is to prepare the Body of Christ for their conquest of the promised land—which means their participation with the Bridegroom in the restoration of all things during His millennial reign on earth.

THE REST OF HER CHILDREN IN THE WILDERNESS

How will the outer court section of the Body of Christ experience the final wilderness? As with the rest of the nation of Israel after the Exodus, their experience will be marked by their inability to see or embrace God's provision. Remember, these will be spiritually immature believers, whether because they have long avoided embracing the lesser trials and difficulties that bring maturity, or because they are new converts just entering the kingdom. In one sense, the very reason that these Christians will still be in the outer court is *because* they have not yet embraced the lesser wilderness trials of life.

Jesus alluded to this category of Christians during the second half of the seventieth week in Matthew 24:

> "Therefore when you see the ABOMINATION OF DESOLATION which was spoken of through Daniel the prophet, standing in the holy place—let the reader understand—then those who are in Judea must flee to the mountains. Whoever is on the housetop must not go down to get things out of his house. And whoever is in the field must not turn back to get his cloak. **But woe to those women who are pregnant, and to those who are nursing babies in those days!**
> —MATTHEW 24:15-19

"Woe to those who are pregnant, and to those who are nursing babies in those days!" In an earlier chapter, I mentioned that the larger warning in this passage is primarily directed at the nation of Israel, but there is a sense in which it also applies to the Church. From the Church's perspective, it is a warning to those spiritual leaders who keep their people weak and dependent upon their ministry (like mothers nursing babies beyond the appropriate time), and by extension, it is also a warning to those immature Christians who are too comfortable as spiritual babies to embrace the challenge of weening found in the wilderness. The great tribulation will be especially difficult for these outer court Christians who have yet to find their legitimacy in Christ's Sonship.

PROTECTION AND NOURISHMENT?

And now we come to a crucial question: We know that the inner court Christians will escape the wrath of the dragon during the great tribulation by virtue of their flight to the wilderness, but will the outer court enjoy the same protection and nourishment afforded by the wilderness?

In the Revelation chapter 12 narrative, the woman flees to the wilderness, the dragon fails in his attempt to pursue her, his attacking flood is consumed (more on that in a moment), and then he goes off to attack her other children. This sequence would suggest that the "rest of the woman's children" do not flee to the wilderness with her and are therefore more vulnerable to the dragon's wrath. But how does that correspond with the Exodus narrative? Wasn't all of Israel together in the wilderness? If Moses represents the male child, and the Levitical priesthood represents the woman, and the rest of the tribes represent the rest of the woman's children, does that suggest that all three parts of the Body of Christ will also be in the final wilderness together?

To ask the question another way, when Jesus pronounced, "Woe to those women who are pregnant, and to those nursing babies in those days," did He mean that they would not be able to flee the wrath of the dragon, or simply that their flight would be more difficult than the rest? I suspect the answer is a bit of both.

Remember that Jesus warned those fleeing the great tribulation not to worry about their worldly possessions: "Whoever is on the housetop must not go down to get things out of his house. And whoever is in the field must not turn back to get his cloak." Many outer court saints will be so wrapped up in the cares of this world that they will be unwilling to leave their comforts behind, and therefore they will not flee to the wilderness at all.

It is possible that some outer court saints will choose to flee, but they will arrive at that decision belatedly and thus incur a much more difficult flight than the inner court saints who willingly embraced the wilderness from the start. Perhaps these will eventually enter the wilderness (and therefore the protection of the inner court) because of their choice to flee. I'll touch on this concept more in the next chapter, but for simplicity, let's just consider the outer court saints to be those who do not flee.

At the end of the day, this is a heart issue, not a location issue. Whether or not the outer court Christians are actually in the wilderness at the end isn't the point. The main thing that makes them outer court saints is that they resist the trials of the wilderness, and to the degree that they resist is the amount they will miss out on its protection, nourishment, and conversion factor. In that light, consider the symbolism of the following passage:

> I was given a reed like a measuring rod and was told, "Go and measure the temple of God and the altar, with its worshipers. **But exclude the outer court; do not measure it, because it has been given to the Gentiles. They will trample on the holy city for 42 months**.
> —*REVELATION 11:1-2 NIV*

These verses are part of a larger narrative describing some of the ways in which the people of God will oppose and overcome the kingdom of darkness during the second half of the seventieth week. It has relevance to both the Church and the nation of Israel. We'll unpack the fuller context in the next book. For now, just consider what this sobering passage suggests about the outer court of the Body of Christ. The outer court will be excluded from the measurement of the temple during the second half of the seventieth week, and as a result, they will not be afforded the same protection and nourishment as those in the fully covered inner court and holy of holies sections. That is why Jesus pronounced woe to this group of immature and distracted believers in Matthew 24.

The main thing that makes them outer court saints is that they resist the trials of the wilderness, and to the degree that they resist is the amount they will miss out on its protection, nourishment, and conversion factor.

This absolutely does not mean that the outer court portion of the Body will be abandoned by Christ, nor that they will miss out on the power of His Unveiling, but their path through the great tribulation will be significantly more difficult, and their overall experience of the second half of the seventieth week will be one of scourging more than divine encounter. Remember, there are difficulties that we willingly embrace when we follow the Holy Spirit into the wilderness, and then there are difficulties that we bring upon ourselves when we embrace the comforts of an Egyptian system of slavery that is destined for judgment by fire.

At the very time that the male child and the woman will be experiencing the temporary light afflictions of the wilderness to align the eyes of their spirit with Christ's Unveiling, God will allow the rest of the woman's children in the outer court to face the brunt of the dragon's wrath, not as punishment from an angry God but as merciful discipline from a loving Father providing one last opportunity for His children to earn the great reward of an overcomer.

R emember, there are difficulties that we willingly embrace when we follow the Holy Spirit into the wilderness, and then there are difficulties that we bring upon ourselves when we embrace the comforts of an Egyptian system of slavery that is destined for judgment by fire.

CHAPTER 23

THE PARABLE OF THE UNVEILING - PART 7:
THE OVERCOMERS

or - "It starts today!"

T o fully appreciate the dichotomy between the experiences of
the outer court Christians represented by "the rest of the
woman's children" and that of the woman herself, we need to
remember what else will be happening during the time of the woman's
wilderness. We've talked about the fasting and isolation that the woman
will be invited to embrace, but those are not the only difficulties she will
face on her journey to divine encounter. Remember the serpent's flood?

> And the serpent poured water like a river out of his mouth
> after the woman, so that he might cause her to be swept
> away with the flood.
>   But the earth helped the woman, and the earth opened
> its mouth and drank up the river which the dragon poured
> out of his mouth.
>   —*REVELATION 12:15-16*

What exactly is the serpent's flood? Consider the serpent in the Garden of Eden. What was his main weapon? Other than generally twisting God's Word, he specifically leveraged the promise of the fruit from the tree of the knowledge of good and evil to create a sense of lack where there was no lack—a mindset of poverty in the face of abundant paradise—to separate humanity from God and then trap us in the shame of our separation. In a sense, Satan was trying to remake mankind in his own image or to cut humanity down to his level. As a result of this abomination, the Lord cursed the serpent:

> The LORD God said to the serpent, "Because you have done this, cursed are you more than all cattle, And more than every beast of the field; On your belly you will go, and **dust you will eat all the days of your life**;
> —*GENESIS 3:14*

Some speculate that this curse had a literal impact on the physiology of snakes. Is it possible that prior to this curse, snakes had legs, or even wings? Either way, consider the more impactful spiritual application of the curse.

Dust is the substance from which Adam was originally formed by God. In that context, dust speaks of the raw material of the human body before God shaped it into His image and enlightened it with the human spirit. In other words, dust is humanity without the breath of God and the divine light of Christ.

If you'll pardon my highly speculative embellishment of the text, when God cursed the serpent to eat dust, it was as if He was saying, "Okay, Satan, you looked at the crown of My creation, formed by My own hands in My own image, and in your pride desired to reform them into your image, to use deception to redefine their essence and to elevate yourself by claiming them as *your* crowning achievement. Very well, henceforth you are cursed to eat the dust from which they came as a reminder that you are utterly powerless to design, or to create, or to establish essence, or to build anything that my own Word has not already conceived. And such lifeless dust will never satisfy you."

Satan can do nothing but chew up, twist, and either spit out or defecate the raw materials of God's creation. He, and all other demonic forces, are forever cursed with an insatiable desire and an unquenchable need to cultivate and feed off "the deeds of the flesh"—the acts of humanity that are driven by the desires of the body, devoid of the influence of the human spirit and inflamed by the effects of the fruit of the knowledge of good and evil.

The apostle Paul described these deeds of the flesh as actions that are in opposition to the kingdom of God, which suggests that they also empower the serpent's kingdom:

> But I say, walk by the Spirit, and you will not carry out the desire of the flesh. For the desire of the flesh is against the Spirit, and the Spirit against the flesh; for these are in opposition to one another, in order to keep you from doing whatever you want. But if you are led by the Spirit, you are not under the Law.
>
> Now the deeds of the flesh are evident, which are: sexual immorality, impurity, indecent behavior, idolatry, witchcraft, hostilities, strife, jealousy, outbursts of anger, selfish ambition, dissensions, factions, envy, drunkenness, carousing, and things like these, of which I forewarn you, just as I have forewarned you, that those who practice such things will not inherit the kingdom of God.
> —*GALATIANS 5:16-21*

THE SERPENT'S FLOOD

The initial form of the serpent's lie in the garden was that humanity could take a shortcut in their calling to become God's suitable companion by eating the forbidden fruit to acquire God's knowledge without embracing the prescribed discipline that leads to His character. This is the lie of humanism in its most subtle, prenatal form. What Eve didn't understand was that God had created her and Adam to eventually receive the fullness of His knowledge through a process that would have required them to work out their calling on earth in relationship with Jesus.

Remember the original commissioning of Adam and Eve: They were placed in a paradise and commanded to unpack the principles that God used when He planted the garden, and then to learn how to apply those principles to extend His paradise to the untamed earth. In that context, the rest of the earth can be seen as a wilderness when compared to the garden of Eden, and it was in the difficulties and trials of that wilderness where Adam and Eve were meant to mature in sonship, and to grow in character, knowledge, and authority. But then Satan offered a shortcut to knowledge that claimed to avoid the difficulties of unpacking God's principles and the pain of working them out in the wilderness.

The serpent's flood at the end of the age will leverage the grown-up version of this humanistic lie without any of the subtlety used in the garden. The lie will be audaciously successful on a broad scale because the shame of the fruit from the tree of knowledge of good and evil will have already grown to full maturity in some portion of humanity, enslaving many in a prison of spiritual darkness

> The initial form of the serpent's lie in the garden was that humanity could take a shortcut in their calling to become God's suitable companion by eating the forbidden fruit to acquire God's knowledge without embracing the prescribed discipline that leads to His character.

where the eyes of their spirits will be so blinded to the light of Christ that they will be left with little inspiration in life beyond the lusts of their flesh. They will have a knowledge that is completely devoid of the light of Christ. We referred to this phenomenon as *the nature of the beast* in a previous chapter, and the serpent's flood will rely upon and proliferate this nature.

Like water vomited out his mouth, these debased humans will unknowingly infest the earth with the same works of the flesh that the serpent has feasted on since the time of the garden. They will make no pretense about seeking the knowledge of God. Instead, they will actively fantasize about overthrowing the natural and spiritual principles that reflect the divine character, and in so doing they will unwittingly become the strength and power of the serpent during the second half of the seventieth week as he attempts to flood the earth with the deep darkness of his own appetites.

This spiritual flood of filth is the same thick darkness prophesied in Isaiah 61, and it will engender the same feckless rage against God's principles described in Psalm 2:

> Arise, shine; for your light has come, and the glory of the Lord has risen upon you. For behold, **darkness will**

cover the earth and deep darkness the peoples; But the Lord will rise upon you and His glory will appear upon you. Nations will come to your light, and kings to the brightness of your rising.
—*ISAIAH 60:1-3*

Why do the nations conspire and the peoples plot in vain?

The kings of the earth rise up and the rulers band together against the Lord and against his anointed, saying, "Let us break their chains and throw off their shackles."

The One enthroned in heaven laughs; the Lord scoffs at them. He rebukes them in his anger and terrifies them in his wrath, saying, "I have installed my king on Zion, my holy mountain."
—*PSALM 2:1-6 NIV*

Whereas the dragon's main weapon in the second heaven was the bully pulpit of soul-decaying accusations he effectively used to twist perceived reality on a mass scale, on earth the serpent's main weapon will be the lawlessness of easily manipulated humans who will, with a seared conscience, fully embrace the nature of the beast while they rage against everything that reflects the divine nature. This mob will attempt to flood the earth with abominable thoughts, words, and actions, also known as the deeds of the flesh.

There is one other aspect of the serpent's flood that is important to mention, though I'm not going to take the time to fully unpack it here. In Matthew chapter 24, while describing the period of the great tribulation (which is directly tied to the serpent's flood), Jesus said the following:

If those days had not been cut short, nobody would be saved. But for the sake of the elect, those days will be cut short. At that time, if anyone says to you, 'Look, here is the Christ!' or 'There He is!' do not believe it. For false Christs and false prophets will appear and perform great signs and wonders that would deceive even the elect, if that were possible. See, I have told you in advance.
—*MATTHEW 24:22-25*

False Christs, false prophets, deceiving signs and wonders—these counterfeits will be the captains of the serpent's flood, meant to obfuscate God's nature, or to muddy the waters as much as possible, to keep the elect of God from seeing what He is really like, because only by seeing Jesus as He is and understanding His character can we be transformed into His image. This insidious attack will be driven by Satan's desire to redefine God's character in our minds in order to erode the very foundation of our reality. In current times these deceptions are an extension of the dragon's voice of accusation in the second heaven, but during the serpent's flood their influence will manifest in more direct ways on earth.

> The best training for spotting a counterfeit is to become deeply and intimately acquainted with the genuine article.

We'll see an Old Testament example of this deception in a moment, and then we'll discuss other facets when we dive into the book of Revelation in book 2, though rest assured that even while unpacking those topics, we will keep our eyes fixed on the true Christ. After all, the best training for spotting a counterfeit is to become deeply and intimately acquainted with the genuine article.

THE EARTH HELPS

Despite the overwhelming depth and persuasiveness of the serpent's onslaught, we know this for certain: the attack will fail, and his waters will perish when the earth opens its mouth to help the woman. In the words of Christ, "But for the sake of the elect, those days will be cut short." But what does that mean? And how will the earth help the woman? Let's look at the verse one more time:

> But the earth helped the woman, and the earth opened its
> mouth and drank up the river which the dragon poured out
> of his mouth.
> —*REVELATION 12:16*

Notice that not only does the serpent's attack come from his mouth, but the corresponding help comes from the earth's "mouth." This juxtaposition is specific and peculiar, and it harkens back to the words of Christ:

> What goes into someone's mouth does not defile them, but what comes out of their mouth, that is what defiles them.
> —*MATTHEW 15:11 NIV*

Defilement will be the central theme of the serpent's flood. The strength of his flood will be in the people who embrace the nature of the beast. The strategy of his flood will be to defile the earth with lawless philosophies and abominable deeds of the flesh, and the main goal of his flood will be to expand his authority across the earth until he can sweep away the woman in her wilderness—a goal which he will epically fail to achieve.

So what could it mean for the earth to open its mouth to swallow the serpent's flood? The answer has some layers that will require the context of book 2 to fully unpack, but for now, let's turn one last time to Israel's wilderness journey in the Old Testament to find a parallel example that ties back to the end of the age and highlights the different ways in which the male child, the woman, and the rest of the woman's children experience and overcome the serpent's flood.

KORAH'S REBELLION

This particular story is excluded from most Sunday school lessons and often ignored from the pulpit, so it may not be as familiar as our other examples from Exodus. The full story can be found in Numbers chapter 16, but since our goal is to find a few relevant principles to complete the topography of our Revelation chapter 12 narrative, we'll skip to the highlights in order to get to the main point:

> Now Korah the son of Izhar, the son of Kohath, the son of Levi, with Dathan and Abiram, the sons of Eliab, and On the son of Peleth, sons of Reuben, took men, and they stood before Moses, together with some of the sons of Israel, 250 leaders of the congregation chosen in the assembly, men of renown. They assembled together against Moses and Aaron, and said to them, "You have gone far enough! For all the congregation are holy, every one of

them, and the LORD is in their midst; so why do you exalt yourselves above the assembly of the LORD?"
—*NUMBERS 16:1-3*

This is the beginning of a story often referred to as Korah's Rebellion. Perhaps you've heard this taught as an object lesson against attempting to organize a coup against godly leadership. I'd like to challenge that narrative a bit. I'm not saying that description is entirely wrong, but it does miss the point.

What was at the heart of Korah's rebellion? On the one hand, falsely accusing Moses and Aaron in front of the entire congregation ("Why do you exalt yourselves above the assembly of the LORD?") was a heinous twisting of reality in an attempt to gaslight their way to greater influence, but that was hardly the worst thing going on here. Korah's core accusation was against God, not man. It wasn't so much an attack against Moses and Aaron as it was a direct assault against God's character. The root iniquity was a rejection of God's design and a rebellion against His principles.

Korah was a first cousin of Aaron and Moses, and likely an elder in the tribe of Levi. As a Levite from the house of Izhar, of the house of Kohath, his family had already been set aside by God to assist the priesthood in the transportation, setup, takedown, and overall care of the most holy tabernacle furniture (see Numbers 3). Items like the ark of the covenant, the golden lampstand, the table of showbread, the various altars, and the inner curtain were entrusted to the Izharites (along with the other descendants of Kohath), of which Korah and his family were chief members. That means Korah was already invited closer to God's presence and gifted more opportunity to observe the physical representations of God's principles in the tabernacle than anyone outside of the priesthood of Aaron's lineage. But none of that was enough for Korah because he had the mindset of a slave rather than a son.

THE ROOT OF HUMANISM

Before we move on with the story, let's take a moment to expound on the concept of the rejection of God's design that was at the root of Korah's rebellion and will be at the root of the final rebellion of the serpent's flood. It is basic Christian theology that our sovereign God appoints a measure of grace to every human. Even before we were formed in the womb He designed our spirit, soul, and body with a unique combination of wonderful attributes, and it is the main honor and adventure of our life to identify and unpack those gifts as resources to be used in His service.

He is under no obligation to distribute His gifts of grace in a manner that is equal or fair according to our judgment. God chooses the complex details of our design according to *His* perfect wisdom. Everything from the time and place of our birth to our DNA, country of origin, gender, familial and social circumstances—the Creator is sovereign over them all. It is His prerogative that not everyone is born with identical spiritual gifting, comparable mental acumen, equivalent physical attributes, or even equal opportunities. In the divine calculus, perhaps He will balance out these inequalities in the new heavens and the new earth, and perhaps in the next phase, there will be greater rewards in store for those who overcome greater obstacles in this life. The blessings of the Beatitudes in Matthew chapter 5 seem to suggest that such a rebalancing is in the cards.

Either way, God is sovereign over our design, and therefore one of the truest forms of worship is simply agreeing with the Creator's design choices, celebrating them as good, and unpacking them so that we can present them back to Him in reverence. Such worship helps us to see Him more clearly, and then to see ourselves more clearly, and then to embrace the trials He gives us as lovingly handcrafted opportunities for growing more like Him.

On the other hand, a mindset of slavery can lead us to reject God's design, or despise the way He made us, or covet the gifts of others, or wish we were something that we are not, and all of those attitudes lead us to avoid the wilderness trials that He presents for our good. This was the root of Korah's rebellion.

Don't get it twisted. Desiring deeper intimacy with God is the birthright

> God is sovereign over our design, and therefore one of the truest forms of worship is simply agreeing with the Creator's design choices, celebrating them as good, and unpacking them so that we can present them back to Him in reverence.

of humanity, as is the drive to better our circumstances through the application of Godly principles, but neither of these was Korah's motivation. It would seem he wanted the priesthood and the perceived legitimacy associated with its position so that he could redefine holiness to fit his poverty mindset rather than embracing the abundant provision God had already given to help him synchronize with His divine character.

If Korah's heart had been pure—if he had appropriately desired to be intimate friends with I AM like Moses, or to be trusted to minister in God's presence like Aaron—perhaps the story would have progressed differently. But based on Korah's venomous accusations, and because neither Korah, nor any of his followers or any other Israelite outside of Moses, responded appropriately when God first offered to make them a kingdom of priests and a holy nation, we must assume that Korah was more interested in avoiding and redefining God's principles than embracing them to his betterment. And that is why he sought more authority.

Does any of this sound familiar? Remember Lucifer's infamous boast in Isaiah 14:

> "But you said in your heart, 'I will ascend to heaven; I will raise my throne above the stars of God, and I will sit on the mount of assembly in the recesses of the north.
>
> 'I will ascend above the heights of the clouds; I will make myself like the Most High.'
>
> "Nevertheless you will be thrust down to Sheol, to the recesses of the pit.
> —*ISAIAH 14:13-15*

In a previous chapter, we compared this passage to the fall of the dragon in Revelation chapter 12. Whether Isaiah was describing a past event, a future reality, or both at the same time, the principle behind the fall is the same. Lucifer's initial folly was in failing to comprehend God's nature, which led him to misunderstand his own design, which led him to think he could outshine his Creator. He must have thought his way was better than God's way, or his own character more worthy of emulation, because he desired a position from which he could redefine the universe around his own will rather than the divine principles of God's character. To dwell in the presence of God without being enthralled by the beauty of His holiness is the ultimate blindness, and to be near Him without desiring to synchronize with Him is the ultimate poverty mindset.

Korah's folly was rooted in this same poverty spirit, and it led to the same perverse desire to rewrite God's design and redefine His principles, which is the ultimate goal of humanism. If you've read the end of his story, you know that God also judged Korah's company in a similar fashion to Lucifer in Isaiah chapter 14 (more on that in a moment). For this reason, Korah's rebellion can be seen as a spiritual foreshadowing of the serpent's flood at the end of the age. All the main players from Revelation are represented in the story. The parallels run rich and deep, but let's just investigate the general shape for now.

DEFILEMENT CONSUMED

In the parallel, Moses and Aaron represent the male child and the woman respectively (the holy of holies and inner court saints). The rest of the congregation represents the rest of the woman's children (the outer court saints). Korah, Dathan, and Abiram represent Satan and his two captains (the two beasts mentioned in Revelation 13, or the false christs and false prophets that Jesus warned about in Matthew 24). In that frame, the accusations that these three brought against God and His anointed are an overall picture of the serpent's flood, and the 250 "men of renown" from among the congregation who stood with Korah's company represent some small percentage of outer court leaders who will succumb to the lies of the serpent's flood.

With all of that in mind, let's skip ahead to the end of Korah's rebellion to see what will happen to the serpent's flood:

> Then Moses said, "By this you shall know that the LORD has sent me to do all these deeds; for it is not my doing. If these men die the death of all mankind, or if they suffer the fate of all mankind, then the LORD has not sent me. But if the LORD brings about an entirely new thing and **the ground opens its mouth** and swallows them with everything that is theirs, and **they descend alive into Sheol**, then you will know that these men have been disrespectful to the LORD." And as he finished speaking all these words, the ground that was under them split open; and **the earth**

opened its mouth and swallowed them, their house-holds, and all the people who belonged to Korah with all their possessions. So they and all that belonged to them went down alive to Sheol; and the earth closed over them, and they perished from the midst of the assembly. Then all Israel who were around them fled at their outcry, for they said, "The earth might swallow us!" Fire also came out from the LORD and consumed the 250 men who were offering the incense.

—*NUMBERS 16:28-35*

"The earth opened its mouth and swallowed them." As far as judgments go, that is about as unambiguous as it gets. How does God feel about someone fomenting rebellion among His covenant people against His divine principles in a hopeless gambit to redefine reality around ungodly desires? Or how will God respond to the enemy's attempt to short-circuit His Bride's final wilderness experience by offering her a shortcut to maturity? Korah, Dathan, and Abiram found out quickly, just as the dragon and his two beastly minions will discover at the end. We'll see more of the details of how that plays out in the next book. Right now we're just taking a fifty-thousand-foot view of the proceedings—the topography of the situation, as it were.

If you read all of Numbers chapter 16, you'll find that neither Moses nor Aaron were deceived by the gaslighting orchestrated by Korah's company. Moses quickly discerned that Korah's hidden agenda was to usurp Aaron's priesthood (see Numbers 16:10), and both Moses and Aaron later interceded that God would not destroy the entire congregation of Israel in response to Korah's defilement (see Numbers 16:22).

Even though only 250 "men of renown" from among the congregation aligned themselves publicly with Korah, Dathan, and Abiram (see Numbers 16:2 and verse 35), the lie was so insidiously persuasive that it threatened to sweep up the entire congregation in its deception. Fortunately, the rest of the congregation heeded Moses's warning by separating themselves from the instigators before judgment came so that when the earth did open its mouth only the households of Korah, Dathan, and Abiram were swallowed alive into Sheol. Their judgment was unprecedented in its eternal finality. The 250 men who publicly aligned themselves with the rebellion were also judged, but their deaths came in the form of a consuming fire.

All these details are relevant to how the outer court, inner court, and holy of holies sections of the Body of Christ will experience the serpent's flood at the end. The holy of holies and inner court portions will neither be deceived nor defiled by the flood of deceptive filth. They will have already embraced the wilderness of God's design, and like Christ in the wilderness of temptation, they will resist the false wisdom of the enemy's shortcuts. And just as it was Moses who directly confronted Korah's attempted twisting of God's design, it will be the sons of God walking in the full authority of Christ Jesus who will call upon the earth to swallow the serpent's defilement before it can overtake the rest of the Body of Christ. The very earth that even now is groaning and travailing for the revealing of the sons of God—the very land that is longing for the true Christ to be Unveiled in and through His people—this physical earth will finally be unleashed at the appropriate time and in the appropriate places to respond with violent prejudice against the ensuing abominations of the serpent while the inner court saints are in their wilderness.

Keep in mind that the serpent's flood probably won't be a singular attack localized to a specific area, but rather a flood meant to overwhelm the earth in a desperate attempt to reach the inner court saints wherever and however they are hidden. In the same way, the earth's help won't be a one-time event. It is difficult to define exactly what I mean without diving deeper into the book of Revelation. Later in the series we'll discuss the severe natural disasters that transpire on earth in response to the blowing of the seven trumpets during the second half of the seventieth week. If you've studied the book of Revelation, you may find my take on the purpose of the seven trumpets to be slightly different than what you've heard in the past, but either way most commentators agree that the resulting natural disasters will greatly reduce the enemy's ability to carry out his evil agenda on earth. When we get to that part of our discussion of the Unveiling, we'll see how the earth's response to the blowing of the seven trumpets corresponds directly to the Revelation chapter 12 sign of the earth opening its mouth to help the woman.

DANGEROUS PLACE TO BE

What about the outer court saints? How will they be impacted by the serpent's flood? Just as the rest of the congregation of Israel was in danger of being swept up in Korah's rebellion, the outer court saints will be in a precarious position. And just as 250 men of renown sided with Korah, some small percentage of the outer court—especially those poverty-minded leaders who value their power and influence above their faith in Christ, and those leaders who keep their congregations in a state of immature dependency like nursing mothers—will succumb to the serpent's tempting shortcuts. These will be trotted out by the enemy in an attempt to gaslight the rest of the Body of Christ into apostasy.

Remember that the serpent's flood is essentially equivalent to the great tribulation Jesus warned about in Matthew chapter 24, and one of the main markers of the great tribulation will be false christs and false prophets that deceive many about the true nature of God. This deception will lead to mass persecution of those outer court saints who refuse to go along with the delusion. That is why Revelation chapter 12 described these faithful outer court saints as "the rest of her children, who keep the commandments of God and hold to the testimony of Jesus."

One quick technical note, in case you are thinking that the dragon's war against the rest of the woman's children must be separate and subsequent to the serpent's flood. Revelation chapter 12 does say that after the earth helped the woman, the dragon was enraged and went off to make war with the rest of her children, but that does not necessarily mean that the war against the outer court saints is a wholly separate offensive. It probably means that the dragon won't switch his focus to the outer court until after he observes the earth beginning to help the woman. It will be the second phase of the same battle.

Again, the earth helping the woman will be a repeating pattern of intervention over a season of time and space, and the serpent's flood will still be raging in places around the world when the earth's help first starts. That is when the flood will be redirected toward the outer court saints, even as the earth continues to protect the woman. Once the sons of God release the earth to open its mouth, the frequency and impact of the earth's help will increase steadily during the second half of the seventieth week until it reaches a crescendo that so decimates the enemy's beastly kingdom that the great tribulation will be cut short.

We'll dive deeper into the great tribulation later in this series. Far from just a deplorable season of defeat, when you view the details of the book of Revelation through the correct lens, you begin to see the great tribulation as a glorious season of intense pressure that leverages the enemy's greatest assault against him to open more hearts to Christ's Unveiling.

THE OVERCOMERS

To tie all of this together and put the finishing touches on the map we've been building throughout this book, let's return to one of the most exciting and encouraging parts of Revelation chapter 12. Remember what happens immediately after the dragon is cast down to earth at the beginning of the seventieth week?

> Then I heard a loud voice in heaven, saying, "Now the salvation, and the power, and the kingdom of our God and the authority of His Christ have come, for the accuser of our brethren has been thrown down, he who accuses them before our God day and night. **And they overcame him because of the blood of the Lamb and because of the word of their testimony, and they did not love their life even when faced with death.**
> —*REVELATION 12:10-11*

As you might expect, there are multiple layers to this proclamation. On one level, this is a description of the threefold strategy implemented by the male child to gain the authority to cast the dragon out of heaven, but that is a discussion for another time. On another level, this is a chronological description of the game plan that the entire Body will use to overcome the dragon even after he is cast to earth. From that perspective, you could say that the dragon is cast down for the sole purpose of being crushed under the feet of the Body of Christ. Sure, Satan is making diabolical plans for his final season because he knows his time will be short, but the whole thing is a baited trap laid by God, and all three portions of the Church have already been given a blueprint for crushing the serpent's head in their respective realms of authority.

The blueprint itself has many applications, but even if we just superficially apply the fractal of three to what we've learned so far of the holy of holies, inner court, and outer court saints, a highly encouraging picture begins to form.

For instance, think of "the blood of the lamb" as the primary force through which the sons of God will cast Satan out of heaven and thus initiate the entire progression of the Unveiling. Just as the first Passover was the crescendo that humiliated the gods of Egypt and opened the way for Israel to leave Egypt, the holy of holies saints will establish an open heavens when they attain the full authority of the Firstborn by fully embracing every aspect of His work on the cross.

Now think of "the word of their testimony" as the primary weapon of the inner court saints. Their entire lives will be a testimony. The very existence and persistence of the woman (as both Israel and the Church) throughout the ages has been a testimony of God's faithfulness, and the power of that testimony will be amplified when God publicly and miraculously protects the inner court saints in the face of the dragon's wrath. The world won't be privy to the details of the woman's encounter with Christ in the wilderness—it is a secluded place for intimate Unveiling after all—but just as the surrounding nations were in awe as they observed from a distance God's miraculous care for Israel in the wilderness, the protection of the inner court saints will be a clarion testimony to the world.

> When you view the details of the book of Revelation through the correct lens, you begin to see the great tribulation as a glorious season of intense pressure that leverages the enemy's greatest assault against him to open more hearts to Christ's Unveiling.

Finally, it is primarily the outer court saints who will overcome by "loving not their lives even when faced with death." They will experience more direct physical persecution with less divine protection than the other two sections of the Body, but their eternal reward will be no less great if they hold fast to the truth in the face of overwhelming deception and violence.

When you add all of this together, Christ's plan for His overcoming Bride during the second half of the seventieth week is glorious on every level. Even in the midst of incomprehensible darkness on earth, the kingdom of God will invade as it is preached and demonstrated with unstoppable authority and power. When the world experiences the open heavens perpetrated by the sons of God (the blood of the lamb), and witnesses the unassailable divine favor so obviously enjoyed by the inner court saints despite the dragon's fiercest attacks (the word of their testimony), and absorbs the courage and sacrifice of the outer court saints in the face of death (loved not their lives even when faced with death), a vast multitude of lost souls will be emboldened to turn to Christ despite the potential persecution. And so Jesus will turn Satan's greatest flex into the failure of the ages that paves the way for His kingdom. And even that is merely a token of the power of His Unveiling, seen through a predominantly old covenant lens. A more dazzling encounter with His divine essence awaits us on the journey ahead.

TODAY IF YOU HEAR HIS VOICE

I'll leave you with one final note on the three sections of the church. I've hammered away relentlessly for many chapters and from multiple angles on the differences between the holy of holies, inner court, and outer court saints, not just because the concept is central to the path we'll take through the book of Revelation in the next book, but because our responses to our Holy-Spirit-led wildernesses today will largely determine if we become the generation that ushers in the Unveiling of Christ.

If we follow Him into these wildernesses whenever and wherever He leads, and if we learn to embrace His trials and trust His provision, we can position ourselves to become the holy of holies company, like Moses entering the Sinai wilderness to be prepared as a son forty years before the rest of the nation.

If we lean on the crutch of our religious systems to avoid the most challenging wilderness invitations, or if we complain our way through our trials, we are positioning ourselves for a steeper learning curve with the inner court saints when the second half of the seventieth week begins.

And if we altogether forsake our wilderness trials in favor of the comforts and acceptance of the world, we may find ourselves facing the wrath of the dragon directly with the rest of the outer court saints.

I don't mean to suggest that the last generation will be absolutely locked into their level of maturity when the final season of the Unveiling begins. After all, Christ's Unveiling is all about transformation. The holy of holies saints will experience varying and gradual degrees of transfiguration during that season. Some inner court saints will find their way into the holy of holies while in the final wilderness, and surely some outer court saints will find grace to persist through the dragon's wrath by belatedly fleeing into the wilderness before their only option is death or apostasy. These categories are organic and fluid. But that doesn't mean we should leave the wilderness trials to the spiritual giants while we bank on having time to grow up sometime in the future when it is more convenient. Our time is now. Let us turn our ears to hear what the Spirit is saying to the Church today.

WHERE DO WE GO NEXT?

We've removed the fallen brush. We've located the journey's entrance. We know how to hold our map, and we are intimately acquainted with the grandeur of its crimson thread, the simple profundity of its legend, the specific scale of its markers, and the general shape of its topography. We've even spied out the path ahead. What's next?

Now we are finally ready to embark on our expedition! We have most of the tools necessary to flourish, and we'll have plenty of opportunities along the way to practice and apply anything that still feels new or underdeveloped.

The journey will begin in book 2 where I will introduce one more tool: the compass. The intro won't take long though because the best way to get acquainted with this compass is to just start walking.

> Jesus will turn Satan's greatest flex into the failure of the ages that paves the way for His kingdom. And even that is merely a token of the power of His Unveiling.

And the compass will immediately steer us down an unexpected path through the book of Revelation, following steps so hidden yet obvious, so complex yet simple, so inevitable yet exciting, that they will defy expectation while further establishing our hope in the stunning glory of our Bridegroom's Unveiling.

You see, the compass we will use in book 2 is the book of the Song of Solomon, and I think you are going to fall in love with the trail it navigates for our spirit, soul, and body to experience unfathomable transformation through Christ's Unveiling. The path will rely heavily upon the fractal of seven to enlarge our perspective and reveal deeper and more tangible purpose to many familiar ideas, such as the letters to the seven churches, the seven seals, the seven trumpets, and the seven bowls of wrath. And just as we largely focused on our male roles as sons of God in this book, our focus will shift to our female role as the Bride of Christ in the next. After all, one of the main tasks of the sons of God is to cooperate with the Holy Spirit to prepare the Body of Christ for her Bridegroom. Are you ready to start?

Notes

[1] Arthur Burk, *The Seven Principles*, "CD02.01 Definition," audio recorded in studio, June 6, 2004, 10 hours 39 minutes, Sapphire Leadership Group, https://theslg.com.

[2] C.S. Lewis, *The Lion, the Witch and the Wardrobe* (HarperTrophy, 1994), 171.

What's Next?

T hank you for reading *Face to Face: The Unveiling of Jesus Christ*, book 1 of *The Unveiling of Jesus Christ* series. Our journey continues in book 2, *Come Up Here: The Unveiling of Jesus Christ*, available today at www.theunveiling.org, and wherever books are sold online.

I'm currently working on book 3, which is tentatively scheduled for a mid-2026 release. Please visit my website at www.theunveiling.org to join my mailing list and stay up to date on my latest news. You can also read my blog, purchase watercolor artwork from my amazing wife, or ask me questions about anything I've written. I'd love to hear from you!

Lastly, would you please consider helping me spread the word about my books by leaving an honest book review? Reviews are one of the most impactful ways to help unknown indie authors like me get noticed. Scan the QR code below to see a list of book review sites from which you can choose.

Until next time, friends …

May the Father of glory give to you a spirit of wisdom and of revelation in the knowledge of Him. (Ephesians 1:18-19)